Civic Agency in Africa

Arts of Resistance in the 21st Century

Civic Agency in Africa

Arts of Resistance in the 21st Century

Edited by
Ebenezer Obadare
& Wendy Willems

Foreword by Patrick Chabal

JAMES CURREY

James Currey
an imprint of
Boydell & Brewer Ltd
PO Box 9, Woodbridge
Suffolk IP12 3DF (GB)
www.jamescurrey.com

and of

Boydell & Brewer Inc.
668 Mt Hope Avenue
Rochester, NY 14620-2731 (US)
www.boydellandbrewer.com

1 2 3 4 5 18 17 16 15 14

British Library Cataloguing in Publication Data
available on request

ISBN 978-1-84701-086-5 James Currey (Cloth)

Papers used by Boydell & Brewer are natural, recycled products
made from wood grown in sustainable forests.

FSC www.fsc.org MIX Paper from responsible sources FSC® C013604

Typeset in 11/12 Photina MT
by Avocet Typeset, Somerton, Somerset
Printed in Great Britain
by CPI Group (UK) Ltd, Croydon, CR0 4YY

Contents

Notes on Contributors vii
Foreword by Patrick Chabal xii
Acknowledgements xix

1 **Introduction**
African Resistance in an Age of Fractured Sovereignty
Wendy Willems & Ebenezer Obadare 1

Part I POSTCOLONIAL STATE FORMATION & PARALLEL INFRASTRUCTURES 25

2 **Global Technologies of Domination**
From Colonial Encounters to the Arab Spring
Sabelo J. Ndlovu-Gatsheni 27

3 **Citizenship from Below**
The Politics of Citizen Action & Resistance in South Africa & Angola
Bettina von Lieres 49

Part II EMBODIED MODES OF RESISTANCE & THE POSTCOLONIAL STATE 63

4 **The Politics of Confinement & Mobility**
Informality, Relocations & Urban Re-making from Above & Below in Nairobi
Ilda Lindell & Markus Ihalainen 65

5 **Overcoming Socio-Economic Marginalisation**
Young West African Hustlers & the Reinvention of Global Capitalism
Basile Ndjio 85

6 **Accepting Authoritarianism?**
Everyday Resistance as Political Consciousness in Post-Genocide Rwanda
Susan Thomson 104

Part III POPULAR CULTURE AS DISCURSIVE FORMS OF RESISTANCE 125

7 **Participatory Politics in South Africa**
Social Commentary from Above & Resistance from Below
Innocentia J. Mhlambi 127

8 **Laughing at the Rainbow's Cracks?**
Blackness, Whiteness & the Ambivalences of South African Stand-Up Comedy
Grace A. Musila 147

9 **'Beasts of No Nation'**
Resistance & Civic Activism in Fela Anikulapo-Kuti's Music
Jendele Hungbo 167

Part IV PUBLICS AS EVERYDAY SITES OF RESISTANCE 183

10 **The Power of Resonance**
Music, Local Radio Stations & the Sounds of Cultural Belonging in Mali
Dorothea Schulz 185

11 **Narrating the Contested Public Sphere**
Zapiro, Zuma & Freedom of Expression in South Africa
Daniel Hammett 204

Index 226

Notes on Contributors

Patrick Chabal joined King's College London following a Research Fellowship at Cambridge where he got his PhD. His earlier education was at Harvard University, where he got his BA, and Columbia University, where he did a Masters in International Affairs. Both in the USA and in Britain, he specialised in the modern history and politics of Africa and in the theory of comparative politics. He has been a Visiting Professor in Italy, France, Switzerland, India and Portugal, a member of the Institute for Advanced Study at Princeton University and a Visiting Researcher in South Africa. He has worked or done research in over a dozen African countries. Patrick Chabal has published numerous books, of which the last three are: *Culture Troubles: Politics and the Interpretation of Meaning* (Hurst & Co, 2006), *Africa: the Politics of Suffering and Smiling* (Zed Books, 2009), and *The End of Conceit: Western Rationality after Post-Colonialism* (Zed Books, 2012).

Daniel Hammett is a Faculty Research Fellow based in the Department of Geography, University of Sheffield, United Kingdom and a Research Associate of the Department of Geography, University of the Free State, South Africa. He is a political and development geographer working primarily on Southern Africa. His research focuses on topics relating to citizenship and belonging and the field of critical geopolitics, notably around negotiations of the meanings and practices of citizenship, the contested processes of democratisation and understandings of nationhood and belonging. He is co-editor (with Sara Rich Dorman and Paul Nugent) of *Making Nations, Creating Strangers: States and Citizenship in Africa* (Brill, 2007). His publications have appeared in journals such as *Political Geography*, *Area*, *Geopolitics*, *Citizenship Studies*, *Politikon* and *GeoJournal*.

Jendele Hungbo is a Senior Lecturer in the Department of Communications, North-West University, Mafikeng, South Africa. He was a Volkswagen Foundation post-doctoral fellow at the Wits Institute of Social and Economic Research (WISER), University of the Witwatersrand, Johannesburg, South Africa. He has been involved in the teaching of various courses on popular culture and media in Africa. Jendele is a researcher on the 'Passages of Culture: Media and Mediations of Culture in African Societies' research project funded by the Volkswagen Foundation, Hanover, Germany. His research interests include media in Africa, African popular culture, life writing and post-colonial studies.

Markus Ihalainen is a Master's student in Development Studies in the Department of Geography at the University of Uppsala, Sweden. He holds a Bachelor's degree in Geography from the University of Stockholm, Sweden and is an intern based in the Urban Economy Branch of UN-Habitat in Nairobi, Kenya. His research interests include urban governance, urban spaces and informality.

Bettina von Lieres is Assistant Professor in the Centre for Critical Development Studies at the University of Toronto Scarborough in Canada. Her current research and teaching focuses on new forms of citizen participation in the global South, poverty, marginalisation and the intersections between political and economic citizenship. She is the co-convenor of a global research network on citizenship and democracy, the Collaboration for Research on Democracy (CORD). From 2007–11, she co-convened the international working group on Building Democracy in States and Localities for the Centre for Citizenship, Participation and Accountability (www.drc-citizenship.org) at the Institute for Development Studies, University of Sussex in Brighton, United Kingdom. From 1992–2006 she was a Lecturer in the Political Science Department at the University of the Western Cape in Cape Town, South Africa. Her publications include *Mobilizing for Democracy: Citizen Action and the Politics of Participation* (co-edited with Vera Schattan: Coelho, Zed Books, 2010), 'Democracy and Citizenship' (co-authored with Steven Robins) in *New South African Keywords* (Jacana, 2008) and 'Rethinking "Citizenship" in the Postcolony' (co-authored with Andrea Cornwall and Steven Robins) in *Third World Quarterly* (2008).

Ilda Lindell is Associate Professor in the Department of Human Geography at Stockholm University in Stockholm, Sweden. Her current research focuses on the politics of informality in urban Africa. She has authored book chapters and journal articles in *Urban Studies, Global Networks, Third World Quarterly* and *Journal of Southern African Studies* among others. She has edited the book *Africa's Informal Workers: Collective Agency, Alliances and Transnational Organizing in Urban Africa* (Zed Books and the Nordic Africa Institute, 2010), as well as thematic journal issues in *African Studies Quarterly* (2010), *Labour, Capital and Society* (2011) and *Urban Forum* (2012, co-edited with Mats Utas). She is also the author of *Walking the Tight Rope: Informal Livelihoods and Social Networks in a West African City* (Almqvist & Wiksell International, 2002, 2006).

Innocentia Jabulisile Mhlambi is a Senior Lecturer in the Department of African Languages at the University of the Witwatersrand, Johannesburg, South Africa. She teaches African-language literatures, Black film studies, popular culture and politics, opera in Black South Africa, visual culture and studies in oral literature. Her current research focuses on Black film in South Africa, cultural connections between people of African descent and in the Diaspora, and developing African-language literary theory. She is the author of *African-Language Literatures: Perspectives on isiZulu Fiction and Popular Black Television Series* (Wits University Press, 2012).

Grace A. Musila is a Senior Lecturer in the English Department at Stellenbosch University in South Africa. Her research interests include East and Southern African literatures, popular media and gender studies. She is co-editor (with James Ogude and Dina Ligaga) of the essay collection *Rethinking Eastern African Literary and Intellectual Landscapes* (Africa World Press, 2012).

Basile Ndjio teaches Social and Cultural Anthropology at the University of Douala in Cameroon. He is currently a Research Fellow at the International Institute of Social History in Amsterdam, Netherlands. He has published widely on topics as varied as Chinese prostitution networks in Africa; migration, architecture and the transformation of the local landscape; African urban spaces, same sex relations and politics; and sorcery and democratisation processes in Cameroon and South Africa. His latest book is titled *Magie et Enrichissement Illicite: La Feymania au Cameroun* (Karthala, 2012).

Sabelo J. Ndlovu-Gatsheni is Head of the Archie Mafeje Research Institute (AMRI) based at the University of South Africa in Pretoria, South Africa, and Professor in the Department of Development Studies at the same university. He has taught in universities in Zimbabwe, the United Kingdom and South Africa and has published extensively on African history and politics. He is the author of *Do 'Zimbabweans' Exist? Trajectories of Nationalism, National Identity Formation and Crisis in a Post-Colonial State* (Peter Lang, 2009), co-editor (with James Muzondidya) of *Redemptive or Grotesque Nationalism? Rethinking Contemporary Politics in Zimbabwe* (Peter Lang, 2011), author of *Coloniality of Power in Postcolonial Africa: Myths of Decolonization* (CODESRIA Books, 2012) and *Empire, Global Coloniality and African Subjectivity* (Berghahn Books, 2013).

Ebenezer Obadare is Associate Professor of Sociology at the University of Kansas in Lawrence, United States. He earned his doctorate in Social Policy from the London School of Economics and Political Science in 2005, and has undergraduate and graduate degrees in History (1989) and International Relations (1992) respectively from Obafemi Awolowo University, Ile-Ife, Nigeria. A former award-winning journalist, Dr Obadare's research interests intersect civil society and the state, religion and politics in Africa, civic service, and citizenship. He has published extensively on these subjects in leading refereed journals, including *Review of African Political Economy (ROAPE), African Affairs, Politique Africaine, Journal of Civil Society, Democratization, Patterns of Prejudice, Africa Development, Critical African Studies, Development in Practice, Journal of Modern African Studies,* and *Journal of Contemporary African Studies.* He is the author of *Africa Between the Old and the New: The Strange Persistence of the Postcolonial State* (UNCW, 2008); *Statism, Youth and the Civic Imagination: A Critical Study of the Nigerian National Youth Service Corps* (CODESRIA, 2010); and co-editor (with Wale Adebanwi) of *Encountering the Nigerian State* (Palgrave, 2010) and *Nigeria at Fifty: The Nation in Narration* (Routledge, 2011).

Dorothea Schulz is Professor in the Department of Cultural and Social Anthropology at the University of Cologne in Germany. Her new book, *Muslims and New Media in West Africa: Pathways to God* (Indiana University Press, 2012), deals with Islamic revivalist movements in Mali that rely on various media technologies to promote a relatively new conception of publicly enacted religiosity. She has also published widely on media practices and public culture in Sahelian West Africa, gender studies, and the anthropology of the state. She is currently researching Muslim practices of coming to terms with death and mourning in a situation of continued ecological and social disaster and irruption in Uganda.

Susan Thomson is Assistant Professor of Peace and Conflict Studies at Colgate University in Hamilton, United States. Her research and teaching interests are in state-society relations in contemporary Africa, lived experiences of conflict and violence, and qualitative research methods, with particular focus on research ethics and doing research in difficult environments. She has published articles in *African Affairs, African Studies Review, Journal of Modern African Studies* and *The International Journal of Transitional Justice,* along with numerous book chapters and a book entitled *Whispering Truth to Power: Everyday Resistance to Reconciliation in Post-Genocide Rwanda* (University of Wisconsin Press, 2013). Susan Thomson received her BA from Saint's Mary University in Halifax, Canada; her LLB from University College London in London, United Kingdom; and her MA and PhD from Dalhousie University in Halifax, Canada.

Wendy Willems is Assistant-Professor in Media, Communication and Development at the London School of Economics and Political Science in London, United Kingdom. Her PhD research at the School of Oriental and African Studies, University of London dealt with politics, performance and popular culture in Zimbabwe. Her most recent research project is concerned with new media, social change and conceptions of space in Zambia. Her additional research interests include media and nationalism, new media cultures, and audience participation. She has published in a range of journals, including the *Journal of Southern African Studies*, *African Identities*, *African Studies*, *Africa Development*, *Telematics and Informatics*, *World Development* and *Popular Communication*. She is Associate Editor of the *Journal of African Media Studies*.

Foreword by Patrick Chabal

The search for meaning in today's African politics involves a dual exercise: an understanding of the nature of power and an exploration of the ways and byways of resistance to power. The former entails a reconsideration of the manner in which power is understood and exercised on the continent. The latter implies the use of methodologies capable of making sense of the behaviour of political actors. The standard approach to these questions has conceptualised power in terms of the state and resistance in terms of civil society – the one being the converse of the other. Much energy has thus been devoted to an analysis of the post-colonial state and to an investigation of the specific texture of civil society in Africa. This conceptual journey has yielded useful conclusions but it has suffered from one fundamental defect: the propensity to define state and civil society with reference to the politics of the West. Yet the analytical limits of this Western bias in the political analysis of post-independence Africa have all too often been exposed. As a result, the most recent scholarship has suggested that the state should be approached from a different, more local, angle and has conceded that the concept of civil society extant fails to explain the workings of societal resistance to the social, political and economic pressure under which Africans live and work.[1]

The most fruitful way of explaining how we can get a better grip on contemporary African politics is to tackle these questions from the perspective of the 'informal' and of 'agency'. But how can we conceptualise these two notions from an African rather than Western perspective? In order to do that, we should start from what can be observed on the ground rather than from the categories employed by Western political theories.[2]

If it is undoubtedly true that the *state* remains the preeminent actor in African politics, what is at stake here is the question of what the state actually is – that is, what are its boundaries and how it operates. The key here is to relate the state to the exercise of power. On the one hand, the state is constructed upon, and works according to, a formal institutional

1 For a more general discussion of these issues, see Patrick Chabal, *Africa: the politics of suffering and smiling* (London: Zed Books, 2009).

2 See here Patrick Chabal and Jean-Pascal Daloz, *Africa works: disorder as political instrument* (Oxford: James Currey, 1999).

logic, which has its origins in the Western liberal or the Eastern authoritarian template. The state does what it was intended to do, namely aggregate and legitimise the exercise of power by the political elite who are deemed to embody legitimate sovereignty. On the other hand, the states operates according to what are best defined as informal codes, which reflect the ways in which the relations between rulers and ruled actually operate. Here, the realities of legitimacy, representation and accountability refer to a separate, more subterranean, exercise of power shaped by the nature of the politics binding the political elite to the population, which sanctions their actions.

Similarly, the meaning and relevance of *civil society* need to be set in their appropriate African context. Civil society became the cardinal concept of political analysis when it came into prominence during the post-Soviet transition of Eastern European countries. Until then, civil society had been part of the analytical armoury of Western political scientists, who had made use of a notion that had taken hold in the slow movement of Western societies towards democracy. The salience of civil society in Africa thus arose from the idea that it embodied the productive resistance of ordinary people against the authoritarian state, which monopolised power and exploited the populace. Since the Washington consensus viewed the state as the main obstacle to development and democracy, the parallel between Eastern European and post-colonial societies seemed relevant. This notion of civil society had a major influence on donor policies, which now viewed African civil society organisations (CSOs) as the harbinger of the 'will of the people'. Yet the similarities were misleading. Not only was it inappropriate to compare the communist polities of Eastern Europe with the post-colonial African states, but it was disingenuous to suggest that there were in Africa civil societies that could channel political resistance in the way it had been done in post-Soviet Eastern Europe.

A more realistic understanding of African politics is to view state and civil society as being intimately connected by means of the *informal* exercise of power. When the state is understood as the concatenation of a formal structure and informal neo-patrimonial relations between the rulers and the ruled, it becomes easier to identify how resistance is most likely to take shape. Resistance is, as we would expect, the exercise of individual or collective agency in opposition to the post-colonial political dispensation as symbolised by the state. However, because of the nature of that state, the channels through which agency travels are those that are available at the interstices of the formal and informal. So, instead of looking for resistance where it lies in the West, in the formally constituted parts of civil society, it is more profitable to approach the question from the bottom up. How do ordinary people resist the totalising tendencies of the state and of the political elite that preside over their destiny? How do they create and maintain the social, economic, cultural and political space they need to operate in the societies in which they live?

How do they express their opposition to what they perceive as the oppressive environment that constrains their lives and activities? How is such resistance determined by the limits of the freedoms they enjoy? How effective is such resistance?

The most recent scholarship on agency in Africa has stressed two main points.[3] The first is that, despite a superficial view that Africans are helpless in the face of the twin evils of state oppression and globalisation, their obvious ingenuity and resilience point to myriad informal instances of successful resistance. The second is that it is through the study of such informal resistance that one can best understand the likely evolution of African societies. For instance, one should analyse the productive potential of informal trading activities when trying to understand how African economies really function. So it is that much new scholarship, as illustrated in this volume, provides social and political examples of informal agency, such as humour, music, ethnic mobilisation, the occupation of public space or delinquency. What these have in common is that they belong firmly to the non-official realm. What they point to is that the politics of formal civil society largely fail to channel the opposition to the state and its ancillary bodies. In other words, the more genuine critique of the ways power is exercised in Africa is not to be found where Western political theory is searching – in the non-governmental organisations (NGOs) and CSOs that are ostensibly constituted to balance the power of the state – but in the more grassroots and unstructured acts of disobedience and avoidance.

This approach is a vast improvement on the perennial presentation of an Africa that is characterised by a long history of resistance – first against colonial rule, then against neo-colonial exploitation, and finally against globalisation. As is evident in the contributions to the present volume, this Manichean view of African politics is highly deceptive. It is in truth the continuation of the view of the continent as the perpetual prey to outside forces, which are allied with the political elite that continue to take advantage of the populace's helplessness. An obsession with resistance of that type is another way of saying that Africans can only be seen as victims, unable to exercise sufficient political agency against this hostile external and internal coalition. The efforts made by those who seek to identify how ordinary people oppose, by-pass, evade, or make use of the forces that limit their autonomy is proof, if such were needed, of the continuously evolving cunning with which they assert initiative and resourcefulness. Not surprisingly, therefore, their resistance is tailored to the oppression they experience. It is less a frontal battle than a multifaceted guerrilla struggle, to use a military metaphor.

Above and beyond this conceptualisation of agency, it is important to

[3] For a more systematic discussion of agency in Africa, see Patrick Chabal, 'Agency in Africa: the domestication of the modern mind', in Dieter Neubert amd Christine Scherer (eds), *Agency and changing worldviews in Africa* (Münster: Lit Verlag [Bayreuther Beiträge zur Afrikaforschung, Bd. 40], 2012).

point to some of the limitations of such an approach. As I have argued elsewhere[4], the flip side of the stress on resilience and ingenuity is the risk that we neglect the *realpolitik* of the relations between rulers and ruled in Africa. A good example of such danger is the present analysis of the hazards of multiparty elections. It is the consensus among Western experts and donors that such electoral contests are a pre-requisite to the emergence of more accountable politics. The many instances of ethnic violence that have damaged competitive elections are seen as the result of the political elites' manipulation of existing social divisions for electoral purposes. In other words, it is assumed that in the absence of such manipulation ethnicity would not interfere so starkly with the conduct of 'proper' multiparty elections. But this interpretation fails to come to terms with the more informal ways in which politics is played out: the importance of neo-patrimonalism means that politicians can only acquire legitimacy if they are seen to favour their natural constituency, which not surprisingly transits through various forms of identity, of which ethnicity often features prominently. In other words, the so-called ethnic 'drag' on the democratic dividend is not merely a question of curbing the misdeeds of the political elite. It is, rather, to understand that elite and populace inhabit a common cultural and moral space within which such patrimonial relations are legitimate; and if that is the case, then it is also likely that the meaning of resistance will have to be revisited.

It is this book's merit to point us in the direction of a more considered notion of agency, which better reflects how actual politics on the ground is organised and functions. For this reason, this volume ought to be seen not as a collection of chapters attempting to give an 'exact' picture of resistance in contemporary Africa but as an example of how a more ground-up approach can enlighten those who wish to make sense of what is taking place on the continent. In other words, it is more enlightening to look at the myriad ways ordinary people cope with and undermine the politics of hegemony pursued by the political elite than it is to classify resistance according to more formal Western categories. What matters is the analysis of that which confronts and constrains the lives of such ordinary people as they seek to acquire greater autonomy within the confines of the informal political dispensation in which they have to labour. How they behave is obviously the result of the way they perceive power to be exercised over them. This varies according to countries but there are commonalities between them. How then should we conceptualise the notion of agency in today's Africa? How are agency and resistance related? Is the nature of agency making it impossible for resistance to bring about substantive political change on the continent?

Agency is usually understood as directed, meaningful, intentional and self-reflective social or political action. In other words, it is not just

[4] Ibid.

the reflex opposition, a mere 're-action' to the actions of the agents of the state. It involves a deliberate act that seeks to oppose or undermine the constraining pressure, which restricts the ability of ordinary people to live, function, work or play as they see fit. Where Western political theory attempts to locate such resistance in the formal political actions of those who suffer oppression, the notion of agency I favour is that which encompasses all the deeds that undermine power. It is because the exercise of power in Africa is largely informal, that we need to turn to the informal if we are to understand what resistance means. Of course, there is a place for an analysis of the formal types of resistance – from trade unions, churches, NGOs, etc. – that exist in all countries. But the core of resistance in Africa must be seen as belonging firmly to the informal, for it is the informal that constitutes the matrix within which formal resistance occurs. So, for example, it is important to understand how the Catholic Church tries to influence politics in Cameroon, but it is equally (if not more) important to study the ways in which witchcraft impinges on the relations of power between elite and populace. Equally, it is necessary to look at how the vocabulary used by ordinary people when they mock or insult the elite is conducive to the undermining of their political legitimacy.

If these informal types of agency rarely threaten the power of the elite, they contribute to a discourse that sets politicians in the cultural context from which they often try to escape. Politicians may engage in savage repression but they can do nothing against the forms of resistance that debase their might and chip away at their will to power. Since the elite's legitimacy is dependent on their ability to manage the realm of the informal, they often need to address the questions raised by those who challenge their hegemony. Failure to do so may not result in their losing power – after all, they do know how to manipulate elections – but it undoubtedly reduces their ability to *exercise* that power in the ways they would want. Witness the chapters in this book that show how Fela Kuti's 'Beasts of no Nation' or Zapiro's cartoon of Jacob Zuma discuss forms of agency that seek to speak truth to power. The example of Zuma, as of many other African leaders, shows how these politicians can manage to stay in power even as their foibles are being exposed publicly. This may appear to suggest that these informal forms of resistance have little practical effect but that would be to misunderstand their purpose. They may not lead to dramatic and overt political change but they do affect people's perceptions of politicians and of their policies; and they help us understand how resistance to hegemony functions on the continent.

These examples suggest that it is important to try to recognise the different types of resistance found in Africa. Whereas books on African politics usually focus on formal political resistance, as it is observed in the West – strikes, protest, petitions, party competition, opposition in parliament – much is to be gained by searching beyond these obvious forms of opposition – such as was displayed elsewhere by the Occupy movement or the Arab Spring. For instance, there are many reasons why Paul Biya has managed to rule Cameroon for so long and some of these reasons undoubtedly have to do with the way in which repression prevents open revolt, or even organised opposition. But if we are to understand the politics of that country, it is obvious that we need to look at the informal, more covert, ways in which power is exercised. In order to do that, it is useful (as the chapter on the *feymen*, or tricksters, of Cameroon shows) to study the various forms of resistance found there, along with the ways in which ordinary people exercise agency in that particular context. Indeed, the role of the 'trickster' is not so much to threaten the government as it is to ridicule the type of political control rulers impose and thereby to try to justify the illicit or criminal activities in which they indulge.[5]

Therefore, the tendency among Western analysts and donors to view African politics merely as a zero-sum game is misleading. Yes, it is true that it serves little purpose in Africa to come second in the elections and to be confined to playing the 'loyal' opposition to the regime in place. What is more profitable for the loser is to use political opposition in order to be co-opted into government. But, and this is often overlooked, the same also applies to the 'civil society' opponents to the regime: NGO members often use their position to acquire status and thus to be invited to join the winning party. Equally, the youth that ridicules politicians is often mobilised to form militias, which are used violently to 'enforce' support for those self-same politicians. This is a by-product of competitive multiparty elections in countries where there are virtually no legitimate outlets for the young, who are unemployed and eke out a living in the informal sector. Political violence becomes a way to acquire prestige and to join in the politics of that country. Although the young are often exploited by the politicians who employ them, they also embody a kind of resistance against the political system that marginalises them so completely. Theirs is not a 'progressive' revolt but it is undoubtedly political agency – however much outsiders may choose to ignore the fact.

One final question arises: are the forms of resistance found in contemporary Africa impediments to the emergence of social movements that would lead to radical political change, or even revolution? In truth, this is a difficult question to answer plausibly. On the one hand, there were in the nineties a wave of 'national conferences', driven by civil society, which led in some instances to profound political and constitutional change – for example in Benin and Congo-Brazzaville. On the other hand, these constitutional 'revolutions' were easily overturned: in Benin the incumbent (Mathieu Kérékou), who had been forced out of office, regained power in the following elections. In Congo, multiparty elections led to a virtual state of civil war, the outcome of which was that the

[5] Even in the West some of the 'traditional' ways of understanding resistance may need to be revised to take account of amorphous movements such as Femen and Pussy Riot, which aim not to dislodge hegemonic power but to undermine it through ridicule.

incumbent (Sassou Nguesso) also managed to regain power. To this day, the only two post-independence 'revolutions' to have taken place in Africa have come, not as a result of civil society revolt, but as a result of a successful guerrilla war (in Uganda) or military coup (in Ghana). It is only in Ghana, where the incumbent (Jerry Rawlings) agreed to stand down after the mandated two terms of office, that regular multiparty elections led to genuine competition between the two main parties. In Uganda, Yoweri Museveni not only initially banned party political competition, but later changed the constitution so that he could enjoy third and fourth terms in office. His political revolution, which appeared promising at the beginning, seems to have resulted in a form of authoritarian and patrimonial politics commonly found elsewhere in Africa. So the question, which we are not in a position to answer at this stage, can legitimately be raised as to whether the current political dispensations found in Africa – of which vertical patrimonial and clientelistic relations between rulers and ruled are the mainstay – make it more difficult for resistance to bring about substantive, let alone revolutionary, political change. Is it the case that, at best, we can expect a slow process of relative democratisation, such as is taking place in Ghana?

In the end, this volume contributes not just to a better understanding of the nature of resistance in Africa but also to an explanation of why agency is not that straightforward to conceptualise. It is a common mistake to assume that revolt and violence necessarily improve the societies where they erupt. They certainly represent a type of opposition to the existing political and economic system in place but they may also partake of types of (individual and collective) agency, which bring about the greater informalisation or criminalisation of society. Africa should not only be seen through well-meaning Western eyes, the vision of which comforts the idea that resistance is always for the better. Why should that be when the opposite has often been the case in the West itself? African societies are dynamic living organisms that are as prone to the nefarious exercise of agency as any other part of the world. Therefore, let us begin to read African politics from a universal and not merely Western perspective.

Acknowledgements

The current volume is a concretisation of our mutual interest in alternative forms of civic agency in Africa. Ebenezer Obadare's interest in political jokes in Nigeria was underpinned by a desire to understand the 'undisciplined' ways in which Nigerians encounter the state, and how they engage, deconstruct and wrestle with it on an everyday basis. Humour, for him, was an integral part of an array of stratagems mobilised by ordinary Nigerians, partly to critique the state, but fundamentally to recuperate dignity and selfhood amid the humiliations and savageries of everyday postcolonial life. As a young reporter in Lagos in the early 1990s, he was a first-hand witness to (and participant in) this eternal struggle of dignity against degradation, conducted against the social backdrop of a deadly military dictatorship. At the same time, he saw how state and society continually criss-crossed, generating evanescent solidarities that confound the axioms of traditional sociological and political science literatures. Fundamentally, his work aims to organise and format these ethnographies as serviceable theoretical taxonomies.

Having worked for a British NGO for several years, supporting a number of social movements and grassroots organisations in Eastern and Southern Africa, Wendy Willems' interest in civic agency and informal resistance is also propelled by her professional background. Troubled by the highly normative and prescriptive notions of 'civil society' floating around – amidst other buzzwords – in an often deeply professionalised and depoliticised 'development industry', she observed how these were frequently reproduced in the practices and discourses of many NGOs in the global South that seemed so detached from the lived experience of their so-called 'target groups' or 'beneficiaries'.

Her academic work connected her with the state of 'civil society' in Zimbabwe, which could count on generous funding from a range of donors in the context of the 'crisis' in the early 2000s, all keen to 'commission' or 'engineer' a civilised form of legal resistance against the state. While numerous accounts narrated how 'real' resistance on the streets failed to materialise, she struggled to equate civic agency with conventional understandings of civil society generally understood to comprise the activities of NGOs, frequently also referred to as the 'Pajero Brigade' in the Zimbabwean context (after the ubiquitous Mitsubishi 4x4, elsewhere known as the Shogun). Living in Zimbabwe in the early

2000s, Wendy's interest was drawn to the less visible ways in which Zimbabweans commented on the state on an everyday basis through political humour, often shared through SMS phone texting.

Our personal, professional and academic backgrounds were therefore strong motivations for this collection on civic agency and informal resistance in Africa. We hope the book offers a broader understanding of the way in which Africans engage, resist, transform and co-opt the state, one whose sovereignty has become increasingly fragile and fractured in the context of global forces of power. We are grateful to all the contributors for their richly textured accounts of civic agency in twenty-first-century Africa, and for their willingness to endure our constant harassment to honour unfair deadlines. We can only be thankful they barely resisted our efforts at disciplining them! We would like to acknowledge Professor Patrick Chabal in particular for kindly agreeing to contribute a foreword at relatively short notice.

Ebenezer is obliged to his colleagues and support staff in the Department of Sociology at the University of Kansas for their generosity of spirit and unstinting collegial and professional support. Wendy would like to thank her colleagues in the Department of Media Studies at the University of the Witwatersrand (which she left in December 2012) and the Department of Media and Communications at the London School of Economics and Political Science (which she joined in January 2013). We value all the support which enabled us to bring this project to fruition. Jaqueline Mitchell and Lynn Taylor at James Currey have been wonderful, and we are grateful for all their assistance. We also appreciate the thoughtful and provocative comments provided by the two anonymous reviewers. The comments were helpful in clarifying the overall argument of our Introduction, and the theses of the individual chapters.

Last but not least, we are indebted to Messrs John Coltrane and Miles Davis who provided the soundtrack to this book and kept us ticking along nicely. Without their soothing tunes, this book would have been exceedingly more difficult to produce.

Ebenezer Obadare, Lawrence, Kansas
Wendy Willems, London, UK

1 Introduction
African Resistance in an Age of Fractured Sovereignty

Wendy Willems & Ebenezer Obadare

> [O]ne of the problems is that our economy fragments us into many parts, two of which would be, for example, consumer and citizen, and these fragments are pitted against each other (Jensen 2002: 102).

For scholars with an abiding interest in the subject of resistance – its enactment, forms, promises, even dystopias – recent global events could not have occurred at a more opportune moment. Across North Africa and the entire 'Muslim World', concerted popular action culminated in the unexpected demise of entrenched dictatorships. In the United States, the Occupy Wall Street movement both epitomised and canalised widespread antipathy toward not just the country's 'one percent', but more significantly the global financial system. Outside the country, 'Occupy' proved a timely banner for those seeking to redress a wide array of local injustices. In Nigeria, to take just one African example, the unlikely coalition of civil society organisations, politicians, professional and interest associations, and student and human rights groups which stormed the streets in January 2012 to protest a sudden hike in the pump price of petroleum christened itself 'Occupy Nigeria' (Obadare and Adebanwi 2013).

That these are instances of resistance is beyond any serious disputation. Less obvious are what *kinds* of resistance they are, and the specific lessons to be drawn from them, not only about resistance qua resistance, but also about politics and political action, oppositional politics, popular empowerment, civic agency, citizenship, subjectivity, and the state. The torrent of recent writings on the 'Arab Revolutions' and 'Occupy' respectively (see for instance McMurray and Ufheil-Somers 2013; Lynch 2013; Gitlin 2012; Graeber 2013; Mitchell, Harcourt and Taussig 2013) only goes to show that these are by no means idle agitations.

Though this book was conceived well before these epochal events occurred, the problems they have given rise to – especially in regards to the epistemologies and praxes of resistance – have made our original questions even more salient. For example: What does resistance mean in the contemporary global nexus? What are the opportunities for resistance today, given the ubiquity of neoliberalism and the financialisation of nearly all aspects of social life? What are the emergent spaces – and methodologies – for resistance, and what kinds of social agents constitute and animate those spaces? What is the impact of global financialisation on subjectivity? Last but not least, how has the experience of liberal democracy and its many formalities conditioned attitudes towards politics, political action and the state? No doubt, each of these questions carries with it a range of subordinate dilemmas.

Our attitude towards these questions was to seek answers primarily in an African context, meaning that we wanted such answers to be inspired by the experiences of contemporary Africans in a variety of rapidly evolving economic, social, cultural and political circumstances. At the same time, we were conscious of having to locate resistance in a global fulcrum: first, as a straightforward admission of the mutual imbrication of the 'local' and the 'global', but also as a methodology to suggest a framing in which 'local' resistance continues to be subjected to –which is not to say absolutely determined by – powerful exogenous economic and political constraints.

As such, the contributions in this book are collectively grounded in a rejection of the austere formalism that appears to be definitive of the dominant approach to the forms and mechanisms of resistance in African societies. Thus, although some of the chapters here may deliberately foreground the shaping of community identities as a sort of validation which is then expressed as agency, while others grapple with acts of solidarity that directly and indirectly confront the state in its various guises and disguises, the recurring motif is a determination to reimagine resistance by tracking its 'parallel infrastructures', i.e. the subtle ways in which it is mobilised, plotted and enacted. The result is a volume in which stand-up comedy, cartoons, local music and everyday social commentary, among other forms of quotidian (sites of) resistance, are fused to produce a very unconventional portrait of African political consciousness.

From anti-colonial resistance to civil society protest

In many ways, histories of resistance in modern Africa have been equated with the history of colonialism. While 'African history' initially was written as history made by Big White Men as part of their mission to 'civilise' the 'natives' stuck in the groove of tradition, a new wave of African historiography emphasised the contribution of Africans to events unfolding on the continent and freeing it of its colonial rulers (see for example Ranger 1977). Postcolonial historiography re-inscribed the agency of Africans and emphasised their heroic attempts in resisting colonial oppression and liberating themselves from the colonial state. This master-narrative of 'domination' and 'resistance' has continued to shape accounts of postcolonial African subjectivity, thereby alternately highlighting the opportunities for agency with more pessimistic paradigms emphasising the structural constraints to African agency.

While anti-colonial resistance dominated African historiography in the 1960s and 1970s, a new paradigm emerged in the 1990s which focused on the way in which Africans contested postcolonial governments, many of which had morphed into intolerant, one-party states, thus reproducing by and large the repressive framework of the colonial state. A crucial concept dominating accounts of resistance in the 1990s was the notion of 'civil society' which gained popularity in the post-Cold War period in the wake of the so-called 'third wave of democratisation' that saw the gradual disappearance of governments under one-party rule and the introduction of multi-party democracies, both in parts of Africa and Eastern Europe (Huntington 1991). In this new paradigm, civil society organisations (CSOs) – also known as 'not-for-profit organisations', 'community-based organisations' (CBOs) and 'non-governmental organisations' (NGOs) – were endowed with an important role in resisting autocratic regimes.

The concept of 'civil society' did not only serve as an explanatory term to describe events then unfolding; it was reified as a normative policy recommendation for African states (Lewis 2001; Obadare 2004). Increasingly, international financial institutions such as the World Bank and the International Monetary Fund blamed the African authoritarian state for poor economic performance. Whilst in the 1960s and 1970s, a strong state was considered to be crucial for economic growth and nation-building, the Washington Consensus that emerged in the 1990s prescribed liberal democracy as the most suitable template for 'good governance' which included the conduct of regular multi-party elections, the withdrawal of the state from the economy and an increasing role for civil society which was seen as both a counterweight to a 'bad state' and a replacement for a 'reduced state' (Abrahamsen 2000; Obadare 2011).

For example, Harbeson, Rothchild and Chazan (1994: 1–2) argued that 'civil society is a hitherto missing key to sustained political reform, legitimate states and governments, improved governance, viable state-society and state-economy relationships, and prevention of the kind of political decay that undermined new African governments a generation ago'. The emphasis on a mystery 'missing key' suggested that Africa did not yet have a 'civil society', and that one therefore needed to be 'established', thus tacitly legitimising a role for foreign donors in helping to 'build' African civil society. Civil society was conceptualised as an intrinsically 'good', power-free essence with a magical capacity to transform the notoriously 'bad African state'.

In the 1990s and 2000s, African resistance was therefore largely equated with the activities of formal civil society organisations which rapidly mushroomed on the continent under the rubric of 'non-governmental organisations'. The typical NGO on the continent was dependent on foreign donor funding, established relatively recently in the 1990s, involved either in advocacy and campaigning targeting the state or in delivering services such as education, health care or social welfare, hereby to a certain extent replacing the state. This narrow, normative discourse on civil society not only profoundly masked the rich historical legacy of civil society organisations and activities on the continent, it also excluded other forms of organising (and dis-organising) which did not neatly fit with the assumptions made about the social composition of civil society and its normative obligations. For example, organisations which were not defined in opposition to the state or organised along the lines of kinship, religion, ethnicity or local 'tradition', were not considered to be part of 'good civil society' (Obadare 2006). Furthermore, the discourse failed to apprehend the power structures within NGOs, and also overlooked the manner in which these were embedded in a global set of power relations due to funding dependencies.

In order to extend the concept of civil society, Mamdani (1996: 19) advocated for 'an analysis of actually existing civil society so as to understand it in its actual formation, rather than as a promised agenda for change'. Similarly, in their edited volume *Civil society and the political imagination*, anthropologists John and Jean Comaroff (1999) also thought it necessary to move away from the Eurocentric tendency to limit civil society to a narrowly defined institutional arena by acknowledging other African forms of association, often perceived as 'uncool', 'partisan', 'parochial' or 'fundamentalist' in donor policy discourses. Instead of asking what the idea of civil society can tell us about contemporary Africa, they proposed to ask what a specific set of African cases can 'tell us about the planetary appeal of the Idea of civil society' (Comaroff and Comaroff 1999: 3; see also Obadare 2004; cf. Chan 2002), thereby hinting at what civil society might mean in an African context.

From formal civil society to informal modes of civic agency

At all events, nearly three decades after its much heralded entrance into academic circles in Africa, disgruntlement with the concept of civil society remains strong. As indicated above, for some scholars (we call them the exceptionalists), the source of dissatisfaction lies in the perceived inapplicability of an idea that emerged within a specific European historical trajectory to Africa's historical specifics and cultural distinctions. For others, a nagging source of agitation is the tendency of most of civil society scholarship itself to normativise the idea as consisting of formal organisations either outside the reach of, or in a permanently conflictive relationship with, the state. The latter has resulted in a widespread equation of civil society activity with the agency (dubious or otherwise) of formal extra-state organisations, especially NGOs.

Although efforts by Mamdani and the Comaroffs to ground the concept of civil society in Africa within a deeper historicity are commendable, for us the way in which African resistance still tends to be seen to reside within the domain of formal and organised spaces – whether understood as anti-colonial liberation movements during the colonial period, or as formal or informal associations in the postcolonial period – remains a nagging source of disgruntlement.

Hence the interest here in the unruly vastness of the non-governmental sphere and the various socio-economic, political and artistic praxes that animate it. We suggest that there is a need for a broader conception and examination of civic agency in Africa which transcends the study of NGOs which have since the 1990s been assigned a key role in processes of social change and frequently been seen as exemplifying agency and resistance on the continent. Drawing on a range of interdisciplinary case studies from different parts of Africa, our book explores a wide range of modes of civic agency. In situating these forms within global, regional and national socio-economic and political milieus, we hope to contribute to a better understanding of processes of 'social change *actually* taking place' on the continent (Chabal 2009: 11).

Most conventional analyses of African politics have often adopted either an oppositional state-centred or society-centred approach in which the state is either rubbished or society celebrated. On one hand, gloomy political scientists have framed the African state through accounts of widespread corruption and misgovernance which were thought to be partly a product of African clientelist practices (Bayart 1993; Bayart, Ellis and Hibou 1999). On the other, upbeat anthropologists have highlighted the creative ways in which Africans have adapted to situations of crisis through inventive livelihood strategies. For example, with the introduction of structural adjustment policies and the rise of multi-party democracy on the continent in the 1990s, African subjectivity was frequently conceptualised as the creative manner in which Africans circumvented the negative economic impact that accompanied the turn to a neo-liberal policy paradigm. Framed within livelihood studies, scholars sought to move away from notions of Africans as victims and shifted attention to their ability to negotiate the ecological, economic and political constraints which they faced (Chabal, Engel and de Haan 2007), the creativity of African urban dwellers in their survival strategies (Konings and Foeken 2006), the notion of local vitality in Africa (Probst and Spittler 2004), and the meaning of violence in different forms of African insurgency (Abbink, de Bruijn and van Walraven 2003).

Resisting the state, resisting the global

We are concerned that both of these sour doomsday scenarios and syrupy celebratory accounts of agency in Africa have almost neutralised the ever-present exogenous constraints – represented for example by the restrictions imposed by international financial institutions and global power relations more broadly – on the agency of individual Africans as well as on the sovereignty of the national state. While African nation-states are often taken for granted as fully fledged, self-governing entities, we are conscious of the fundamentally inequitable global system within which African states are situated (see also Comaroff and Comaroff 2006; Mbembe 2006). Hence, it seems fair to us to argue that African states largely operate as 'quasi-states' (Jackson 1990) within a context of what we call 'fractured sovereignty'. Too often, African resistance has been understood as reacting to domination exerted by the nation-state.

However, resistance, even when ostensibly 'local', is frequently transgressive, and engages with or is targeted at powerful global forces (Obadare 2005a). In this regard, the idea of fractured sovereignty is deployed not just as a convenient nod to the complexity of things. That goes without saying. At the same time, however, we are eager to posit the fundamentally disruptive influence of the global economic system on ordinary African agents, and the ways in which this reality of persistent rupture puts the very idea of agential autonomy (and holism) that is signified by the notion of sovereignty under pressure. Seen in this light, the idea of fractured sovereignty speaks eloquently to the situation of the ordinary African, and theorises the varieties of ways in which (as registered by different contributions to the volume) agency is fragmented and dispersed into individual acts of 'accommodation' and 'getting by'.

This has implications for power, which we imagine as a network of relations which can be both constraining and enabling. The subjects which power relationships constitute are always both experiencing and exercising power. Here, we draw inspiration from Foucault (1980: 122) who advocated for an analytical approach beyond the state, thus:

> I don't want to say that the State isn't important; what I want to say is that relations of power, and hence the analysis that must be made of them, necessarily extend beyond the limits of the State. In two senses: first of all because the State, for all the omnipotence of its apparatuses, is far from being able to occupy the whole field of actual power relations, and further because the State can only operate on the basis of other, already existing power relations.

Hence, it is important that the African nation-state be not understood as a force which primarily exercises power, hereby inviting simple resistance, but as an actor that is also subject to power. In advancing this understanding of power, we are eager to distance ourselves from the idea dominant in mainstream political theory that power is predominantly vested in the nation-state. By contrast, Foucault's concept of power enables us to discuss the multiple levels at which power is reproduced and contested.

Neither adopting a state-centred nor a society-centred approach, we treat agency and resistance therefore as practices dialogically produced in the interaction between state and society situated within a global system of power relations. *Pace* Achille Mbembe (2001: 103), we aim to eschew 'the binary categories used in standard interpretations of domination, such as resistance v. passivity, autonomy v. subjection, state v. civil society, hegemony v. counter-hegemony, totalisation v. detotalisation'. For Mbembe (2001: 110), it is unnecessary to insist 'on oppositions (*dédoublement*) or, as does conventional analysis, on the purported logic of resistance, disengagement, or disjunction. Instead, the emphasis should be on the logic of "conviviality", on the dynamics of domesticity and familiarity, inscribing the dominant and the dominated within the same *episteme*'. The relation between rulers and ruled in the postcolony cannot be understood through dichotomies of domination and resistance, but is characterised by a more intimate form of co-existence.

Hence, this book does not explore agency or resistance as practices situated outside power. Rather, it is fundamentally oriented at apprehending how these practices engage, transform, co-opt, undermine, reproduce or reinforce the postcolonial African state, ultimately further shedding light on the nature of the state. We treat power and resistance as mutually constituted categories that cannot always be easily separated. While the empirical focus in the book is on Sub-Saharan Africa, the issues interrogated in the collection automatically resurrect and complicate broader conceptual debates on agency, resistance and state formation in postcolonial or post-transitional settings. As Lila Abu-Lughod (1990: 41–2) has noted, some scholars read 'all forms of resistance as signs of the ineffectiveness of systems of power and of the resilience and creativity of the human spirit in its refusal to be dominated' but we are concerned that '[b]y reading resistance in this way, we collapse distinctions between forms of resistance and foreclose certain questions about the workings of power.'

Beyond the unified and heroic subaltern subject

Related to this is another idea that we aim to contest in this volume: the tendency to associate resistance with heroic, successful, large-scale revolutions and rebellions (cf. Tilly 1978; Skocpol 1979, 1994). As it happens, the recent wave of protests across North Africa and the Middle East provides a timely empirical foil for our cogitations and raises a number of important issues for our book. These popular protests have stimulated debates worldwide on the meaning and strategies of resistance in the 21st century. A key theme emerging in these debates is the profound absence of formal organisations coinciding with effective forms of resistance that ultimately transformed the state. Another theme that has recurred through these events is the idea that the classic concept of civil society understood as formal organisations is no longer able to explain processes of social change. But above all, the events arguably still unfolding in North Africa and the Middle East have also profoundly demonstrated the seductiveness of outwardly rapid, large-scale revolutionary processes of social change. However, what popular media brandings of these events as 'Twitter or Facebook revolutions' have failed to investigate is the long-term historical trajectory out of which the seemingly sudden uprisings have materialised.

In this book, we do not solely define resistance as organised, wide-scale, effective rebellion against the state; *per contra*, we are interested in understanding everyday forms of resistance that are often implicated in, or positioned at, the nascent stage of processes of social change, thereby engaging with previous arguments developed in the vast literature on 'subaltern studies'. Founded by the Indian historian Ranajit Guha and drawing major inspiration from Antonio Gramsci's work, the Subaltern Studies Group responded to the elitist bias of particularly Indian historiography and its focus on the agency of 'Big Men'. Instead, subaltern studies scholars emphasised the role of women, peasants, industrial workers and low-caste labourers in bringing about changes in power. As indicated earlier in relation to the enormous attention attracted by the so-called 'Arab Spring', many scholars have indeed been drawn to the role of ordinary people in rebellions and insurgencies:

> Dramatic confrontations between the dominant and the dominated – manifest in riots, rebellions, revolutions and organised political movements – have always constituted a major source of attention for social historians, sociologists and political scientists, particularly those keen to find among the oppressed the universal urge toward liberation (Haynes and Prakash 1991: 1).

However, as we argue in this book, the focus on these 'extraordinary moments of collective protest' has precluded scholars from examining the 'more enduring, "everyday" forms of resistance constantly present in the behaviours, traditions and consciousness of the subordinate' (Haynes and Prakash 1991: 1). In his influential book *Weapons of the weak*, James Scott (1985: xvi) conceptualised everyday forms of resistance as 'the prosaic but constant struggle between the peasantry and those who seek to extract labour, food, taxes, rents and interest from them. Most forms of this struggle stop well short of outright collective defiance'. Resistance should therefore not strictly be understood as referring to physical and material protests in the streets, but comprises a broader set of practices, often hidden and invisible, used by the dominated to contest those who make attempts to dominate them (Scott 1990).

Our understanding of resistance encompasses a wide-ranging collection of cultural practices such as rituals, gossip, humour, dress and behavioural codes which is also how we have understood the practice in our work on the role of popular humour in the Nigerian and Zimbabwean contexts respectively (Obadare 2009, 2010a, b; Willems 2010, 2011a, b, c, 2012). However, while we are sympathetic to the heterogeneous forms in which subaltern studies scholars have conceptualised resistance and the manner in which they have emphasised its 'everyday' character, we are wary at the same time of the way in which subaltern studies has tended to celebrate subaltern agency. Like Achille Mbembe (2001: 5), we are concerned about 'the rediscovery of the subaltern subject and the stress on his/her inventiveness' which has 'taken the form of an endless invocation of the notions of "hegemony", "moral economy", "agency" and "resistance"'. This has often resulted in a dichotomy of 'the noble, heroic subaltern' in sharp opposition to 'the corrupted, malicious state'. Furthermore, there is a tendency to ascribe a coherent identity to the subalterns who are frequently far from a homogenous mass but instead are differentiated through complex, overlapping and multiple markers of identity, including class, race, ethnicity, gender, age and sexual orientation.

The collection: basic objectives

One key aim of this book, then, is to expand the thematic, agential, cultural and intellectual possibilities as far as thinking about civil society, agency and resistance in Africa is concerned. Contra the predominant focus on what formal NGOs (whether civil or not) do or do not, we turn instead to the dialogical ways in which Africans contend with, challenge, subvert, reproduce or even collaborate with the state, and how this in return impacts on processes of postcolonial state formation. Our book privileges politics and political praxes. Part of the (legitimate, in our view) criticism of the existing literature on civil society is that the almost exclusive focus on the African organisational landscape has led to the elision of issues that affect the everyday lives of ordinary people across the continent, the spaces where the seeds of resistance are sown, and particular modes of protest. By 'bringing politics back in', our volume emphasises instead the different forms of agency that animate the public sphere. Finally, we examine African forms of popular agency while transgressing disciplinary boundaries. We articulate various dimensions and expressions of public action, from sociology, anthropology, history, political science, human geography, geopolitics, cultural and literary studies.

Postcolonial state formation and parallel infrastructures

Part I of this volume considers emerging forms of African resistance in the context of a frail neo-liberal nation-state. Because of the way in which the postcolonial state has to a large extent reproduced the colonial state, it lacks a certain legitimacy and rootedness in society, thereby provoking parallel processes of state formation. The persistent global constraints within which the African nation-state operates and the imposition of neoliberal structural adjustment programmes forced the state to deregulate its economy and curtail bureaucratic control. The frail and ineffective postcolonial state has provoked citizen action channelled via a range of organisations but this has not always resulted in a more responsive state.

This section starts with a historical exploration by Sabelo Ndlovu-Gatsheni of different understandings of African resistance in previous scholarly work (Chapter 2). The key argument of this chapter is that while anti-colonial resistance has been well-documented, less attention has been devoted to the way in which Africans have resisted postcolonial domination, thus appearing to suggest that decolonisation marked the end of Africa's history of domination and resistance. While African(ist) historians narrated history as a sequence of instances of domination and resistance, postcolonial scholars subsequently emphasised the complex, hybrid, entangled encounters between the coloniser and the colonised. Engaging with the work of Latin-American scholars, part of the decoloniality school, Ndlovu-Gatsheni argues that African resistance in the postcolonial period should be located within the context of global imperial designs and colonial matrices of power, reinforced by the way in which the postcolonial state has largely reproduced its colonial predecessor and its lack of embeddedness in society, thereby continuously provoking struggles between political elites and ordinary citizens.

Bettina von Lieres's contribution in Chapter 3 concentrates on 'mediated citizen mobilisation', which she understands as the way in which marginalised citizens come to rely on mediators or interlocutors to trigger their actions and strategies. Comparing instantiations of citizenship in the fragile democracy of Angola and the more established democracy of post-apartheid South Africa, she demonstrates the way in which citizenship is practised in cases where the state is absent, ineffective, distant and unable or unwilling to provide services. With her analysis, von Lieres shows that in contexts where there is a longer history of citizen mobilisation, such as in South Africa, the HIV/AIDS advocacy group, the Treatment Action Campaign (TAC), acts as an important mediator between political actors with access to medical knowledge and state/political networks, and the vast majority of the organisation's working and poor membership who do not. While the TAC's actual forms of mobilisation, South Africa's existing political culture, and its distinct history of social mobilisation enabled the organisation to provoke greater state responsiveness to citizens' demands and better access to anti-retrovirals, the activities of the Angolan umbrella body of local associations representing small-scale farmers, the Federation of Representative Associations of Dombe Grande (NRA), did not provoke greater responsiveness from the state but primarily increased citizens' knowledge of their rights and enhanced their capacity to mobilise for their rights. By stressing the need to move beyond a focus on formal organisations, Von Lieres highlights the importance of taking into account diverse forms of citizen action, ranging from highly localised and often spontaneous grassroots mobilisations to more considered engagements with powerful actors such as local states or national governments.

Embodied modes of resistance and the postcolonial state

Part II examines forms of resistance emerging in the aftermath of the severe disruptions to African livelihoods that have been the result of structural adjustment and conflict. While economic deregulation, liberalisation and privatisation forced many Africans into retrenchment, leaving them with no option but to survive as vendors or traders in the informal economy, global neo-liberal principles were also expressed through the desires of the postcolonial state to create 'world class cities' and the aspirations of ordinary people to become 'world class consumers'. The deregulation of the economy coincided with a re-regulation and confinement of space so as to create 'orderly' urban centres. Similarly, the commercialisation of agriculture resulted in a forced re-arrangement of arable land away from food to cash crops. However, apart from these constraints imposed on the allocation of space, the rise of the internet resulted in a doubling of physical and virtual space, enabling young Africans to directly confront global sources of power through newly emergent transnational networks. Within these spatial re-arrangements, which have been both constraining and enabling, the body has emerged as a powerful site of resistance, defying regulations imposed by state bureaucrats, challenging conventional norms around youth behaviour and dress, and refusing submission to commercial modes of agricultural production.

In the first contribution in this section, Ilda Lindell and Markus Ihalainen examine the subaltern practices of insurgent space-making by street traders in the context of Western-inspired models of urban planning in Nairobi, Kenya. Challenging romantic accounts of subaltern, subversive urban agency, the chapter offers a more nuanced account of the way in which street traders relate to local authorities as well as the power relationships they forge among themselves. Lindell and Ihalainen's analysis proceeds from the contestations around the construction of Muthurwa hawkers market in Nairobi's central business district. The market constituted an attempt by the City Council of Nairobi to gain control over large numbers of street vendors who were perceived as unruly subjects, incompatible with the idea of a 'modern, orderly city'. Spatially fixing the hawkers and tying them down to specific slots would not only make them traceable and legible, but also enable the authorities to more effectively tax an otherwise mobile population, potentially increasing the revenues of the local government. While informal traders are often considered to be autonomous from the state, circumventing its regulations, the authors demonstrate that the construction of the hawkers market was partly initiated by, and derived support from, a street trader association, thus problematising binary accounts of domination and resistance and demonstrating the entangled relationship between local authorities and street traders. However, as the disadvantages of the new spatial regulations were increasingly felt and the limited capacity of the state and its agents to systematically enforce those regulations became evident, street vendors not only ignored market regulations, but also reclaimed the city streets as their space of operation. As the account shows, resistance did not take the form of a collective, well-organised movement, but, à la James Scott (1990) and James Holston (2009), of quiet insurgent practices that nevertheless carry political relevance. Furthermore, Lindell and Ihalainen's study also narrates the highly divergent experiences of the relocation among vendors in both economic and political terms, thus problematising the idea that the subaltern can be ascribed with a distinct and coherent identity anchored in an easily identifiable subject position.

In Chapter 5, Basile Ndjio analyses the flamboyant lifestyle of young Cameroonian tricksters, known as *feymen*. He contends that African youths are far from being hapless victims of corrupt and clientelist governments but instead have managed to invent new opportunities for enrichment in a context of austerity and drastic structural adjustment measures. Through sophisticated business frauds, large-scale deceptions and confidence tricks, marginalised African urban youth have succeeded in gaining access to material and financial resources from which they were previously excluded (cf. Obadare 2007). Many young Cameroonian tricksters experienced social and economic marginalisation in their home country, either because of their underprivileged social backgrounds or because of their ethnic origins. Due to dwindling employment as a result of the imposition of structural adjustment programmes, young Cameroonians saw their chance of finding a permanent job in the formal sector, and most notably in the public service, narrowed considerably. In this context, *feymania* became a prime means of gaining access to financial and material resources, enabling people to enjoy full citizenship while bypassing the role of the postcolonial state in both the production and (re)distribution of wealth. While initially *feymen* primarily targeted politico-bureaucratic elites or wealthy businessmen connected to the Cameroonian ruling party, they increasingly began to direct themselves to white middle-class politicians, professionals, businessmen or entrepreneurs in the mid-1990s. Hence, as Ndjio points out, young professional tricksters perceived their actions as constituting a form of resistance, not only to African postcolonial politico-bureaucratic elites, but also to global capitalism. Instead of mimicking the criminalisation of the state in Africa (as conventional accounts tend to argue), *feymania* has challenged the rules of global capitalism and questioned the ethical codes, principles and laws that govern economic activities and commercial transactions at both local and international levels. This reinvention has compelled many Western governments to set up anti-fraud units and forced many international banks to invest millions of dollars in tightening their banking security against the theft of identity, thus destabilising the hegemonic order that Western developed countries have always maintained in their commercial and economic transactions with African countries.

Susan Thomson's contribution traces the ways in which rural (southern) Rwandans navigate their lives against the background of a top-down state-imposed official narrative of national unity and reconciliation in which only Tutsi are victims of the genocide and Hutu are morally responsible for it, hence silencing individual lived experiences. In post-genocide Rwanda, state power is primarily exercised at the local level in the form of directives from the central government and through the strict monitoring of the ability and willingness of local leaders to implement government orders effectively and efficiently. Rural Rwandans are subject to the exercise of the power granted to local leaders and must conform to the government's authoritarian directives in the name of national unity and reconciliation. Central to the exercise of oppressive state power at the level of the Rwandan rural resident are the government's ambitions to transform a predominantly subsistence agricultural sector into a large-scale engine for economic growth. Based on a detailed textual analysis of interview transcripts, Thomson concludes that rural Rwandans are far from being apolitical, passive and ignorant individuals who need government officials to teach them how to behave in the 'new' Rwanda. Instead, they exercise tactical forms of compliance to give the appearance of obedience to elite policy directives. While these practices have yet to translate into collective political consciousness, Thomson argues that Rwandans at the lower rungs of the social hierarchy are becoming aware of their personal ability to challenge government through their everyday acts of resistance to its many demands. These findings point to a nascent political activism that, whilst cognisant of potential missteps, struggles to demand a more equitable distribution of wealth.

Popular culture as discursive forms of resistance

While Part II highlighted the body as a crucial site of resistance, Part III's emphasis is on disembodied forms of resistance powerfully mediated through a range of texts, words and expressions. Arguably the body is still essential in communicating and performing these discursive forms of resistance, but words are more crucial in conveying their meaning. While formal mass media such as television, radio and the press in Africa have often been constrained in resisting state or corporate power due to censorship practices or specific – often transnational – ownership patterns, popular culture has been a crucial space allowing for occasional 'moments of freedom' (Fabian 1998), enabling the ruled to resist their rulers. In the context of an authoritarian state such as Nigeria under military dictatorship, the musician Fela Kuti not only offered powerful social commentary on postcolonial political elites but also targeted the global, fundamentally unequal system of power relations produced by histories of slavery, colonialism and apartheid, and reproduced through the United Nations system. Similarly, in post-apartheid South Africa – described by many as a 'liberal democracy' irrespective of the existence of major social and economic inequities – stand-up comedy and humour have been important in ridiculing the state but also in challenging the remnants of coloniality as inherited through histories of racism. While race often continues to be part of the 'unspeakable' in formal mass media, stand-up comedy has been able to confront this taboo topic more readily.

In the first contribution to this section, Chapter 7, Innocentia Mhlambi examines political laughter by South African comedians such as Eugene Khoza and serious political commentary by political analysts such as Andile Mngxitama. Her chapter assesses the extent to which 'comic discourses' either constitute forms of resistance which underscore a new mode of participatory politics, or represent a reinvention of old forms of resistance to which officialdom has grown immune. In South Africa, according to Mhlambi, the post-1994 neoliberal policy shift of the ruling African National Congress (ANC) had far-reaching repercussions in all spheres of life, to such an extent that the disaffected group's attempts to find a common voice by reversing to known forms of rallying consciousness around common aspirations have run into difficulties because of the rampant expansion of a conspicuous consumerist culture and concomitant depoliticisation of discourse. Mhlambi argues that South African comedians' performances largely work within the broader frameworks of depoliticising politics, neutralising the public sphere through laughter and contributing to the disappearance of a critical discourse in the popular imagination. While Khoza's jokes can be viewed as redirecting listeners' criticism away from contentious issues, Mngxitama's political commentary, on the other hand, firmly locates him within a space where new forms of resistance could be engineered through collaboration with the masses. Mhlambi concludes that whereas there is no lack of resistance to the power abuses of the post-1994 ANC-led government in South Africa, a large section of the population that would have normally represented the subaltern has been subsumed into mainstream political thinking through concession and other modes of ideological control that have brought them into a conspicuous consumerist culture. Echoing Lindell and Ihalainen, she demonstrates that the subalterns are not always situated in opposition to those in power, but instead continuously face co-optation by those in power.

Grace Musila interrogates South African stand-up comedy's engagement with the thorny question of race relations in public life and explores the possibilities of humour as a vehicle of transgressive engagement with a problematic racial status quo in South Africa. Beneath the seemingly clichéd deployment of racial stereotypes, elements of popular lore and fragments of the everyday, South African comedians use ambivalence as a strategic self-location that facilitates the breaking of the various silences around 'taboo' questions of race relations, while allowing them to articulate alternative readings that challenge hegemonic 'common senses' at the core of South African public life. The combination of stereotypes and ambivalence enables stand-up comedians to convene conversations about elements of race relations in South Africa, which are often wrapped up in the thick silence of political correctness and implicit forms of censorship which police the boundaries of 'the speakable'. As such, Musila argues, stand-up comedy surfaces the cracks that fracture the rainbow nation project by using laughter to ease these 'taboo' issues into the terrain of 'the speakable'. However, ironically, it is precisely in its deployment of stereotype and ambivalence at the moment of 'speaking the unspeakable' that much South African comedy paradoxically opens up 'the unspeakable' to the risk of secondary silencing in form of discursive containment and co-option. Musila's contribution therefore offers a more complex account of the workings of power and resistance by arguing that while the practice of taboo-breaking can be seen as an act of resistance, it simultaneously reproduces power through the invoking of stereotypical accounts of race and gender associated with South African stand-up comedy.

In Chapter 9, Jendele Hungbo examines the way in which popular Nigerian musician Fela Anikulapo-Kuti's 1989 song, 'Beasts of No Nation' undermined the production and reproduction of dominant power structures at both the local and the global levels. He shows that music has the potential not just for cultural agency but also for playing a pedagogical role in the lives of those who consume it. In his music, Hungbo contends, Fela recalls the role of the agentic popular performer who never keeps quiet whenever he sees things go amiss around him but who bears the responsibility of alerting society to dystopian developments which have implications for its growth and direction. 'Beasts of No Nation' touches on three major historical moments that have dealt major blows on the African continent: slavery, colonialism and apartheid (in South Africa), presenting his audience with a dramatic re-enactment of collective agony applicable to colonised and oppressed people across Africa. The song reconstructs the agonies of liberation struggles in different parts of Africa in a show of solidarity with subalterns throughout the continent. In this way, it can be interpreted as a response to the oppression of the defenceless masses that characterised colonial rule as well as post-independence dictatorships in Africa. However, as Hungbo demonstrates, 'Beasts of No Nation' does not merely challenge profound injustices on the African continent but also calls into question the relevance of the United Nations as a global mediator among states, chiefly by drawing an analogy between 'beastly' nature and 'human' behaviour, by pointing to the hypocrisy inherent in the very idea of nations which are ordinarily not at peace with one another claiming to come together to form a 'united' front in an organisation, and by highlighting the skewed power relations among member states expressed in the veto power of members of the UN Security Council. In exposing these hypocrisies, especially as they concern the experience of struggling postcolonial countries in Africa, through his music, Fela extends his radical evaluation of the power relations at multiple levels. Emphasising the crucial relevance of popular culture, Hungbo deftly demonstrates the importance of moving away from the normative search for civil society within the praxis of formal non-state institutions to a more nuanced appreciation of the potential of music as embodying civic agency and resistance.

Publics as everyday sites of resistance

In the context of processes of political and economic liberalisation in the aftermath of the Cold War, the abolishment of state censorship, the liberalisation of the airwaves and the emergence of private media institutions have been important in constituting new publics in Africa, enabling citizens to partake in new platforms of political participation and to debate the performance of the state on an everyday basis, thereby gaining the opportunity to converse with strangers beyond their immediate physical location. New publics have emerged around phone-in radio programmes broadcast by local stations and through online discussion platforms on the internet. These are potential sites and spaces through which new forms of resistance could be mediated (as was also powerfully demonstrated by the catalytic role of social networks in the context of the Arab Spring) but as the chapters in Part IV demonstrate, these platforms do not in themselves always mobilise resistance. More than anything, they constitute important arenas through which people shape identities and imagine communities of belonging.

In the first contribution, Dorothea Schulz explores the interlocking of mass media technologies, call-in radio programmes, and conventions of social interaction and debate against the backdrop of a new politics of local identity and belonging in Mali. Whereas most studies assess the potential of local radio stations to foster a democratic culture and offer political-critical information, Schulz's chapter examines how local radio broadcasts resonate with listeners' everyday concerns on one side, and with long-standing expectations about the community-building effects of debate and public interaction on the other. Based on normative, Habermasian notions of the public sphere, media scholars often focus attention on the 'alternative' spaces that media institutions create for civic activism, and the platform they provide for the sharing of political information and debate. Music and talk radio are considered mostly with regard to their potential to extend beyond 'mere entertainment' by clearing a space for democratic debate. Such an analysis would be tempting in the Malian context given the way in which political liberalisation coincided with the mushrooming of local radio broadcasting, hereby offering new possibilities for popular participation, democratic access and transparency afforded by local radio stations. However, although local radio stations certainly contributed to the disruption of a former state monopoly over media discourse and promotion of national culture, in her ethnographic study of rural radio listeners in southern Mali, Schulz found that they often criticised what they deemed the 'political' uses of local radio that, they felt, would not foster 'political participation'. To them, the principal goal of local radio was to broadcast 'conversation' and 'our music' for the purpose of 'furthering social bonds'. 'Political information' and 'critical speech' were considered the antitheses of this kind of sociable conversation. Conversely, Schulz explains that the tremendous popularity of local talk-radio broadcasts and music programmes in Mali was because of their deep resonance with the aesthetic preferences and moral concerns of radio listeners. Consumption of these radio broadcasts generates, if only temporarily and fleetingly, experiences of a collective 'we'. Local radio stations allow listeners to express and reflect on their positions within a national 'community'. Deviating from Habermas' rational account of the public sphere, Schulz thus demonstrates the importance of bringing closer attention to the affective dimensions of the processes by which listeners identify themselves with and attach themselves to a broader community. A narrow focus on resistance or political subversion would not capture the complex resonances that interactive radio formats and music broadcasts generate as a medium for feelings of attachment and belonging.

Echoing the importance of the affective dimension of cultural products – in this case political cartoons, in the final chapter Daniel Hammett explores the diachronical account formed by South African cartoonist Zapiro's depictions of President Jacob Zuma and popular responses to these images as expressed in responses posted to social networking sites and South African online newspapers. As Hammett explains, the production of meaning from a cartoon involves not only the conceptualisation and construction of the image by the cartoonist but also the viewer's decoding and processing of the image. Hence, audiences cannot be viewed as passive or reactive recipients of cartoons, but are in fact active agents. For Hammett, more detailed engagements with audience responses to political cartoons and satire are vital in order to gain a deeper understanding of the ways in which resistance and opposition may be mobilised, as well as the ways in which ideas and ideologies are received and contested by different audiences. Such consideration moves beyond the assumption that satire mobilises and/or reflects resistance and dissent, to question how the processes implicit in critical engagements and citizenship are engaged and played out. He argues that the vibrancy of the responses posted in reaction to Zapiro's cartoons reflects the existence of a dynamic public sphere, emphasising the socially subjective nature of the decoding of cartoons (as acts of resistance), although the demagogy and intolerance of certain posters towards differing viewpoints, as well as calls for a less critical media, indicate potential challenges to this space. The multiplicity of engagements and competing readings of a political cartoon contribute to a heterogeneous array of resistances – including resistance to the expression of resistance. For Hammett, it is in these complexities that nuanced understandings of the contested practices, power and performance of resistance need to be understood, not only in relation to state-society relations but also between and within communities and society.

Power and powerlessness in a neo-liberal age

At the heart of this book is an attempt to understand contemporary forms of resistance in Africa, focusing, through multi-disciplinary lenses, on the manifold ways in which power is experienced, exercised, absorbed and resisted. By departing from the received wisdom in which civil society and/or the public sphere are understood in, and assumed to be always expressive through, organisational and formal terms, we present readers with interesting, but often overlooked, interstices of power and powerlessness as they manifest in the push and pull of resistance in contemporary Africa.

The significance of this volume lies in its engagement with the exuberant interest in civil society and the public sphere in Africa since the end of the Cold War. While most works on state-society relations in

Africa during this period have focused on organised, wide-ranging and widespread forms of confrontation, struggle, conflict, opposition or defiance, the chapters in this volume not only examine compelling examples of such forms of resistance, but also invite engagement with everyday forms of resistance which do not necessarily provoke immediate or highly-visible change. We valorise such forms of resistance not only because they create the space for personal and social autonomy for the actors, but more importantly because they validate the humanity of those who have been short-changed, up-staged, or displaced (socially and spatially) by the economic and political ideologies imposed and promoted by an ascendant neo-liberalism.

Furthermore, we use existing social realities in Africa to speak simultaneously to both the elite and subaltern literature; while providing important perspectives both on macro and micro social processes that determine, establish, endorse, encourage, advance and promote power; or social processes that contest, deconstruct, oppose, invalidate, demote, contain/constrain and defame power. At the macro–level, whether in terms of the 'global technologies of domination' which endorse and advance the interest of global power (based on Euro-Christian-Modernist imaginary) and the resistance they provoke (Chapter 2), or in the 'politics of citizen action and public engagement' (Chapter 3), we see manifold instantiations of resistance and how such resistance and the particular modes in which they are performed are *always already* determined by historical forces, yet re-determinable, and indeed, re-determined by new realities. For us, as stated earlier, power in the postcolony is relational and state sovereignty is fractured. Power is not only vested in the nation-state but crucially constrained by a set of global factors – whether implicitly via inherited ethnic or racial forms of power associated with the colonial state, or directly by international financial institutions such as the World Bank and the International Monetary Fund through the economic and political constraints they imposed via structural adjustment and the concomitant regimes of neo-liberalism that on many occasions have been internalised and domesticated by the postcolonial state. Thus, given the nature of power, resistance should be understood within a much broader context than simply responding to factors confined within the boundaries of the nation-state.

On a positive note, we also recognise the natural predilection of human beings to seek dignity, even while engaged in the mess of the fundamental preoccupation with *living life* as it can be lived in the everyday context. At the micro-level, this volume reveals the embodied nature of resistance in the postcolony through, for instance, 'the politics of confinement and mobility' in Kenya (Chapter 4) and through resistance in post-genocide Rwanda, not so much through action, but more fundamentally, through 'political consciousness' (Chapter 6), thus revealing how what Foucault calls 'capillary of power' can also produce in Africa a *capillary of* resistance. We also show how young West Africans face up to, and sometimes face-down, global capitalism through crime, or what is called 'hustling' (Chapter 5) – thus intervening in the sociological discourse about crime and criminality as a product of social inequalities, rather than as pathology. In considering musicality as civic activism (Chapter 9), and the comedic (Chapters 8 and 11) and the dialogic (Chapter 11) as spaces and instances of resistance, we go beyond either exclusively state-centric or exclusively society-centric approaches which castigate the African state and/or celebrate the African society.

In so doing, we show that because (i) power exists both in the state and in society, and because (ii) power is both enabling and constraining (as evident in the relationships among social institutions), it is imperative to focus on relationships brought about by social processes and the relationships between the powerful and the powerless. When all else fails, even in the face of awesome power, we see in this volume that the powerless can not only preserve the power of the comedic but they can also apprehend reality at the level of their consciousness – even if they are unable to alter the fundaments of actually existing social relations.

The book presents not just different perspectives on the fundamental and contingent nature of non-organisational responses to power in contemporary Africa, but also the manifold ways in which Africans and social formations in the continent mobilise or utilise their agencies in responding to, endorsing, encouraging, advancing and promoting power, while also contesting, deconstructing, invalidating, demoting, constraining and defaming it. The volume instructs that power and powerlessness should be understood less as binaries in actual social processes in Africa, but more as social action simultaneously instanced in the everyday experiences of Africans in the global age.

References

Abbink, J., de Bruijn, M. and van Walraven, K. (eds) (2003). *Rethinking resistance: revolt and violence in African history*. Leiden: Brill.

Abrahamsen, R. (2000). *Disciplining democracy: development discourse and good governance in Africa*. London: Zed Books.

Abu-Lughod, L. (1990). The romance of resistance: tracing transformations of power through Bedouin women. *American Ethnologist*, 17(1), 41–55.

Bayart, J.-F. (1993). *The state in Africa: the politics of the belly*. London and New York: Longman.

Bayart, J.-F., Ellis, S. and Hibou, B. (eds) (1999). *The criminalization of the state in Africa*. Oxford: James Currey.

Chabal, P. (2009). *Africa: The politics of suffering and smiling*. London: Zed Books.

Chabal, P., Engel, U. and de Haan, L. (2007). *African alternatives*. Leiden: Brill.
Chan, S. (2002). *Composing Africa: civil society and its discontents*. Tampere, Finland: Tampere Peace Research Institute Occasional Paper 86.
Comaroff, J. L. and Comaroff, J. (eds) (1999). *Civil society and the political imagination in Africa: critical perspectives*. Chicago, IL: University of Chicago Press.
Comaroff, J. L. and Comaroff, J. (2006). Law and disorder in the postcolony (pp. 1–56). In J. Comaroff and J. L. Comaroff (eds), *Law and disorder in the postcolony*. Chicago, IL: University of Chicago Press.
Fabian, J. (1998). *Moments of freedom: anthropology and popular culture*. Charlottesville, VA: University of Virginia Press.
Foucault, M. (1980) (ed. & trans. Colin Gordon). *Power/knowledge: selected interviews and other writings, 1972–1977*. Brighton: Harvester Press.
Gitlin, T. (2012). *Occupy nation: the roots, the spirit, and the promise of Occupy Wall Street*. New York: HarperCollins.
Graeber, D. (2013). *The democracy project: a history, a crisis, a movement*. New York: Spiegel & Grau.
Harbeson, J. W., Rothchild, D. S. and Chazan, N. (1994). *Civil society and the state in Africa*. Boulder, CO: Lynne Rienner.
Haynes, D. and Prakash, G. (1991). *Contesting power: resistance and everyday social relations in South Asia*. Oxford: Oxford University Press.
Holston, J. (2009). *Insurgent citizenship: disjunctions of democracy and modernity in Brazil*. Princeton, NJ: Princeton University Press.
Huntington, S. P. (1991). *The third wave: democratization in the late twentieth century*. Norman, OK: University of Oklahoma Press.
Jackson, R. H. (1990). *Quasi-states: sovereignty, international relations and the Third World*. Cambridge: Cambridge University Press.
Jensen, D. (2002). *The culture of make believe*. New York: Context Books.
Konings, P. and Foeken, D. (2006). *Crisis and creativity: exploring the wealth of the African neighbourhood*. Leiden: Brill.
Lewis, D. (2001). *Civil society in non-Western contexts: reflections on the 'usefulness' of a concept*. London School of Economics Civil Society Working Paper 13. London: London School of Economics, Centre for Civil Society.
Lynch, M. (2013). *The Arab uprising: the unfinished revolutions of the New Middle East*. New York: Public Affairs.
Mamdani, M. (1996). *Citizen and subject: contemporary Africa and the legacy of late colonialism*. Princeton, NJ: Princeton University Press.
Mbembe, A. (2001). *On the postcolony*. Berkeley, CA: University of California Press.
Mbembe, A. (2006). On politics as a form of expenditure (pp. 299–335). In J. Comaroff and J. L. Comaroff (eds), *Law and disorder in the postcolony*. Chicago, IL: University of Chicago Press.
McMurray, D. and Ufheil-Somers, A. (eds) (2013). *The Arab revolts: dispatches on militant democracy in the Middle East*. Bloomington, IN: Indiana University Press.
Mitchell, W. J. T., Harcourt, B. E. and Taussig, M. (2013). *Occupy: three inquiries in disobedience*. Chicago, IL: University of Chicago Press.
Obadare, E. (2004). The alternative genealogy of civil society and its implications for Africa: Notes for further research. *Africa Development*, 29(4) 1–19.
Obadare, E. (2005a). A crisis of trust: history, politics, religion and the polio

controversy in Northern Nigeria. *Patterns of Prejudice*, 39(3), 265–84.
Obadare, E. (2005b). Second thoughts on civil society: the state, civic associations and the antinomies of the public sphere in Africa. *Journal of Civil Society*, 1(3), 267–81.
Obadare, E. (2006). Playing politics with the mobile phone: civil society, big business and the state in Nigeria. *Review of African Political Economy*, 33(107), 93–111.
Obadare, E. (2007). White collar fundamentalism: interrogating youth religiosity on Nigerian university campuses. *Journal of Modern African Studies*, 45(4), 517–37.
Obadare, E. (2009). The uses of ridicule: humour, 'infrapolitics' and civil society in Nigeria. *African Affairs*, 108(431), 241–61.
Obadare, E. (2010a). Resistance through ridicule (Africa) (pp. 444–6). In J. Downing (ed.), *Encyclopaedia of social movement media*. London: Sage.
Obadare, E. (2010b). State of travesty: jokes and the logic of socio-cultural improvisation in Africa. *Critical African Studies*, 2(4), 92–112.
Obadare, E. (2011). Civil society in sub-Saharan Africa (pp. 183–94). In M. Edwards (ed.), *The Oxford handbook of civil society*. Oxford: Oxford University Press.
Obadare, E. and Adebanwi, W. (2013). Introduction: Democracy and prebendalism: emphases, provocations, and elongations (pp. 1–22). In W. Adebanwi and E. Obadare (eds.), *Democracy and prebendalism in Nigeria: critical interpretations*. New York: Palgrave Macmillan.
Probst, P. and Spittler, G. (2004). *Between resistance and expansion: explorations of local vitality in Africa*. Munster: Lit Verlag.
Ranger, T. (1977). The people in African resistance: a review. *Journal of Southern African Studies*, 4(1), 125–46.
Scott, J. (1985). *Weapons of the weak: everyday forms of peasant resistance*. New Haven, CT: Yale University Press.
Scott, J. (1990). *Domination and the arts of resistance: hidden transcripts*. New Haven, CT: Yale University Press.
Skocpol, T. (1979). *States and social revolutions: a comparative analysis of France, Russia and China*. Cambridge: Cambridge University Press.
Skocpol, T. (1994). *Social revolutions in the modern world*. Cambridge: Cambridge University Press.
Tilly, C. (1978). *From mobilization to revolution*. London: Longman.
Willems, W. (2009). Joking via SMS: new publics and convergence culture in Zimbabwe, conference paper presented at 'Hidden Dimensions of the Zimbabwe Crisis Conference', University of the Witwatersrand, Johannesburg, 1–2 July 2009.
Willems, W. (2010). Beyond dramatic revolutions and grand rebellions: everyday forms of resistance during the 'Zimbabwe crisis'. *Communicare*, 29, 1–17.
Willems, W. (2011a). At the crossroads of the formal and popular: convergence culture and new publics in Zimbabwe (pp. 46–62). In H. Wasserman (ed.), *Popular media, democracy and development in Africa*. Abingdon: Routledge.
Willems, W. (2011b). Comic strips and 'the crisis': Postcolonial laughter and coping with everyday life in Zimbabwe. *Popular Communication*, 9(2), 126–45.

Willems, W. (2011c). Political jokes in Zimbabwe (pp. 410–12). In J. Downing (ed.), *Encyclopaedia of social movement media*. London: Sage.

Willems, W. (2012). Interrogating public sphere and popular culture as theoretical concepts on their value in African Studies. *Africa Development*, 37(1), 11–26.

Part I

POSTCOLONIAL STATE FORMATION & PARALLEL INFRASTRUCTURES

Part I

2 Global Technologies of Domination

From Colonial Encounters to the Arab Spring

Sabelo J. Ndlovu-Gatsheni

Introduction

Resistance in Africa is primarily a response to the coloniality reproduced by the postcolony and global multilateral institutions such as the World Trade Organisation, the International Monetary Fund, and the World Bank. Coloniality is the location of power within which resistance emerges, radiates and is disciplined into emancipatory reformism bereft of revolutionary transformation. It is itself a central motif of global imperial designs, but it must not be confused with colonialism. Colonialism entails a political and economic relation in which sovereignty of a nation and a people 'rests on the power of another nation, which makes such a nation an empire' (Maldonado-Torres 2007: 243). Coloniality emerged as a result of colonialism but it survives it. It is a power structure that defines and permeates 'culture, labour, intersubjective relations, and knowledge production well beyond the strict limits of colonial administrations' (Maldonado-Torres 2007: 243). Coloniality is embedded in books, cultural patterns, common sense, self-image, aspirations of self, and other various aspects of African experience since the time of colonial encounters, and '[i]n a way, as modern subjects we breathe coloniality all the time and every day' (Maldonado-Torres 2007: 243).

Coloniality operates through assumption of various disguises and markers including religion, ethnicity, epistemology, and even notions of beauty and its opposites. As such it forms an ideal entry point to analyse the unfolding character and dynamics of African forms of resistance. Because coloniality operates on a world scale, resistance too must be pitched on this level as well as on a local scale where are featured such dynamics as domination and repression, negotiation and complicity, conversations, conversions and contestations, blending and bricolage, mimicry and hybridity, partnerships and patronage, as well as Orientalising and Occidentalising processes. Coloniality encapsulates global historical and discursive processes/events such as mercantilism, the slave trade, imperialism, colonialism, apartheid, decolonisation, neo-colonialism, the Cold War, structural adjustment programmes, neo-liberalism, the Washington Consensus, the end of the Cold War, 9/11 and the War on Terror, as well as globalisation and the current capitalist financial crisis.

Africans have actively played a part in and responded to all these global events as they impinged on their bodies, minds and spaces, most often not as they intended and with diminished powers of determination. Resistance emerges as African people struggle to make sense of the murky present and thrusting out into the mysterious future, within the confines of a historically-structured capitalist, patriarchal, Western-centric, Christian-centric, hetero-normative, racially hierarchised and asymmetrically organised postmodern world system, created by global imperial designs and underpinned by colonial matrices of power (Mignolo 2007; Quijano 2007; Grosfoguel 2011). Today African forms of resistance have to contend with global coloniality that is manned by global financial institutions as well as industrial-military complexes such as the Pentagon and the North Atlantic Treaty Organisation (NATO).

This chapter adopts coloniality as the entry point into understanding the broader dimensions of power, domination, *subjectivation* and resistance in Africa. The Arab Spring is a recent example of how ordinary people are seeking freedom within the state. However, global imperial designs, which are always hovering above the continent monitoring African activities, soon intervened – particularly in Libya to depose and kill Colonel Muammar Gaddafi under the cover of humanitarian intervention and furtherance of the agenda of democratisation. This example indicates beyond doubt that African forms of resistance are always entangled in coloniality as a global power structure that dilutes, truncates and influences the direction of resistance away from direct confrontation with global imperial designs that have been in place from conquest up to reformism.

Previous conceptualisations and articulations of African forms of resistance have tended to ignore the fact that resistance takes place within a discursive terrain of coloniality, which works as a surveillance tool to prevent any form of revolutionary change. Within coloniality, every art of resistance is either disciplined into emancipatory reformism or criminalised as anti-systemic and barbaric, if not terroristic. Those forms of resistance like the Arab Spring that received global support often take the neo-liberal format and do not shake the foundations of Euro-American hegemony. Their grammar is pro-global neo-liberal equilibrium and offers opportunities for global technologies of domination to sneak in under the guise of humanitarianism, the 'right to protect' and the mission to export democracy and human rights to those areas designated by Euro-American power as outposts of tyranny. Therefore, reading African forms of resistance from a decolonial perspective reveals their entrapment within coloniality which explains their limits and failure to result in real change that transforms the present global power structures.

This chapter is organised in four sections. The first section provides a broad outline of global imperial designs that created colonial encounters that provoked African arts of resistance, ranged against such inimical processes as the slave trade and colonialism. The section also reveals the ideological and epistemic limits of previous forms of resistance that remained deeply interpellated by coloniality. The second section interrogates arts of resisting the postcolonial state which has largely reproduced coloniality. The third section analyses how the freedom of manoeuvre, that is freedom of the state, locked horns with ordinary people's struggles for human rights in the postcolony. The final section examines the Arab Spring and briefly assesses the future of resistance in Africa.

Resisting global imperial designs and colonial encounters

Archie Mafeje (2011: 35) posited that without 'prior existing exclusivist ontologies such as white racist categorisation and supremacist European self-identities in particular' there would be no Afrocentric forms of resistance taking the form of a 'vindicationist intellectual tradition'. Global imperial designs refer to the core technologies of modernity that underpinned its expansion into the non-Western parts of the world from the fifteenth century onwards. Race and Euro-American epistemology (particularly its techno-scientific knowledge claims) were used to classify and name the world according to Euro-Christian-Modernist imaginary (Magubane 2007). African peoples whose cultures and ways of life were not informed by the imperatives of Euro-Christian modernity were deemed to be barbarians or people who did not belong to history and had no history. Mapping, naming and representations of Africa and Africans as well as constructions of African identities were informed by a conception of humanity that was differentiated into binaries of inferior and superior, irrational and rational, primitive and civilised, traditional and modern (Mudimbe 1998).

Global imperial designs are a description of how '[i]t was from the West that the rest of the world is described, conceptualised, and ranked: that is, modernity is the self-description of Europe's role in history rather than an ontological historical process' (Mignolo 2005: 35). Simply put, global imperial designs are those processes that drove the making and reproduction of the current unequal world order and they are traceable to the European Renaissance and Christianisation in the fifteenth and sixteenth century. This was followed by the Enlightenment, mercantilism and the maritime trade in the sixteenth and seventeenth century. Industrialisation and imperialism in the eighteenth and nineteenth centuries commenced and were followed by modernisation and developmentalism in the mid-twentieth century. Neo-colonialism, neo-liberalism, the Washington Consensus and structural adjustment programmes dominated in the late twentieth century. United States super-power imperialism and NATO-driven imperial designs hidden behind the mantras of humanitarian interventions, fighting global terrorism and discourses of exporting democracy and human rights dominate at the beginning of the twenty-first century (Mignolo 1995, 2000; Ndlovu-Gatsheni 2012).

Of course, global imperial designs and colonial matrices of power emphasise the emergence of the Euro-American world as a sole Eurogenic creation and minimise the fact that Africa is embedded in the material and discursive foundations of Europe and America as embodiment of modernity. This is why it is important to situate arts of African resistance within the context of global imperial designs and colonial matrices of power as technologies of *subjectivation* that produced both the Euro-American world and the African world simultaneously (Miller 1990).

Since global imperial designs and colonial matrices of power were complex and diverse, African resistance had to be equally complex and diverse too. Early active and overt violence ranged against imperial and colonial violence which is exemplified by the Ndebele War against British South Africa Company forces in 1893 and the Ndebele-Shona Risings of 1896–97 in Zimbabwe; the Bambata Rebellion of 1906 in South Africa; the Maji Maji Rising of 1905–07 in East Africa and many others. These forms of resistance were depicted by nationalist historians as 'primary resistance' that laid the foundation for the modern mass nationalist and armed struggles of the 1960s and 1970s (Ranger 1968). Many scholars have dealt with how Africans resisted and 'participated' in the slave trade, how Africans resisted and 'collaborated' with the colonialists, how Africans actively prosecuted decolonial struggles including launching armed struggles against stubborn white settler regimes in Kenya, Algeria, Guinea-Bissau, Mozambique, Angola, Zimbabwe, Namibia and South Africa (Ranger 1985, 1967; Rodney 1989). The active resistance by Africans against slavery, colonial encroachment and established colonial regimes culminated in nationalist-inspired scholarship that reduced the African experience to a matter of 'domination and resistance' (Ranger 1986; Glassman 1995; Walraven and Abbink 2003).

This scholarship was dominant during the 1960s when African colonies were increasingly gaining political independence. A nationalist school of history emerged in Nigeria, Tanzania and Mozambique which read religious, labour, agrarian and other African protests as part of resistance to colonial domination. The British liberal historian Terence Ranger became a leading voice and able articulator of nationalist historiography with his *Revolt in Southern Rhodesia* (1967), which became a nationalist bible in Zimbabwe and beyond. But the key crisis in nationalist historiography of the 1960s was that African resistance was reduced to a political dimension and causally connected with nationalism and the politics of decolonisation. In the process, the complexities of colonial encounters that did not fit into domination and resistance were ignored. In short, an inflexible Manichean structure was created, informed by binaries of coloniser and colonised as fixed identities (Zeleza 1997; Ndlovu-Gatsheni 2007).

African forms of resistance never followed a direct or linear trajectory from primary resistance to nationalism to decolonisation and political independence. Some agitations were merely localised responses to concrete challenges posed by colonialism. Some Africans responded by embracing Christianity and modern education. Others appropriated global and Diaspora ideological resources such as liberalism, republicanism, trade unionism, Garveyism, pan-Africanism, and civil rights movements (Padmore 1956; Esedebe 1982; West 2002).

But the interventions of postcolonial theorists such as Edward Said (1978), Homi K. Bhabha (1994) and historians like Frederick Cooper (2003) and anthropologists such as John L. Comaroff and Jean Comaroff (1991, 1997) revolutionised studies of resistance and opened up colonial encounters to questions of power and discourse, and challenged meta-narratives of anti-colonialism. They introduced new concepts of mimicry, bricolage, hybridity, alienation, and other ambiguities and contradictions that were ignored by the orthodox nationalist historiographies of the 1960s. These new interventions transcended the old tendency of studying African resistance as always informed by materialism and made visible various dimensions of African people's agency.

The work of postcolonial theorists revealed how African resistance took complex forms including admixtures of tacit accommodation to the hegemonic colonial order while at the same time trying to appropriate some aspects of global imperial designs to advance the cause of African freedom and dignity. The example of the emergence of African Christians within the colonial terrain was part of how Africans appropriated ideological resources within the colonial order to advance the cause of their improvement (Ranger 1994). For instance, where colonial state coercion stifled overt political expression, the polysemic metaphors of the Bible offered a haven for the critical imagination (Comaroff and Comaroff 1991, 1997; Ndlovu-Gatsheni 2007). Postcolonial theorists deployed discourse analysis to demonstrate that global imperial designs and colonial matrices of power invented Africans as the 'other' and understood the colonial encounter as characterised by ambivalences and slippages which enabled negotiations, co-presence and even co-invention of the colonial order.

However, postcolonial interventions have come under serious criticism from historians like Paul Tiyambe Zeleza (2006). The genealogy of postcolonial studies is in the first place traced to intellectuals who were located inside the empire and is seen as part of imperialism's ideological armoury aimed at caricaturing African resistance and suggesting that Africans took an active part in their own enslavement and colonisation. Postcolonial thought's emphasis on hybridity, contingency, decentredness and ambivalence is said to result in stripping all cultures of historicity and density (Ahmad 1992). Zeleza (2006: 110) understood

African resistance as deep-rooted in nationalist humanism, enabling African struggles to recover and reaffirm their history and humanity that was arrested and seized by Euro-American hegemony through global imperial designs and colonial matrices of power.

To Zeleza (2006: 111), the aim of the nationalist imaginary of African resistance was to attain political, cultural, and economic liberation. This entailed seeking political independence and the creation of sovereign postcolonial nation-states as well as attempts to mobilise cultural and ideological resources from both pre-colonial pasts and Euro-American modernity as they actively engaged in 'modernizing their indigeneities and indigenizing their modernities' (Nyamnjoh 2006: 293). Nationalist-inspired African scholars are sceptical of postcolonial theorists' antipathy towards ideas of resistance, revolution, nation, class, history and reality as well as attempts to present imperialism and colonialism as 'shared cultures, negotiated discursive spaces' rather than violent impositions (Zeleza 2006: 124). The reality is that imperialism and colonialism have been upheld by physical force and epistemic violence rather than 'by ideas and images' (Zeleza 2006: 124).

The ubiquity of coloniality and the reality of incomplete decolonisation has given rise to a rather ironic but animated debate between nationalist historians and postcolonial theorists. The latter are criticised for 'the fixation on colonialism' as 'one of the greatest metanarratives of African history that nationalist historians worked so hard to decentre' (Zeleza 2006: 125). Postcolonial theorists criticised nationalist historians for nativism and the peddling of a metaphysics of difference that creates a neurosis of victimhood and leads to intellectual dead-ends. For example, Achille Mbembe (2002a, 2002b) blamed both Afro-Marxists and nationalist historians for a fixation on 'slavery, colonisation, and apartheid'. What emerges from these debates is a simple reality that coloniality constitutes the foundational problem lurking at the centre of the modern world system. Even if one cannot reduce the history of Africa to a seamless continuity in a long track of subjugations, there is no doubt that since the time of colonial encounters in the fifteenth century, colonialism and coloniality have continued to provoke diverse African responses and forms of resistance. The attainment of political independence (juridical freedom) did not amount to the end of coloniality. This is a point well captured by Grosfoguel (2007: 219):

> One of the most powerful myths of the twentieth century was the notion that the elimination of colonial administrations amounted to the decolonization of the world. This led to the myth of a 'postcolonial' world. The heterogeneous and multiple global structures put in place over a period of 450 years did not evaporate with the juridical-political decolonization of the periphery over the past 50 years. We continue to live under the same 'colonial power matrix'. With juridical-political decolonization we moved from a period of 'global colonialism' to the current period of 'global coloniality'.

In line with the above argument it becomes clear that analysis of technologies of domination and African resistance cannot be limited to the colonial order only. The postcolonial order became another theatre of *subjectivation* which resulted in the continuation of technologies of domination and resistance. New technologies of domination cascading from the postcolony provoked and engendered new arts of resistance, pitting the ordinary citizens against ruling elites in charge of the postcolonial state (Ndlovu-Gatsheni 2013).

The arts of resisting the postcolonial state

To gain a deeper understanding of the vicissitudes and tensions within the politics of juridical freedom and popular freedom, it is important to briefly analyse the nature and character of the post-1945 normative order within which the postcolonial state was born and under which ex-colonised peoples were expected to graduate from being subjects to citizens (Mamdani 1996). The end of the Second World War in 1945 witnessed the birth of a new global normative international order. The right of national self-determination was inscribed in the United Nations Charter. By 1948, a Universal Declaration of Human Rights was adopted that codified human rights as another major ingredient of the post-1945 global normative dispensation.

It was within this context that decolonisation gained a further boost from the fact that the post-1945 international system became dominated not by major colonial powers like Britain and France but by the United States of America and the Soviet Union as superpowers. Despite the fact that the two post-war superpowers became engrossed in complex Cold War rivalry, 'both of [them] by different logics favoured the dissolution of the colonial order' (Foltz 2002: 28). During this period, African freedom was simplistically defined in relation to ending direct colonial rule. This conception of freedom was articulated by Kwame Nkrumah (1963: 175) who stated: 'When I talk of freedom and independence for Africa, I mean that the vast African majority should be accepted as forming the basis of government in Africa'.

Most studies of decolonisation, with the exception of the work of Frantz Fanon (1968) and a few others produced in the 1960s, failed to capture the crucial fact that the departure of direct colonial rule resulted in the birth of undemocratic postcolonial states that inherited repressive structures and oppressive institutions created by colonial rule. African nationalists 'sought no other formula; even as they fought colonial power, their own education and socialisation had schooled them to hold the institutions of the imperial occupant in high regard as exemplary models of freedom' (Young 2002: 29). A state-centric concept of freedom emerged that ran counter to popular discourses of freedom. This conception of freedom by the African elites in charge of the postcolonial state marked the beginning of the crisis of the postcolonial nation-state project. One after another, the postcolonial states 'abandoned the multi-party political framework on the basis of which freedom from direct colonialism was attained and adopted single party rule or slid into military rule' (Laakso and Olukoshi 1996: 13–14). Once this process was on course, the state increasingly became predatory and unrepresentative. A majority of ordinary citizens struggled to free themselves from predatory postcolonial states. Victor Azarya and Naomi Chazan (1998: 110–11) argued that this struggle involved a shift from an 'engagement paradigm' to a 'disengagement paradigm' as the state failed to afford ordinary people material welfare and freedom.

But even the cataclysmic changes of the 1990s, described by Larry Diamond (1998: 263–71) as the 'second wind of change', did not succeed in facilitating the gaining of sovereignty by the ordinary people. Despite the so-called 'third wave of democracy' that swept Africa in the 1990s, extreme disdain for the sovereignty and freedom of ordinary people continued in countries like Libya, Egypt, Tunisia, and Zimbabwe. Citizens continued to be treated as subjects. As a result of the failure of the postcolonial state to afford former colonial subjects real citizenship rights, democracy and development, many African scholars have been very harsh on the African founding fathers of postcolonial states. African leaders have been criticised for being sell-outs that sold every ordinary African down the colonial drain and diluted the agenda of decolonisation.

However, a key limitation that is often ignored is that the postcolonial African state suffers from a lack of embeddedness in African society. It is not thoroughly decolonised. It is not imbued with African values. It is therefore largely irresponsive, unaccountable, and illegitimate in the eyes of those Africans who have endured its violence and vindictiveness. Ira William Zartman (2007: 30) posed the following question regarding the postcolonial state: 'Is there an African state now? Where is it headed? Is its trajectory similar to that on the other side of the Atlantic? And then, what is the alternative?'. Pita Ogaba Agbese and George Klay Kieh (2007) have emphasised the urgent need to democratise postcolonial states as part of their reconstitution and to make them relevant to the needs and aspirations of the majority of the peoples of Africa.

A body of critical literature, by such scholars as Tukumbi Lumumba-Kasongo (1994), Pierre Englebert (2000), Claude Ake (2000), Mueni wa Muiu and Guy Martin (2009) and others, has focused attention on the problems emanating from the character and structure of the postcolonial African state. For example, Ake emphasised how the postcolonial state was shaped by colonialism into an all-powerful and arbitrary political formation that set it on a collision course with the citizens from the time of its birth. The triumphant African nationalist leadership continued the colonial practice of turning against democracy. This was so because the achievement of political independence only changed the composition of the managers of the state but not the character of the state which remained much as it was in the colonial era.

Consequently the postcolonial state emerged as an apparatus of violence; its embeddedness within society was very shallow, its rootedness in popular social forces remained extremely narrow and this made it to rely for compliance on coercion rather than consent (Ake 2000). Ake's central argument and observations were echoed by Lumumba-Kasongo (1994: 58) who depicted the postcolonial African state as 'an institution of domination *par excellence*'.

Ake's interventions were also reiterated by Crawford Young (1994) and Mahmood Mamdani (1996) who closely studied the character of the colonial state which formed the template for the postcolonial state. They noted that it lacked three essential attributes that were found in other modern states and these were sovereignty, nationalism and external autonomy. Its crisis emanated from the fact that the colonial state was imposed by force of arms on African societies. At initial construction level, the colonial state did not even pretend to serve the interests of the colonised African people in terms of provision of services. Coercion became the DNA of the postcolonial state. As argued by wa Muiu and Martin (2009), the colonial state was 'essentially a foreign construct that could not possibly take root on African soil'. It even destroyed existing African indigenous civil society that had taken the form of age-set groups, etc. The postcolonial state was merely a deracialised and Africanised colonial formation that was never structurally decolonised to enable it to suit African demands and aspirations.

The situation was worse in Francophone Africa where with the exception of Guinea under Sékou Touré, postcolonial states were born with diminished sovereignty as they did not work to delink from French colonial tutelage. At birth the former French colonies had no control over foreign, economic, monetary and defence policies. In Anglophone Africa, Chinweizu (1975) noted that African nationalists had to sign agreements to uphold some negotiated neo-colonial compromises, including safeguarding primitively accumulated properties in the hands of white colonialists such as land and mines even before entering new offices.

Independence constitutions were written for the African leaders by the departing colonial masters. Wa Muiu and Martin (2009: 56) argue that Duncan Sandys – who was Britain's Secretary of State for Commonwealth Relations in 1960 – became a notorious expert in persuading African leaders to sign independence constitutions which did not favour the aspirations of the black majority through keeping African negotiators talking until they signed highly compromised decolonisation documents out of sheer exhaustion. Wa Muiu and Martin (2009: 56) concluded that:

> Thus decolonization was just a façade barely disguising the continuation of colonization by other means and leading to the mere 'flag' (or juridical) independence of utterly impotent and powerless quasi-states lacking the substance of sovereignty.

Uncritical celebrations of decolonisation as the proudest moment in African history have negatively impacted on ordinary people's lives, silencing them, and giving them false hope that through hard work they would harvest the fruits of freedom that were denied by colonialism. The postcolonial state itself was not free because multinational corporations and erstwhile metropolitan governments continued to control African economies in cohort with African leaders who ran African affairs on behalf of global capital. African leaders were themselves 'remote controlled' by the powerful leaders of Europe and America who governed the world. The difficult question to answer is whether it was really possible for African leaders to pursue an autonomous political, ideological and economic path without provoking a reaction from the ex-colonial powers?

This question is pertinent because those scholars who argued for the reconstitution and reconstruction of African postcolonial states on the basis of indigenous knowledges and institutions seemed to imply that Africa's founding fathers of postcolonial states had a choice not to ignore indigenous institutions as the template (wa Muiu and Martin 2009). At the same time they point to the cases of such leaders as Patrice Lumumba, Modibo Keita, Thomas Sankara, Mirien N'Gouabi, Samora Machel and Laurent-Désiré Kabila who lost their lives for the sin of trying to radically transform African states to serve the interests of their citizens (wa Muiu and Martin 2009). Those radical African leaders who survived assassination suffered sponsored military coup d'états like the one that toppled Nkrumah in 1966. This means that African leaders had to operate within an imperially created cul-de-sac where they had to act carefully, including choosing to suppress African people's aspirations and demands rather than provoking the anger of the Euro-American political league that was capable of disciplining those who deviated from the given script on governance and state management. Instead of delivering services to the people, African leaders engaged in deluding their own people by pretending to be in charge and inviting the hungry and angry population to partake annually in celebrations of flag independence that did not change their well-being.

Having inherited the colonial state together with its repressive apparatus, African leaders presided over a leviathan that was active in suffocating alternative popular struggles for freedom. The first group of people to react against the postcolonial state was the excluded elite who found themselves at the mercy of those who controlled the state. According to Ake (2000: 37), the excluded elite fought for incorporation, adding that 'Africa is in constant turmoil from struggles between people who must secure power and those who must access it by incorporation'. It was often the excluded elite that resorted to the mobilisation of ethnicity to build a political constituency to use in bargaining for power. On the other hand, there were ordinary masses of peasants and workers who struggled for economic incorporation and this demand propelled them to seek what became known as 'second independence', not from colonial masters but from the indigenous elite (Ake 2000: 47).

Ordinary citizens' struggles for freedom took various forms involving disengagement from the state, agitating for internal democratisation of the state, supporting opposition parties, trying to take control of the state, outright emigration, mocking the state, trying to influence state policy from within, agitating for secession and other more subtle and softer forms of resistance and engagement such as conviviality and use of music, jokes, comic strips and satire to reveal the vulgarity, debauchery and buffoonery of those in control of state power (Mbembe 1992a, 1992b, 2001).

In the face of internal opposition, the postcolonial state developed various survival techniques. Mbembe's work (1992b, 2001) focused on the ideological production of power within the postcolony and how this configuration of political power impinged on the development of relations between the state governors and the governed. Mbembe (1992a: 4) noted that postcolonial hegemony was created through the invention of new technologies and ideas of *subjectivation*, involving a selection of cultural repertoires and the dramatisation of power's magnificence. He further argued that the relations between leaders and citizens was shot through by a 'promiscuous' relationship, mediated by 'convivial' tensions as well as a 'zombification' of both the dominant and the dominated (Mbembe 1992a). The net effect of this relationship was that 'each robbed the other of their vitality and has left them both impotent' (Mbembe 1992a: 5). Resistance took the form of continuous bargaining and improvisation, strategic and tactical deployment of fluid identities as well as constantly undergoing metamorphosis and mitosis in the face of 'plurality of legitimising rubrics, institutional forms, rules, arenas and principles of combination' deployed by naked authoritarian modality *par excellence* (Mbembe 1992a: 5, 1992b: fn 7).

The postcolony therefore existed to create a fiction of a society devoid of conflict, a form of state power that was indistinguishable from society, a pedagogical state that acted as the promulgator and articulator of history, an upholder of law and repository of truth, and finally a form of vulgarised power embodied in one person – the postcolonial African president (Mbembe 1992a: 6). In this context, forms of resistance became equally complex, circulating within 'the simulacral regime *par excellence*' where ordinary people simulated 'adherence to the innumerable official rituals of life in the postcolony', including carrying party cards, wearing party uniforms with portraits of the President, chanting party slogans, and performing public gestures of support for the President (Mbembe 1992a: 11). All this was done to avoid trouble in the postcolony where opposition was considered anathema and where 'mere indifference is blasphemous' (Mbembe 1992a: 16).

But scholars like Mikael Karlstrom (2003: 57) have criticised Mbembe for overestimating the ideological power of the postcolonial state and for 'unjustifiably' creating a pessimistic portrayal of state-society relations in postcolonial Africa 'as terminally mired in inherently dysfunctional political dispositions and practices'. Karlstrom (2003: 57–8) attempts to demonstrate that 'the disabling paradoxes of postcolonial politics identified by Mbembe do not arise out of any inherent pathology of the African political imagination, but rather out of the postcolonial state's tendency to deploy local models and practices of the public sphere in ways that evacuate them of much of their legitimating content'. While Karlstrom tries to create a positive image of the postcolony as characterised by harmonious state-society relations based on his particular case study of Uganda, there is overwhelming counter-evidence that reveals what Mbembe has un-covered.

But Mbembe's interventions on resistance seem to also indicate an African people trapped in a post-resistance predicament where they simply ridicule and reinstate state power (Robins 2004: 18–26). Nationalism as a form of resistance is caricatured as an empty myth and mirage of liberation. Africans are presented as a conniving and ingratiating mass lacking any clear liberatory project. To Mbembe (1999: 3), cultural nationalism in particular results in nativism and 'territorialization of the production of knowledge'. Mbembe's work seems to deny value to both political and epistemological resistance cascading from Marxist and nationalist critical interventions. In the end, Mbembe encourages African scholars to embrace what he considers to be international scholarship and Africans to embrace globalisation. This 'solution' is faulty because Africa suffers not from isolation from the world but from too much indulgence in world affairs that are structured by coloniality.

The fact that the postcolonial state was not well-embedded in society meant that state-citizen relations were not stable and political elites and ordinary citizens were constantly engaged in struggles. Those who did not control the state remained closed out of economic, civil and political benefits within the postcolony in the same manner that colonial regimes excluded Africans from the economic, civil and political sphere. As such the general thesis that postcolonial state-society relations have not been characterised by deep and horizontal comradeships running across interactions of ruling elites and the governed is very plausible. Tensions rather than 'ritualised dialogics' have remained a common factor in state-society relations across postcolonial Africa. Only during the first decade of independence which was dominated by false hopes and euphoria were there some cordial relations. This legitimacy crisis led Ali Mazrui (1989: 476) to offer the following ground-breaking explanation:

> In situations where the leaders are identified too readily as people who have arisen from the ranks, it is easier for those who remain in the ranks to become envious of the privileges enjoyed by their former peers. Long-established elites are sometimes forgiven luxurious living more easily by 'lower classes' than newly successful members of the privileged classes. Those who have been rich for generations have consolidated their social distance and made it appear natural if not deserved. But the newly opulent are more easily accused of 'giving themselves airs' – and are more easily resented as a result. Resentment arises not from a defined social distance but, on the contrary, from the persistent residual social *nearness* between these newly opulent and the power fold from whom they spring. The Africa of the first generation of independence was an Africa bedevilled by precisely this close interpenetration between the elite and the masses (emphasis added).

Mazrui's intervention is very important as it challenges the common intellectual wisdom which generally explained tensions between the governed and the governors in terms of the widening distance between the ruling elites and the ordinary citizens. To Mazrui (1988), the issue of the postcolonial legitimacy crisis must not be sought in 'social distance' but in 'social nearness' that breeds envy among the ordinary members of society and other elites excluded from the corridors of power.

Praise texts that emerged during the independence euphoria of the 1960s, and which were less critical of the denials of freedom to citizens by the postcolonial state, contributed to the hiding of myths of decolonisation and illusions of freedom (Robins 1996; Ndlovu-Gatsheni 2009). Freedom for the African state was celebrated as freedom for the ordinary people. Those people who questioned whether decolonisation bequeathed freedom on ordinary citizens were quickly branded as traitors and enemies of the postcolonial state. They were either forced to flee to exile or were detained, if not liquidated completely. The earliest targets were excluded elites who were trying to create oppositional political formations and critical intellectuals who were easily branded as counter-revolutionaries.

What has not received adequate scholarly attention in this scheme of things is how ordinary citizens fought and resisted being captured, dominated, exploited, and being used to indulge in an officially imposed postcolonial order that did not benefit them. Eric Worby (1998) argues that postcolonial African leaders rarely enjoyed undisputed power, meaning that their hold on power has always been tenuous and contested. This forced them to opt for and try to depend on the performance of quotidian ceremonies underpinned by extravagant dramaturgical and improvisational content, aimed at fostering popular collusion and eliciting citizen consent.

The question of freedom has always been a central aspiration of colonised peoples and decolonisation was supposed to and expected to bring it to ordinary people. Robert H. Taylor (2002: 7) argues that:

> Freedom is an idea which was not merely discovered once and then spread around the world like a new commodity. Rather, freedom and its institutions emerge and re-emerge out of concrete circumstances of individuals' lives in history. The story of freedom knows no cultural barriers and continues to unfold in unexpected ways.

With specific reference to Africa, freedom was basically understood in its relationship to those processes that denied it. To Young (2002: 9), in Africa freedom is generally understood in relation to 'its negative other', '[t]he ultimate sources of unfreedom, in much of the reflection upon it, are external to Africa: the Atlantic slave trade; colonial subjugation; great-power imperial pretensions, globalising capitalism'. The chances of African people enjoying freedom were compromised by technologies of domination that dominated both the colonial and postcolonial orders.

Freedom of manoeuvre versus ordinary people's struggles for human rights in the postcolony

Foltz (2002: 40) characterises the struggles for freedom of the state as 'freedom of manoeuvre' that became imbricated with ordinary people's struggle for human rights within the postcolony. Freedom of the African state entailed, among other things, admitting it to membership in the international society of sovereign states. The immediate struggle by the elite in charge of the young postcolonial states was to consolidate 'freedom of the state' into 'freedom for the state' (Foltz 2002: 40). This form of resistance developed within a terrain of emergence of African states as unique 'quasi-states' which were recognised as sovereign and independent units by other states within the international system, but which could not meet the demands of 'empirical' statehood (Jackson 1990).

What provoked postcolonial forms of African resistance was that the postcolonial state assumed the character of the proverbial goat that grazed where it was tethered – preying upon the people, capturing, dominating, exploiting and squeezing the local citizenry. Examples include Ghana and Guinea under Kwame Nkrumah and Sékou Touré respectively, closely studied by Azarya and Chazan (1998). These two West African states were practising socialism that was used to justify extreme forms of centralisation and politicisation of every aspect of society. Youth movements, trade unions, women's movements and other voluntary associations became integrated within the ruling parties. At the end of it all: 'Every citizen had to be a party member, and every village, neighbourhood, factory, and office had its party committee' (Azarya and Chazan 1998: 110).

The underlying logic was to bring larger and larger segments of the population into the state domain of surveillance, repression, domination and exploitation. The failure by the postcolonial state to deliver material benefits and freedom to the ordinary people resulted in a problematic relationship between the state and the citizens. Those in control of the state became the only full citizens together with their clients and cronies. The majority of the ordinary people became subjects once more after the end of colonial rule (Mamdani 1996). Instead of governing, the elites in charge of the state became rulers in the crudest sense of the term whereby their words became law and they reduced citizens not only to subjects but also to powerless sycophants and hungry praise singers (Mazrui 1967).

The 1990s also witnessed the mobilisation and organisation of Africans into civil society organisations (CSOs), ranging widely from churches, trade unions, women's movements and student movements to ethnic-based pressure groups. Comaroff and Comaroff (2000: 331) noted:

> Civil Society has served as a remarkably potent battle cry across the world. During inhospitable times, it reanimates the optimistic spirit of modernity, providing scholars, public figures, poets, and ordinary people alike a language with which to talk about democracy, moral community, justice, and populist politics; with which, furthermore, to breathe life back into, 'society', declared dead almost twenty years ago by powerful magi of Second Coming.

Africa-based CSOs worked closely with Western non-governmental organisations (NGOs) and aid agencies to campaign for freedom. In Francophone Africa the embers of freedom culminated in what became known as 'the national conference phenomenon' that began in Benin as a convergence zone of those groups fighting for an end to authoritarianism practised by one-party regimes (Robinson 1994).

Indeed a few one-party authoritarian regimes that had come to power in the 1960s crumbled under the weight of a combination of civil society and opposition forces' resistance to oppression and exploitation. The examples include Mathieu Kérékou in Benin, Haile Mariam Mengistu in Ethiopia, Kenneth Kaunda in Zambia, and Kamuzu Banda in Malawi. These regime changes were celebrated by Samuel P. Huntington (1991) as the 'third wave of democratisation' in the late twentieth century. Despite the chequered history of the freedom struggles of the 1990s, with some proving to be false starts and others hijacked by incumbent dictators thirsty for relevance and re-birth, they formed a strong background for the current push for transparency, accountability, predictability, good corporate management and good political governance. By 2000, a new continental and global consensus had emerged on the complementarities of democracy and development.

The authoritarian developmentalism of the 1960s and 1970s was replaced by a strong belief in democratic developmentalism in the 1990s and 2000s (Sen 2000). Those fighting for freedom were no longer calling for the death of the state but for its restructuring to serve the interests of the people rather than that of the elites. Issues of corruption, kleptocracy, clientelism and patronage were identified as obstacles that needed to be removed if the African state was to serve the interests of the ordinary people. Some of the most corrupt and kleptocratic states like that of Mobutu Seseko in Zaire (now Democratic Republic of the Congo) could no longer rest until Mobutu himself was forced to leave the country to die in shame in exile. These realities led Young (2002: 37) to conclude that:

> The democratic era of the 1990s, in spite of its disappointments and limitations, situated ideas of freedom in a multiplicity of sites, opened many new debates, and revived older ones on making freedom authentic by rooting it in an indigenous heritage.

The new millennium witnessed the continuing struggles of ordinary people for widened frontiers of freedom consonant with the millenarian mood of hope for new life. The voices range from those of women and girls still pushing the remaining frontiers of patriarchy into the dust bin of history, the youth claiming their space as a new generation, ethnic groups flexing their muscles for recognition and calling for decentralised forms of governance, and religious congregations creating a niche for their flock. What is common among these voices is the clarion call for democracy that would free them from control of the centre and how to make the centre serve the ordinary people.

The Arab Spring and the future of African resistance

Since 2000 an increasing number of voices have called for new African states that exist to serve the ordinary people, and promoted popular freedom. In some literature this type of state is described as a democratic developmental state (Mkandawire 2001). It is a state that is capable of working to fulfil the democratic and developmental aspirations of the majority of the people within its borders. The envisaged democratic developmental state is to be defined by its institutional characteristics. The first key feature is that of its embeddedness in African society, that is, a state that has formed strong and broad-based alliances with society and ensures effective and active citizen participation in decision-making. The second is that of building autonomous institutions free from control by capricious and venal cliques. Such a state is expected to be totally freed from the trappings of the autocracy of the 1960s and 1980s (Mkandawire 2001).

This new agenda could not be carried forward by the old guard leaders like those of Egypt, Libya, Tunisia, Zimbabwe and others who have been in power for over 30 years. These leaders have presided over some of the most predatory and corrupt states. They have used both religion and nationalism to silence political dissent and to justify closure of spaces for freedom of speech. The other contributory factor was the coming to power of a 'new generation of African leaders'. Leaders like Thabo Mbeki of South Africa, Yoweri Museveni of Uganda, Paul Kagame of Rwanda, Meles Zenawi of Ethiopia, Isaias Afewerki of Eritrea and Olusegun Obasanjo of Nigeria were depicted as examples of 'new leaders' who were less authoritarian and less dogmatic, but they also have been a disappointment (Ottaway 1998).

What distinguished these so-called new leaders was their attempt to reconstruct the African state in the direction of fulfilment of popular demands for economic development and democracy. In combination, or as individuals, they engaged and toyed with bigger plans for Africa such as the New Partnership for African Development (NEPAD), the Pan-African Parliament (PAP), and the African Peer Review Mechanism (APRM). These pan-African institutions were meant to create a new moment for Africa characterised by economic development and democratisation. As put by Timothy Murithi (2005: 166):

> With the creation of the African Union, African governments and their societies are expressing the desire, as yet unfulfilled, to address the unjust practices of the past which led to the social and economic marginalization of members of their societies. In so doing it is also an expression that Africa wants to play a constructive role in international relations as an equal partner and that the first step towards achieving this is to put its own house in order.

The drive for building pan-African institutions as part of the concretisation of African aspirations for economic development and democracy is happening in tandem with the return of the state as the legitimate driver of development and democratisation. The Nigerian scholar Eghosa Osaghae (2010) noted that it has dawned on many researchers that the state remains the sole anchor for citizenship. It has also been realised that the state is the only institution that can carry and drive the distribution of resources. The continuing struggle is over the nature and the type of state that will not be a menace to the people but a facilitator of economic development and a provider of freedom and security.

These developments are taking place within a crisis of the neo-liberal project and the capitalist system. Liberal democracy has proven to be elitist and not facilitative of the passage from juridical freedom to popular freedom. Instead it has become associated with the current capitalist crisis. Throughout the world low wages, high food prices and high unemployment have become the order of the day. North Africa, which had somehow escaped the so-called third wave of democratisation and continued to subsist under well-known dictatorships, became the theatre of new arts of resistance.

In 2011, the Maghreb became the focal point of popular resistance ranged against autocratic regimes on the one hand and railing against the failures of neo-liberalism on the other (Joya *et al.* 2011). The mode of resistance this time involved the effective use of information and communication technologies (ICT) including mobile phones, Facebook, Twitter and others that were hard to censor by cornered authoritarian regimes. The youth became the torchbearers of the Arab Spring and its ripple effects ignited similar protests in Sub-Saharan Africa, the Middle East and Europe. Forms of resistance included picketing, demonstrations, riots, burning of shops, as well as outright warfare as was the case in Libya where global imperial designs intervened to topple and kill Gaddafi.

While the Arab Spring fits into long-standing and continuing struggles for popular sovereignty and real democracy, coloniality intervened to further Euro-American strategic interests. The year 2011 became a climax of these forms of resistance – a year of democratic ferments and reformist changes in Egypt, Libya and Tunisia (Africa Centre for Strategic Studies 2011: 3). The mass protests that rocked North Africa were quickly followed by similar forms of resistance in Burkina Faso, Uganda, Senegal, Benin, Malawi, Kenya, Djibouti, Mauritania, Cameroon, Gabon, Guinea-Bissau and Swaziland. While this was taking place, some African leaders like Robert Mugabe in Zimbabwe continue to push state sovereignty ahead of popular sovereignty.

The question which remains is why the Arab Spring could not be fully replicated in Sub-Saharan Africa? Perhaps part of the answer is that Sub-Saharan Africa already experienced its own 'African spring' in the 1990s that swept away some of the dictators. Those dictators that survived have perfected the art of domination and surveillance, making it very difficult for popular forces to mobilise for successful civil disobedience. But preconditions for popular uprisings and resistance exist in Sub-Saharan Africa albeit in different forms to those that obtained in North Africa. Unemployed youth remain a potential time-bomb.

Africa and the world at large have entered an era of the 'end of the end of history'. It is clear that ordinary people can still mobilise their agency and deploy resistance to make new history through deposing long-time autocratic leaders. The Arab Spring has demonstrated the efficacy of 'people's power' to effect political change as well as the active interventions of coloniality in African affairs. While the passage from juridical freedom to popular freedom is opening up and the era of dictatorship is receding into the past, coloniality continues to put speed-traps on resistance. Euro-American military and other interventions are poised to continue to dilute the content and spoil popular bases of African resistance. This reality calls for more vigilance among resisters and careful selection of allies.

References

Africa Center for Strategic Studies (2011). *Africa and the Arab Spring: a new era of democratic expectations*. Washington, DC: African Center for Strategic Studies.

Agbese, P. O. and Kieh, G. K. (2007). Introduction: democratizing states and state reconstitution in Africa (pp. 3–29). In P. O. Agbese and G. K. Kieh (eds), *Reconstituting the state in Africa*. New York: Palgrave Macmillan.
Ahmad, A. (1992). *In theory: classes, nations, literatures*. London: Verso.
Ake, C. (2000). *The feasibility of democracy in Africa*. Dakar: CODESRIA.
Azarya, V. and Chazan, N. (1998). Disengagement from the state in Africa: reflections on the experience of Ghana and Guinea (pp. 98–120). In P. Lewis (ed.), *Africa: dilemmas of development and change*. Boulder, CO: Westview Press.
Bhabha, H. K. (1994). *The location of culture*. London: Routledge.
Chinweizu (1975). *The West and the rest of us: white predators, black slavers and the African elite*. New York: Vintage Books.
Comaroff, J. L. and Comaroff, J. (1991). *Of revelation and revolution, Volume One: Christianity, colonialism and consciousness in South Africa*. Chicago, IL: University of Chicago Press.
Comaroff, J. L. and Comaroff, J. (1997). *Of revelation and revolution, Volume Two: The dialectics of modernity on a South African frontier*. Chicago, IL: University of Chicago Press.
Comaroff, J. and Comaroff, J. L. (2000). Millennial capitalism: first thoughts on a second coming. *Public Culture*, 12(2), 291–343.
Cooper, F. (2003). Conflict and connection: rethinking colonial African history (pp. 13–37). In J. Le Sueur (ed.). *The decolonization reader*. New York: Routledge.
Diamond, L. (1998). Africa: The second wind of change (pp. 263–71). In P. Lewis (ed.), *Africa: dilemmas of development and change*, Boulder, CO: Westview Press.
Englebert, P. (2000). *State legitimacy and development*. Boulder, CO: Lynne Rienner.
Esedebe, P. O. (1982). *Pan-Africanism: the idea and movement, 1776–1963*. Washington, DC: Macmillan.
Fanon, F. (1968). *The wretched of the earth*. New York: Grove Press.
Foltz, W. J. (2002). African states and the search for freedom (pp. 40–61). In R. H. Taylor (ed.), *The idea of freedom in Asia and Africa*. Stanford, CA: Stanford University Press.
Glassman, J. (1995). *Feasts and riot: revelry, rebellion, and popular consciousness on the Swahili coast, 1856–1888*. Portsmouth, NH: Heinemann.
Grosfoguel, R. (2007). The epistemic decolonial turn: beyond political-economy paradigms. *Cultural Studies*, 21(2–3), 211–23.
Grosfoguel, R. (2011). Decolonizing post-colonial studies and paradigms of political-economy: transmodernity, decolonial thinking, and global coloniality. *Transmodernity: Journal of Peripheral Cultural Production of the Luso-Hispanic World*, 1(1), 1–37.
Huntington, S. P. (1991). *The third wave: democratization in the late twentieth century*. Norman, OK: University of Oklahoma Press.
Jackson, R. H. (1990). *Quasi-states: sovereignty, international relations and the Third World*. Cambridge: Cambridge University Press.
Joya, A., Bond, P., El-Amine, R., Hanieh, H. and Henaway, M. (2011). *The Arab revolts against neoliberalism*. Socialist Project: Socialist Intervention Pamphlet Series, available from: www.socialistproject.ca/documents/ArabRevolts.pdf (last accessed: 15 September 2012).
Karlstrom, M. (2003). On the aesthetics and dialogics of power in the post-

colony. *Africa*, 73(1), 57–76.
Laakso, L. and Olukoshi, A. O. (1996). The crisis of the post-colonial nation-state project in Africa (pp. 7–39). In A. O. Olukoshi and L. Laakso (eds), *Challenges to the nation-state in Africa*. Uppsala: Nordic Africa Institute.
Lumumba-Kasongo, T. (1994). *Political re-mapping of Africa: transnational ideology and re-definition of Africa in world politics*. Lanham, MD: University Press of America.
Mafeje, A. (2011). Africanity: a combative ontology (pp. 2–44). In R. Devisch and F. B. Nyamnjoh (eds), *The postcolonial turn: re-imagining anthropology and Africa*. Bamenda and Leiden: Langaa and African Studies Centre.
Magubane, B. M. (2007). *Race and the construction of the dispensable other*. Pretoria: UNISA Press.
Maldonado-Torres, N. (2007). On the coloniality of being: contributions to the development of a concept. *Cultural Studies*, 21 (2–3), 240–70.
Mamdani, M. (1996). *Citizen and subject: contemporary Africa and the legacy of late colonialism*. Princeton, NJ: Princeton University Press.
Mazrui, A. A. (1967) *On heroes and uhuru-worship: essays on independent Africa*. London: Longman.
Mazrui, A. A. (1989) Growing up in a shrinking world: a private vantage point (pp. 469–87). In J. Kruzel and J. N. Rosenau (eds). *Journeys through world politics: autobiographical reflections of thirty-four academic travellers*. Lexington, MA and Toronto: Lexington Books.
Mbembe, A. (1992a). The banality of power and the aesthetics of vulgarity in the postcolony. *Public Culture*, 4(2), 1–30.
Mbembe, A. (1992b). Provisional notes on the postcolony. *Africa: Journal of the International Africa Institute*, 62(1), 3–37.
Mbembe, A. (1999). Getting out of the ghetto: the challenge of internationalization. *CODESRIA Bulletin*, 3–4, 1–10.
Mbembe, A. (2001). *On the postcolony*. Berkeley, CA: University of California Press.
Mbembe, A. (2002a). African modes of self-writing. *Public Culture*, 14(1), 239–73.
Mbembe, A. (2002b). On the power of the false. *Public Culture*, 14(3), 629–641.
Mignolo, W. D. (1995). *The darker side of the Renaissance: literacy, territoriality and colonization*. Ann Arbor, MI: University of Michigan Press.
Mignolo, W. D. (2000). *Local histories/global designs: coloniality, subaltern knowledges, and border thinking*. Princeton, NJ: Princeton University Press.
Mignolo, W. D. (2005). *The idea of Latin America*. Oxford: Blackwell.
Mignolo, W. D. (2007). Delinking: the rhetoric of modernity, the logic of coloniality and the grammar of de-coloniality. *Cultural Studies*, 21 (2–3), 449–514.
Miller, C. (1990). *Theories of Africans: Francophone Literature and Anthropology in Africa*. Chicago, IL: University of Chicago Press.
Mkandawire, T. (2001). Thinking about the developmental state in Africa. *Cambridge Journal of Economics*, 25(3), 289–314.
Mudimbe, V. Y. (1998). *The invention of Africa: gnosis, philosophy and the order of knowledge*. London: James Currey.
Muiu, M. wa and Martin, G. (2009). *A new paradigm of the African state: Fundi wa Afrika*. New York: Palgrave Macmillan.

Murithi, T. (2005). *The African Union: pan-Africanism, peace-building and development*. Hampshire: Ashgate.
Ndlovu-Gatsheni, S. J. (2007). Re-thinking the colonial encounter in Zimbabwe in the early twentieth century. *Journal of Southern African Studies*, 33(1), 173–91.
Ndlovu-Gatsheni, S. J. (2009). *Do 'Zimbabweans' exist? Trajectories of nationalism, national identity formation and crisis in a postcolonial state*. Oxford: Peter Lang.
Ndlovu-Gatsheni, S. J. (2012). Fiftieth anniversary of decolonization in Africa: a moment of celebration or critical reflection? *Third World Quarterly*, 33(1), 71–89.
Ndlovu-Gatsheni, S. J. (2013). *Coloniality of power in postcolonial Africa: Myths of decolonization*. Dakar: CODESRIA.
Nkrumah, K. (1963). *I speak of freedom: a statement of African ideology*. New York: Vintage.
Nyamnjoh, F. B. (2006). Re-thinking communication research and development in Africa (pp. 393–416). In P. T. Zeleza (ed.), *The study of Africa, volume 1: disciplinary and interdisciplinary encounters*. Dakar: CODESRIA.
Osaghae, E. (2010). *Citizenship and reconstruction of belonging in Africa*, unpublished paper presented at the Department of Political Studies, University of the Witwatersrand, 11 August.
Ottaway, M. (1998). *Between democracy and personal rule: new African leaders and reconstruction of the African state*. Washington, DC: Brookings Institute.
Padmore, G. (1956). *Pan-Africanism or communism? The coming struggle for Africa*. London: Dennis Dobson.
Quijano, A. (2007). Coloniality and modernity/rationality. *Cultural Studies*, 21(2–3), 168–178.
Ranger, T. (1967). *Revolt in Southern Rhodesia, 1896–7: a study in African resistance*. London: Heinemann.
Ranger, T. (1968). Connexions between 'primary resistance' movements and modern mass nationalism in Eastern and Central Africa. Parts I and II. *Journal of African History*, 9(3–4), 437–53, 631–41.
Ranger, T. (1985). *Peasant consciousness and guerrilla war in Zimbabwe*. Harare: Zimbabwe Publishing House.
Ranger, T. (1986). Resistance in Africa: from nationalist revolt to agrarian protest (pp. 34–57). In G. Y. Okihiro (ed.). *In resistance: studies in African, Caribbean and Afro-American history*, Amherst, MA: University of Massachusetts Press.
Ranger, T. (1994). Protestant missions in Africa: the dialectics of conversion in the American Methodist Episcopal Church in Eastern Zimbabwe (pp. 123–156). In T. D. Blakely, W. E. van Beek and D. L. Thompson (eds), *Religion in Africa: experience and expression*. London: James Currey.
Robins, S. (1996). Heroes, heretics and historians of the Zimbabwe revolution: a review article of Norma Kriger's *Peasant Voices* (1992). *Zambezia, The Journal of Humanities of the University of Zimbabwe*, 23(1), 31–74.
Robins, S. (2004). 'The (Third) World is a ghetto?' Looking for a third space between 'postmodern' cosmopolitanism and cultural nationalism. *CODESRIA Bulletin*, 1–2, 18–26.
Robinson, P. (1994). The national conference phenomenon in Francophone Africa. *Comparative Studies in Society and History*, 36(3), 575–610.
Rodney, W. (1989). *How Europe underdeveloped Africa*. Harare: Zimbabwe

Publishing House.
Said, E. (1978). *Orientalism*. London: Routledge and Kegan Paul.
Sen, A. (2000). *Development as freedom*. New York: Anchor Books.
Taylor, R. H. (2002). Introduction (pp. 1–7). In R. H. Taylor (ed.), *The idea of freedom in Asia and Africa*. Stanford: Stanford University Press.
Walraven, K. V. and Abbink, J. (2003). Rethinking resistance in African history: an introduction (pp. 1–23). In J. Abbink, M. D. Bruijn and K. V. Walraven (eds), *Rethinking resistance: revolt and violence in African history*, Leiden and Boston: Brill.
West, M. O. (2002). The seeds are sown: the impact of Garveyism in Zimbabwe in the interwar years. *International Journal of African Historical Studies*, 35(2–3), 335–62.
Worby, E. (1998). Tyranny, parody, and ethnic polarity: ritual engagements with the state in Northwestern Zimbabwe. *Journal of Southern African Studies*, 24(3), 561–78.
Young, C. (1994). *The African colonial state in comparative perspective*. New Haven, CT: Yale University Press.
Young, C. (2002). Itineraries of the ideas of freedom in Africa (pp. 31–57). In R. H. Taylor (ed.), *The idea of freedom in Asia and Africa*. Stanford, CA: Stanford University Press.
Zartman, I. W. (2007). The African state (pp. 17–34). In J. C. Senghor and N. K. Poku (eds), *Towards Africa's renewal*. Aldershot: Ashgate.
Zeleza, P. T. (1997). *Manufacturing African Studies and crises*. Dakar: CODESRIA.
Zeleza, P. T. (2006). The troubled encounter between postcolonialism and African history. *Journal of the Canadian Historical Association*, 17(2), 89–129.

3 Citizenship from Below

The Politics of Citizen Action & Resistance in South Africa & Angola

Bettina von Lieres

Introduction

In many contexts of the global South, ideas and practices around citizenship extend beyond the liberal notion of citizenship as primarily about the vertical relations between individual citizens and rights-recognising states. For marginalised communities, citizenship is often not experienced primarily in relation to the state, but instead through highly localised processes of horizontal identification and mobilisation. Collective and horizontal forms of 'citizenship' practices often emerge in reaction to unresponsive states which are unable or unwilling to provide key services such as health, water and housing. Basic services are often provided not by states, but by non-state actors such as transnational donor agencies, non-governmental organisations (NGOs) or humanitarian and relief agencies. In addition, non-state institutions such as chiefly courts, religious movements, social movements and local associations continue to form an important part of the social and political landscape and may become alternatives to the absent state. As a consequence, citizenship is often an inherently 'messy' practice that may involve participation in, and resistance to, a wide range of political institutions and societal spaces. In the daily scramble for livelihoods and security, ordinary people tend to adopt diverse strategies and draw on multiple political identities, discourses and social relationships to navigate daily life. In the context of unresponsive or absent states, citizenship practices, then, are often more about 'the right to have rights' and the right to participate in new and multiple public spaces than they are about struggles to access individual rights. These new forms of citizen action often produce uneven political outcomes and are by no means the result of linear processes of resistance. The trajectories of citizen mobilisation often involve gains and reversals, especially in political contexts where there are competing forms of political authority such as rights-based authority and clientelism, and where states are hostile to citizens' demands. However, despite the sometimes uneven political outcomes of citizen mobilisation, citizen action – both informal and formal – can also build crucial practices of resistance to unresponsive states. In this chapter resistance is understood as the 'construction of citizenship practices', i.e. as civic mobilisation practices aimed at empowering marginalised people to formulate new political claims and to act on these in contexts where states are non-responsive to the demands of ordinary people. 'Resistance-as-citizenship' speaks to the construction of political agency aimed at engaging state power and building civic agency in the spaces between state and society. It often involves localised forms of civic mobilisation through which marginalised communities and people act to claim new rights and to create new public spaces for participation. Citizen action as resistance speaks to those moments in which ordinary people mobilise to confront states not as individuals, but as rights-demanding citizens with public claims. These new forms of civic action are by no means straightforward and their efficacy is never guaranteed. They encounter state power and are often profoundly shaped by these encounters. There are always positive and negative political outcomes of civic action as it can profoundly challenge state power in its demands for new forms of state-society relations.

But under what conditions can resistance in the form of citizen action lead to more responsive states, more inclusive societies and a greater capacity of citizens to shape their own societies? In exploring this question, I examine two case studies from Angola and South Africa and discuss how different forms of citizen mobilisation and agency (formal and informal) shape resistance, political agency and new political outcomes. Drawing on existing case studies from a global research network, the Development Research Centre on Citizenship, Participation and Accountability (Citizenship DRC[1]), I focus on 'mediated citizen mobilisations' in which marginalised citizens rely on third-party mediators or interlocutors to trigger their actions and strategies. In focusing on 'mediated' forms of citizen action, I locate the politics of citizen action against the increasing shift of governance in the global South away from the state into civil society which is increasingly viewed as the source of democratic deepening as a counterbalance to state and market. The growing diffusion of state power and the proliferation of alternative

[1] During the first decade of the millennium, the Citizenship-DRC network (C-DRC) brought together over sixty researchers and practitioners working in twenty countries to develop deeply grounded, empirical insights into the meanings of inclusive citizenship (Kabeer 2005), the politics of rights and participation (Newell and Wheeler 2006) and how citizens mobilise for democracy (Coelho and von Lieres 2011). Broadly speaking, its research suggests that democracy is often made real through the claims and active struggles of citizens and their organisations, and that strategies are needed that focus on the relationship between states and societies. Much of the work has focused on new forms of citizen mobilisation that look to enhance the access of poor and marginalised groups to public goods. Its research focused on the global South, as it is here that much innovative practice by activists, organisations and communities has emerged. The work of the CDRC has tended towards a methodology that focuses on citizens rather than institutions, and tries to understand democratic politics from the citizen's point of view. Embarking from this more 'bottom-up' view of democracy has yielded dividends in that it has become very clear in case after case that for many poor communities democracy is made real through the claims and active struggles of citizens and their organisations, and that popular organisation and mobilisation can make a real and substantive difference to citizens' lives. See www.drc-citizenship.org (last accessed: 24 September 2012).

actors and sources of power mean that coordination and mediation must become more important for collective action. The rise of mediating actors and practices is also related to the increasing importance of informal institutions in governance. These include 'traditional' forms of social order, kinship and ethnic identities and practice, and the complex interaction between informal and formal institutions. The enduring 'contest over public authority' in civil society makes forms of mediation for citizen action a necessity or inevitable as there can be no systemic response without changing the logic of the system, and hence the poor rely on various kinds of intermediaries to access their rights from, through or despite the state, and these often exploit the poor in many ways, but not always.

The actors involved in these mediated forms of mobilisation are both urban and rural, and include a national social movement in South Africa, the Treatment Action Campaign (TAC) and a federation of local associations in Angola, the Federation of Representative Associations of Dombe Grande (NRA), in the *comuna* of Dombe Grande, a small town near the provincial capital, Benguela. These two cases provide examples of citizen action in two political contexts that vary significantly in terms of constitutional and legal frameworks, state capacities and histories of citizen mobilisation. I argue that each of these contextual factors leaves distinctive traces of how citizens and their organisations mobilise for rights and inclusion, and also shapes the choice of forms of mobilisation. I argue that in Angola, a context with a history of civil war, a largely unresponsive state and a fragmented civil society, the most important actors of civic agency and resistance are not formal civil society organisations such as NGOs, but local associations whose relations with local states are usually mediated by third-party interlocutors. These mediated forms of local civic action can result in marginalised communities acquiring new knowledge of rights, the capacity to mobilise for rights, and deepening their capacity for democratic participation. These 'softer' political and civic outcomes are important as they lay the ground for deeper and more effective forms of wider public participation, mobilisation and resistance to disempowering state practices. However, the Angolan case also shows how these localised forms of citizen mobilisation often fail to impact in any significant way on the state's actions and its exercise of power. Localised forms of mediated citizen mobilisation can have little impact on the local state's wider public policies and its responsiveness to citizens' claims and demands. They often fail to re-define state-society relations in any significant way. By contrast, in contexts where there is a longer history of citizen mobilisation and a higher level of state responsiveness, such as in South Africa, social movements play a key role in mobilising citizens, and there is a better chance of larger-scale gains – such as greater state responsiveness to citizen demands, the crafting of new national agendas for citizen participation or sustained access to economic resources, rights and accountable institutions. These larger gains, however, are by no means permanent and are themselves subject to new and emerging forms of state power.

The politics of citizen action and resistance in the global South

This chapter takes as its starting point the 'deepening democracy' approach in current debates on democracy (Gaventa 2006; Fung and Wright 2001). Scholars and activists who take this approach argue that citizenship should mean far more than just the enjoyment of legal rights and the election of representatives. Many of them view citizenship as involving the building of broad coalitions, and mobilisation with the potential to frame new agendas and to provide a counterbalance to state power by encouraging citizens to voice their demands, to advocate for special interests and to play a 'watchdog' role (Appadurai 2002: 21–47). For others, deepening democracy involves being heard by the state and participating directly in deliberation and decision-making on political and policy issues or else having direct relations with government institutions, as opposed to relations that are brokered by citizens (Cornwall and Coelho 2007: 1–29). In short, the deepening democracy approach highlights the importance of citizen engagement in shaping the opportunities for wider democratic change. Within this approach, however, there is a growing body of literature that focuses on the challenges inherent in actually getting citizens involved in democratic change.

A key challenge concerns a tendency by some commentators to automatically equate the growth of civil society organisations (CSOs) with increased democratisation. In contrast to this view, others – among many – call attention to the fact that there is often nothing inherently democratic about CSOs and movements (Houtzager and Lavalle 2010: 6). They focus attention on the possible disjunctures between the practices of democracy, as advocated by CSOs, and the everyday realities of clientelism, patronage and authoritarian local politics experienced by their members and ordinary citizens. Citizens' mobilisations are shaped not only by the organisations which mediate them but also by existing local power dynamics and cultures of politics. Citizens often straddle multiple relations in their quest for more empowered participation – with local power brokers on the one hand, and with mediating organisations such as CSOs on the other.

This chapter's focus is on ordinary people's mobilisations which are mediated but not led by third-parties, and which involve the active participation of unorganised marginalised communities. The actors who mediate on behalf of citizens are often diverse, ranging from local civil society organisations mediating between citizens and local states, to national advocacy non-governmental organisations which campaign on behalf of citizens around social issues to influence public policy, and social movements which broker the inclusion of poor communities in decision-making around investments by transnational corporations. These mediating actors often engage in diverse mediating practices, ranging from advocacy for the inclusion of representatives of marginalised groups to the advocacy of the interests of marginalised groups themselves. The emergence of new forms and actors of democratic mediation challenge some of the assumptions that seem to be implicit in relation to many dominant policy drives in the global South and North: assumptions about the likelihood that poor citizens and marginalised communities will necessarily benefit from policies to promote decentralisation and citizen engagement, for example, without access to sources of democratic mediation, facilitation, capacity building and empowerment (Piper and von Lieres 2011).

Mediating practices and actors can trigger deeper forms of citizen empowerment. Their strategies for engaging citizens in action can produce important political outcomes related to the construction of empowered notions of citizenship, the strengthening of practices of participation, the strengthening of responsive and accountable states and the development of inclusive and cohesive societies, as well as tangible material benefits for poor and marginalised groups (Gaventa and Barrett 2010: 25). In particular, they can trigger non-instrumental outcomes such as a strengthened sense of citizenship and more effective citizenship practices, greater political awareness of rights and of one's agency. It is important to consider that these political outcomes are often uneven and by no means guaranteed. Mediated civic mobilisation often results in violent reprisals from states in entrenched power relations and in new closures of public spaces. In addition, citizen mobilisation triggered by mediating actors can sometimes entrench institutional solutions that favour the 'organised marginalised' – those whose claims are mediated through CSOs– as opposed to less organised citizens with weaker links to civil society and state actors.

I now turn to a discussion of the cases from Angola and South Africa. Here the focus is not so much on a detailed description of the overall trajectory of the mobilisations, but more on the actual mobilisation strategies of actors, the political outcomes of the mobilisations and the consequences of these mobilisations for practices of resistance and state power.

South Africa: building state responsiveness

South Africa, a middle income state, with relatively well-functioning democratic institutions and an enabling legal framework for citizen participation, has a long history of social mobilisation which cut its teeth in the struggle against apartheid. In post-apartheid South Africa, emerging social movements such as the TAC built heavily on this history. South Africa is a country of around 50 million people characterised by massive inequality between rich and poor due largely to the legacy of the apartheid system. Despite better economic growth in the range of 3–5 percent per annum, and better provision of basic infrastructure and public services, the quality of life of most South Africans has not improved dramatically since the advent of democracy in 1994, and unemployment and inequality remain very high (Aliber*et al.* 2006: 49–50). The post-apartheid political order was ushered in with the first non-racial elections of 1994. Shortly followed by the Constitution of 1996, a single state was created with most of the institutions typical of a liberal democracy, including constitutional sovereignty, a bill of rights, regular free and fair elections, and a weak form of federalism. In addition, the constitution provides for an independent judiciary and a number of formal checks and balances on executive power. Despite this, the practice of politics is rendered much more centrifugal through the electoral dominance of the former liberation movement, the African National Congress (ANC). Since 1994 and especially the rise of Thabo Mbeki, the ANC has pursued a centre-left policy of 'third way' politics (Piper 2006: 149). This involves being 'pragmatic' about the model of economic development by embracing a conservative, inflation-targeting, fiscal-discipline-based, investment-led growth model, whilst accommodating the demands for social justice in terms of an expanded programme of basic service delivery and welfare provision. Third way politics, and the trend towards market provision of key 'public goods', has had the consequence of bifurcating citizenship in South Africa such that members of the middle class and above purchase their 'goods' through the market (health, education, security, transport) and the vast majority of working and poor people must rely on the state for these goods. Moreover, it is typically the former who design and run the latter. Superficially this contrast is one between a small group of 'consumer citizens' and a large group of 'conventional' citizens (Piper, Bafo and von Lieres 2012).

The TAC was established on 10 December 1998 when a group of about fifteen people protested on the steps of St. Georges Cathedral in Cape Town to demand medical treatment for people living with the HIV virus that causes AIDS. By the end of the day, protesters had collected over 1,000 signatures calling on the government to develop a treatment plan for all people living with HIV/AIDS. Over the next ten years, the TAC developed into one of South Africa's most effective post-apartheid social movements, mobilising citizens in multiple arenas – the courts, the streets, the media and global forums – and succeeding in winning important reforms in national policy on access to treatment, and with it, greater state responsiveness to citizens' demands (Robins and von Lieres 2004: 584–5).

From 1998 to 2001, the TAC focused its mobilisation strategies on building grassroots support and organisational capacity through local treatment literacy campaigns and widely publicised acts of civil disobedience. It also used global and national media campaigns to force the global pharmaceutical industry to allow developing countries to manufacture antiretroviral (ARV) generics. From 2001 to 2006, the TAC used the courts to argue that the South African government had a legal obligation to promote access to health care, including access to AIDS drug treatment. This was at a time when the South African government, under the leadership of Thabo Mbeki, propagated a discourse of AIDS denialism, questioning the link between HIV and AIDS. In 2001, in direct opposition to the government's policies on access to ARV treatment, the TAC, together with Médecins Sans Frontières (MSF), opened South Africa's first ARV treatment programme in Khayelitsha, Cape Town. In 2004, in response to pressure from the TAC and other citizens' organisations, the Constitutional Court ruled in support of a comprehensive roll-out plan for ARVs. After this significant national policy victory, from 2007 to 2012, the TAC has continued strengthening grassroots mobilisation and education as well as engaging in numerous formal policy processes and dialogues (Piper, Bafo and von Lieres 2012).

The TAC has significantly shaped the identity of civil society in South Africa through a dual strategy which involved strengthening grassroots resistance and, simultaneously, building engagements and collaborations with powerful political actors, including the state. On the one hand, the TAC succeeded in building a strong grassroots organisation with the capacity for multiple forms of citizen action from below, including spontaneous acts of civil disobedience, mass protests as well as organised literacy and education campaigns. On the other hand, the TAC partnered with multiple interest groups, including professional and/or international organisations to enhance campaigning on specific issues. For example, the TAC joined with professional medical associations and, in this one case at least, the Department of Health, in advocating for the removal of patent rights for HIV/AIDS treatments in South Africa. The TAC also built alliances with sympathetic organisations in civil society, including the churches and unions, and engaged with organisations aligned with the ANC: the Congress of South African Trade Unions and the South African Communist Party (Piper, Bafo and von Lieres 2012). The coalition built by the TAC involved complex and highly developed mobilising structures which linked national reformers to local and faith-based groups, the media and repositories of expertise (Piper, Bafo and von Lieres 2012). In bringing together practices of grassroots resistance and political collaborations with powerful interest groups, the TAC acted as an important mediator between political actors with access to medical knowledge and state/political networks, and the vast majority of the organisation's working and poor membership who do not.

As regards the construction of empowered notions of citizenship, the TAC did clearly empower its members through a treatment literacy programme that explicitly linked living with HIV/AIDS to one's rights as a citizen. Further, many members would have directly experienced various aspects of issue-based politics from politicising an issue through to popular mobilisation and protest. In addition, ordinary members both directly shaped the policy agenda and were genuinely empowered as medical citizens (i.e. both in terms of knowledge and the capacity for agency). This is not to say there were no problems, many of which remain. As regards the strengthening of practices of participation, a key objective of the TAC's politics was to open the closed and unstructured processes of HIV/AIDS policy to include civil society, which it achieved. At the same time, the TAC clearly assisted in the development of inclusive and cohesive societies through effecting a policy change that would positively affect the lives of hundreds of thousands, if not millions, of people. Further, the TAC did reinforce certain civil society relations although it remains to be seen how enduring those will be, and certainly has enhanced local solidarities and networks, and has promoted a subjective sense of citizenship. Lastly, as regards tangible, material benefits for poor and marginalised groups, the TAC made clear gains for people living with HIV/AIDS, not just in terms of symbolic recognition brought about by policy change but through its practical implementation. While there are still problems in this regard, the lives of hundreds of thousands of people have been touched positively by the TAC's work (Piper, Bafo and von Lieres 2012).

The TAC is an example of a new social movement that has constructed its own possibilities for citizen action in multiple spaces in civil society. The strength of the TAC as a social movement lies in its capacity to mobilise the poor in a variety of spaces, ranging from once-off campaigns to more formal policy engagements. Its campaigns have legitimised diverse forms of citizen action in civil society, not only in the eyes of ordinary citizens, but also in the eyes of sections of the state. The TAC's interventions in these multiple spaces have allowed ordinary citizens to engage in a rights-based, grassroots activism which, linked to the TAC's work in more formal policy arenas, has significantly shaped the identity of South Africa's civil society as an arena for both formal and informal social mobilisation and citizen action.

Angola: building associational capacity

Angola has a long history of civil war, high levels of social fragmentation and a weak state. Angola became independent from the Portuguese in 1975 after a costly liberation war. Twenty-seven years of civil war followed. Multi-party elections were held in 1992, but the period between 1992 and 2002, when peace broke out, was marked by ongoing civil war, widespread displacement of people from rural to urban areas and a high level of state centralisation with the President and elite able to control extra-budgetary revenues for their own accumulation and clientelistic purposes (Sogge 2006: 8). During the civil war much of the infrastructure, agriculture and rudimentary health services were destroyed. War also meant excess mortality of one million deaths – roughly a tenth of Angola's population, and displacement/urbanisation with about half of all Angolans, perhaps seven million people, living in cities and towns, one-third in Luanda. The agrarian system collapsed as did the health and education services – only 37 percent of primary-aged children were enrolled in school whilst most of the health budget went to hospital-based curative services, including elite spending in South Africa and Portugal. Since 2002 Angola has had a substantial economic growth rate, largely fuelled by oil resources. Despite its mineral wealth, Angolan poverty indicators remain high. Thirty-seven percent of the population lives below the poverty line and poverty is a major issue affecting urban and rural development and welfare. Today at least a third of Angola's population lives in *musseques* (slum settlements) in urban areas. Multi-party elections were held in 2008, but did not in any significant way weaken the dominant position of the ruling party, the People's Movement for the Liberation of Angola (MPLA). In recent years the state has attempted various forms of decentralisation in order to build local government, but has yet to show evidence of a coherent urban strategy. There is growing NGO-initiated citizen engagement in demanding improved public service provision and horizontal communal networks focusing on conflict resolution and citizen control over water services. The outcomes of citizen engagement have been limited, however, by the absence of public institutions mediating the relation between state and civil society. They have also been limited by relatively weak institutions and practices of communal solidarity amongst marginalised people living in the vast urban informal settlements. In a study of communal solidarity in the *musseques*, Robson and Roque (2009) found that social heterogeneity has had negative consequences for the density and extension of social solidarity networks. Where solidarity and communal networks exist, they are largely organised around churches.

In their case study on associational mobilisation, Ferreira and Roque (2010) describe how they worked with a federation of fifteen local associations in Angola, the majority of which represented small-scale farmers, while a few offered civic education services. The study shows how, in the context of fragile democratic institutions and strongly centralised states, both rural and urban NGOs and the associational networks they spawn can make a difference in fostering civic virtues, in teaching political skills and in nurturing a growing ability and willingness on the part of grassroots leaders to check abuses of power at the local level. In the realm of welfare outcomes, Ferreira and Roque (2010) report increases in the capacity of small-scale farmers' associations to protect the livelihoods of their poor members.

In this case, the key mediating actor is a federation of fifteen local associations, the Federation of Representative Associations of Dombe Grande (NRA), in the *comuna* of Dombe Grande, a small town near the provincial capital, Benguela, Angola. The NRA is a network of local associations which organise their members at the village or neighbourhood level. The majority of these local associations represent small-scale farmers. Some of the NRA's local associations are civic associations, offering civic education services to citizens and members of the police force.

Within the NRA there are multiple levels of mediation. The network of associations, the NRA, mediates between communities and local and municipal government. One of its primary functions is to mediate between local government and representatives of local associations. It also mediates between member associations and international NGOs and development agencies. It mediates between civic associations of different municipalities. Member associations of the NRA themselves mediate between community leaders and ordinary citizens. Within the NRA itself a set of more organised associations act as mediators between the association and newer, less organised associations.

The NRA aims to bring together and represent the demands of its member associations to local government and to donors. It also provides services for its member organisations such as training, advice on constitutions, mediation with donors, access to technical expertise and monitoring of the associations' credit activity. Central here are attempts to build citizen capacities for participation through strengthening connections between local associations and engaging the local state. The mediating actor, the NRA, plays a coordinating role, linking civil society organisations to each other, mediating relations with the state and coordinating collective action (Ferreira and Roque 2010).

The case shows how associations have played a key role in fostering a greater knowledge of rights and in building up their members' confidence and capacity to participate politically. Ferreira and Roque, for example, report how increases in the membership of associations in Angola resulted not only in material improvements in the livelihoods of association members brought about by credit schemes but also led to an increased sense of citizenship, self-esteem and capacity to intervene in public life. A member of the federation of local associations that they studied told the authors:

> One of the biggest achievements of my experience with the association is to have become aware that I am somebody like any other person; that I am seen as a person as much as a police officer is; that I am considered as a person as much as a prominent person is. This means that I have the same status as somebody who holds a prominent position [in society]. My rights are similar to those of this other person. If there is something that goes against my dignity, I can place the complaint next to an official entity that will respond to my concern (Ferreira and Roque 2010: 82–3).

In response to current literature asking for evidence of the capacity of associations to stimulate democratic attitudes (Bratton *et al.* 1999: 807–24), this case shows that associations can make a difference in building democratic citizenship by increasing people's knowledge of their rights and by bolstering their capacity for political action. While the existence of associations does not, in itself, lead to democratisation, their everyday practices and deliberate programmatic interventions can and do contribute to shaping active citizenship at the grassroots level.

At first glance,the Angolan case seems to have less obvious outcomes in terms of tangible, material benefits for poor and marginalised groups. However, the case does show how, in contexts with fragile democratic institutions and unresponsive states, these forms of mediated associational mobilisation can also result in more tangible developmental outcomes associated with improvements in livelihoods and challenges to local political abuses of power. The NRA and affiliates report greater access to funding, to building sustainable engagements between associations and ordinary citizens, and the economic and political empowerment of farmer associations. There are clear increases in the capacities of small farmers to support the livelihoods of their poor members.

Many theories of democracy discuss the importance of an empowered citizenry who can actively participate in democratic life, hold the state to account and exercise their rights and responsibilities effectively. Learning these skills involves the development of citizens as actors, capable of claiming rights and acting for themselves. As Gaventa and Barrett (2010: 27) argue, 'an important first-level impact of citizen engagement is the development of a greater sense of rights and empowered self-identity, which serve as a prerequisite for action and participation'. An important part of building more effective citizenship practices is to develop greater political knowledge, awareness of rights and agency, and developing social organisations and networks. Gaventa and Barrett (2010: 32) argue that 'there is a great deal of evidence to suggest that the construction of knowledgeable and empowered citizens is one of the most important sets of outcomes produced by citizen engagement'. Building such 'citizenship' capacities can facilitate other democratic and developmental outcomes. The Angolan case study speaks to these possibilities.

Despite these positive outcomes, however, Ferreira and Roque (2010) also highlight limits in the capacity of localised civic action to influence broader democratisation processes, state power and public policies. While there has been some success in promoting dialogue between local citizens and local government, they point out that overall these interactions seem to have had little impact on state's overall responsiveness to citizens' demands. The NRA's local successes have not been translated into longer-term sustained access to state resources or more sustained state responsiveness at the local level. Longer-term political outcomes have not included increased and more robust institutionalised channels for citizen-state interaction which link the local state to local citizens. While the claim-making capacity of local communities was enhanced, this has not led to a deeper transformation of state-society relations and state power.

Conclusion: citizen action, resistance and civil society

The two case studies discussed in this chapter illustrate the limits and possibilities of civic action as forms of resistance. Citizens and their civic mobilisations can lead to greater state responsiveness and can re-shape state-society relations, but they can also result in deepening the disconnect between state and society. The two cases in this chapter address two issues: the important role of mediating actors in mobilising ordinary people into civic action and the potential political outcomes for state-society relations associated with citizen action. The cases call attention to the fact that the meaning and relevance of the political outcomes achieved through citizen mobilisation depend on the context in which the mobilisations occur. In Angola, a context with deep social fragmentation and a history of weak civil society/state engagement, associational citizen action can achieve political outcomes related to building marginalised communities' capacities for making new claims and accessing rights and services. The case also illustrated the limits of localised civic action in contesting state power and re-defining state-society relations. The South African case shows how social movements can contribute to building citizenship as well as press successfully for state responsiveness to citizens' demands for rights, services and agendas. It is important to bear in mind that the form of mediated citizen mobilisation that showed the greatest capacity to promote state responsiveness – social movements – is characterised by a prior history of citizen mobilisation. Social movements acted and delivered when they could rely on previous forms of social mobilisation (Coelho and von Lieres 2010).

While the cases suggest different patterns of citizen mobilisation in settings with weaker and stronger democracies, they also call for more research on both the mechanisms that combine these different forms of citizen mobilisation, and on the different democratic outcomes generated by these combinations. Civil society mobilisation can play a crucial role in building the institutions and cultures of democratic citizenship and for citizen involvement in public participation, a crucial aspect of the deepening democracy project. However, citizen action does not produce automatic political outcomes that favour marginalised communities. The political outcomes of civic action as a form of resistance are profoundly shaped by the actual forms of mobilisation, existing political cultures and distinct histories of social mobilisation.

Both cases highlight the importance of understanding civil society not simply as the arena of formal organisations. The existence of formal civic society organisations does not in and of itself bring about change. In some cases formal CSOs simply reinforce unequal political and economic relations. Civil society's capacity to hold states accountable is shaped significantly by informal citizen action from below, especially in contexts in which states are non-responsive and unaccountable. Citizen action can range from highly localised and often spontaneous, grass-roots mobilisations to more considered engagements with powerful actors such as local states or national governments. In understanding state-society relations we need to move beyond the focus on formal organisations in civil society towards a broader understanding of the distinct modalities and strategies of diverse forms of citizen action, and how these shape state-society relations. We need to shift our focus to the actual, everyday practices of grassroots civic mobilisation, as well as to the distinct and diverse types of mediated engagement between citizens and powerful actors if we want to understand ordinary citizens' emerging capacities for resistance-as-citizenship vis-à-vis states.

References

Aliber, M., Kirsten, M., Maharajh, R., Nhlapo-Hlope, J., Nkoane, O. (2006). Overcoming underdevelopment in South Africa's second economy. *Development Southern Africa*, 23(1), 45–61.

Appadurai, A. (2002). Deep democracy: urban governmentality and the horizon of politics. *Public Culture*, 14(1), 21–47.

Avritzer, L. (2010). Democratizing urban policy in Brazil: participation and the right to the city. In J. Gaventa and R. McGee (eds), *Citizen action and national policy reform: making change happen*. London and New York: Zed Books.

Bratton, M. P., Alderfer, P., Bowser, G. and Temba, J. (1999).The effects of civic education on political culture; evidence from Zambia.*World Development*, 27(5): 807–24.

Chandhoke, N. (2009). Participation, representation and democracy in contemporary India. *American Behavioural Scientist*, 52(6), 807–25.

Chatterjee, P. (2006). *The politics of the governed*.New York: Columbia University Press.

Coelho, V. S. and Lieres, B. von (eds) (2010).*Mobilizing for democracy: citizen action and the politics of public participation*. London: Zed Books.

Cornwall, A. (2002). *Making spaces, changing places: situating participation in development. IDS Working Paper 170*. Brighton: Institute for Development Studies, University of Sussex.

Cornwall, A. and Coelho, V. S. (eds) (2007). *Spaces for change? The politics of citizen participation in new democratic arenas*. London: Zed Books.

Houtzager, H., Acharya, A. and Lavalle, A. (2007). *Associations and the exercise of citizenship in new democracies: evidence from Sao Paulo and Mexico City. IDS Working Paper 285*. Brighton: Institute for Development Studies, University of Sussex.

Ferreira, I. and Roque, S. (2010). Building democracy and citizenship at the

local level: the Núcleo Representativo das Associações do Dombe Grande (pp. 72–98). In V. S. Coelho and B. von Lieres (eds), *Mobilising for democracy: citizen action and the politics of public participation*. London and New York: Zed Books.
Friedman, S. (2010). Gaining comprehensive AIDS treatment in South Africa: the extraordinary 'ordinary'. In J. Gaventa and R. McGee (eds), *Citizen action and national policy reform: making change happen*. London and New York: Zed Books.
Fung, A. and Wright, E. O. (2001). Deepening democracy: innovations in empowered participatory governance.*Politics and Society*, 29(1), 5–41.
Gaventa, J. (2006). *Triumph, deficit or contestation? Deepening the 'deepening democracy' debate*. IDS Working Paper 264. Brighton: Institute for Development Studies, University of Sussex.
Gaventa, J. and Barrett, G. (2010). *So what difference does it make? Mapping the outcomes of citizen engagement. IDS Working Paper 347*. Brighton: Institute for Development Studies, University of Sussex.
Gaventa, J. and McGee, R. (2010) (eds). *Citizen action and national policy reform: making change happen*. London and New York: Zed Books.
Houtzager, P. and Lavalle, A. (2010). Civil society's claim to political representation in Brazil. *Studies in Comparative International Development*, 45(1), 1–29.
Kabeer, N.(ed.).(2005) *Inclusive citizenship*. London and New York: Zed Books.
Newell, P. and Wheeler, J. (eds) (2006). *Rights, resources and the politics of accountability*. London and New York: Zed Books.
Piper, L. 2006. Beyond neo-liberalism; beyond the ANC: South African politics as 'progressive governance'. In T. Marcus and A.Hofmaenner (eds), *Shifting the boundaries of knowledge: a view on social sciences, law and humanities in South Africa*. Pietermaritzburg: University of KwaZulu-Natal Press.
Piper, L., Bafo, K. and Lieres, B. von (2012). *Opening policy space in the dominant party: the Treatment Action Campaign, HIV/AIDS, and the reinvention of the ANC in South Africa*. Unpublished research report.
Piper, L. and Lieres, B. von (2011). *Expert advocacy for the marginalised: how and why democratic mediation matters to deepening democracy in the global South. IDS Working Paper 364*. Brighton: Institute for Development Studies, University of Sussex.
Robins, S. and von Lieres, B. (2004). Remaking citizenship, unmaking marginalization: new social movements in post-apartheid South Africa. *Canadian Journal of African Studies*, 38(3), 575–86.
Robson, P. and Roque, S. (2001).'Here in the city, everything has to be paid for': locating the community in peri-urban Angola. *Review of African Political Economy*, 28(90), 619–28.
Sogge, D. (2006). Angola: global good governance also needed'. Working Paper 23: 8. Madrid: FRIDE.

Part II

EMBODIED MODES OF RESISTANCE & THE POSTCOLONIAL STATE

4 The Politics of Confinement & Mobility

Informality, Relocations & Urban Re-making from Above & Below in Nairobi

Ilda Lindell & Markus Ihalainen[1]

Introduction

Informal modes of earning a living are expanding rapidly in cities in Africa and beyond. This has its most evident physical expression in the vast unplanned settlements in the peripheries of cities. But a large number of urban residents also daily invade central areas of the city and operate in its interstices in the pursuit of their livelihoods. Their growing numbers are often understood as a problem by many city authorities. Concerned with projecting an image of a modern and orderly city and influenced by ideals of 'cityness' circulating internationally, urban authorities in many cities feel urged to deal with what they consider a growing menace. This chapter illustrates how authorities in Nairobi intervened to 'clean up' the city centre from undesirable informal actors through the creation of a hawkers market and a ban on communal minibus traffic. It uncovers the disciplinary technologies deployed in an attempt to govern these 'unruly' populations as well as the ways in which vendors resisted and engaged with these interventions.

Expanding urban informality has often been seen as a sign of urban involution, an abnormal form of urbanism whose dark future will only lead to further decay and abjection (see Davis 2004). In contrast to such dystopian views, a growing and diverse body of work distances itself from such doomsday interpretations and provides more positive readings of urban informality. James Holston (2008) depicts informal housing areas in the peripheries of São Paulo as sites of an emerging insurgent citizenship. Such insurgency disrupts unequal regimes of citizenship that have forced the urban poor into illegal habitation. Their enaction of counter-politics contests categorisations of illegality, articulates the legitimacy of their urban practices and claims their right to the city. In Holston's work, urban informality occupies a central place in understanding broader issues of citizenship. His writings have inspired

[1] The authors wish to thank Winnie Mitullah and Mary Kinyanjui for sharing their knowledge on the research topic in Nairobi, Ananya Roy for comments on an early oral presentation of this chapter and the anonymous reviewers for their comments. We are grateful to all the respondents who took time to share their experiences. The study was conducted within the framework of a programme on Poverty, Inequality and Social Exclusion in Africa funded by the Swedish International Development Cooperation Agency, under the auspices of the Nordic Africa Institute.

other work where informality and insurgence are seen as closely associated.

Urban informality is represented by a number of scholars as a manifestation of an urban re-making from 'below'. This is often referred to as vernacular or subaltern urbanism, driven by a shared subaltern rationality or spatial logic and characterised by creativity and flexibility (Simone 2002). Marginalised groups appropriate and produce urban space through urban spatial practices that embody their own conceptions of the city. Asef Bayat (2004: 579) conceives the politics of the subaltern as taking a particular form, namely 'the encroachment of the ordinary' and the 'habitus of the dispossessed', marked by 'flexibility, pragmatism [...] constant struggle for survival and self-development'. In a similar vein, Nihal Pereira (2009: 52) refers to a process of familiarisation of space whereby the subalterns, 'by means of accommodation, adaptation, redefinition, and negotiation of space [...] transform extant space [...] into milieus that can accommodate and support their everyday activities and cultural practices'. He points to the significance of such space-making from below in the context of colonial Colombo. In his view, processes of familiarisation of space are linked to subject formation. People reinterpret and give new meanings to the extant spaces of dominant power, and in the process, both spaces and subject positions are changed. He emphasises the transformative capacities of the subaltern and the subversive nature of their space-making practices. Their 'clandestine' practices, he argues, undermine and frustrate the plans and intentions of power holders. Like Bayat, he sees resistance by the subaltern as taking mainly the form of small-scale, everyday ordinary acts rather than large-scale and organised claim-making.

Some authors have expressed concern that some of the work within the strand of informal or subaltern urbanism tends to essentialise subalterns' logics of urbanism and to romanticise their autonomy, resilience and potential (Myers 2011; Byerley 2011). Urban residents are not unconstrained in their city-making practices and the spaces they create are continuously contested (Lefebvre 1991; Mitchell 2003). While they re-work the city from below and take over urban spaces, dominant actors may reclaim those spaces, resulting in unending territorial struggles. These conquests and defeats are of political import, as the citizenship of disadvantaged urban groups is often dependent on their claiming of urban space (Holston 2008; Mitchell 2003; Brown 2006). Through making themselves visible in public space, marginalised groups gain recognition from the larger public. Therefore, measures that erase already marginalised groups from public space potentially deepen their exclusion from society (Mitchell 2003). On the other hand, subaltern groups may also respond to attempts to exclude them from urban spaces that they value.

In her recent critique of the 'subaltern urbanism' paradigm, Ananya Roy (2011: 224) interrogates 'ontological and topological understandings of subaltern subjects and subaltern spaces'. She finds problematic the simplistic assumptions often attached to 'subaltern agency'. Conceptions reliant on notions such as 'habitus of the dispossessed' and 'occupancy urbanism' tend to ascribe to the urban poor a distinct kind of political agency, one which is depicted as being necessarily politically subversive, autonomous from dominant power and developmentalist interventions. Drawing on postcolonialist theorists Spivak and Guha, she warns against representing the subaltern in terms of a coherent identity. 'At best', Roy (2011: 230) argues, 'subaltern politics can be seen as a heterogeneous, contradictory and performative realm of political struggle'. In Spivak's words, 'subalternity is a position without identity' and it does not constitute 'a recognizable basis of action' (quoted in Roy 2011: 231).

Lindell's (2010a) work on the politics of informality has advanced similar arguments about the political subjectivities and agency of disadvantaged people living through informality. A long-standing tradition tends to understand their politics in terms of a sharp and clear-cut opposition between these actors and dominant power. The informal realm has often been described as being state-free and informal actors as always circumventing the state, resisting it, or slowly but relentlessly pushing it back. Seen as autonomous from and against the state, these actors are also represented as occupying a similar structural location and subject position, and as bearers of singular and coherent identities. Such views risk portraying 'informals' as an undifferentiated mass, sitting uneasily with the great variety of actors that today engage in informal economic practices. It has been emphasised that informal actors experience various forms of injustice, occupy multiple subject positions, and carry multiple and fractured identities (Lindell 2010b). Their political subjectivities and behaviour cannot thus be pre-determined. Furthermore, the political modalities of disadvantaged informal actors are more diverse than often is assumed, including both individual everyday acts and more organised forms (Lindell 2010c).

This chapter addresses an official intervention to constrain and eliminate the space-making and familiarising practices of informal operators in Nairobi's central business district (CBD). With a particular focus on street vendors, it explores some of the political processes leading up to their relocation into a new market in 2007 and the long-term outcomes. It describes the forms of spatial and temporal discipline which dominant power sought to impose and how these in turn led to new insurgent spatial practices. The case illustrates the complexity of these territorial struggles, the diverse and contradictory forms of agency employed, and the complex political subjectivities at work. This is complicated by the differentiated experiences of the relocation and of its consequences among the vendor population.

There is considerable work on similar interventions and popular responses in other regions of the global South (for example, see Crossa

2009 and Bromley and Mackie 2009). In Africa, while displacement and relocations of street vendors are on the increase and have been noticed by a few (see for example Tranberg-Hansen 2004), the agency and political processes surrounding such interventions deserve greater problematisation. The ways in which informal actors resist, negotiate or engage with such interventions are still under-researched in the urban African context.

The case presented in this chapter is based on an exploratory study carried out in Nairobi in 2010. While that study focused on the planning of the new hawkers market and on the effects of the relocation as experienced by the vendors, it is used here as a basis for drawing some reflections upon issues relating to 'subaltern politics'. The study draws on interviews carried out with a range of relevant actors. First, open interviews with key informants provided a general overview of the studied area, of the market-place and of the process of relocation. Second, five urban planners and key officials in several departments of the City Council of Nairobi (CCN) and two in relevant departments of the Ministry of Local Government were interviewed. Third, semi-structured interviews were conducted with twenty vendors operating at Muthurwa market as well as with a group of hawkers who had abandoned the market to return to the CBD streets, to learn about the vendors' perspectives and experiences of the relocation. In order to capture the experiences of a heterogeneous group, vendors of different genders and scales of operation were interviewed. Several representatives of vendors associations were also interviewed. Interpreters were used for the interviews which hopefully enabled the vendors to give more elaborated answers.

Containing informality

Nairobi's CBD is the prime location of headquarters of corporations, hotels and important government functions in the city. Through the years, the area has also attracted a growing number of people who pursue their livelihoods on the CBD streets where income opportunities are higher than elsewhere. Street vending has become a prominent source of income for Nairobi residents (Mitullah 2003a, 2003b; Lyons and Snoxell 2005) and, according to estimates of the Ministry of Local Government, there were 15,000–20,000 hawkers operating in the CBD area, prior to their removal. Street vending has been a long-standing activity in Nairobi's CBD and has increased through the years. The street vending population has been described as being quite heterogeneous, in terms of the goods they sell, their locational strategies and scales of operation. For example, men tend to sell goods of higher value than women, have larger stocks and hire assistants to a greater extent (Mitullah 2003b: 6; Muiruri 2010). Although the level of collective organising among the street vendors has been described differently by different authors (see Mitullah 2003a; Muiruri 2010), it can be said that, prior to the relocation, a number of associations operated in the CBD area – often small rotating savings and credit associations that worked as an insurance scheme for member traders. There have also been initiatives to create larger or federated organisations of informal operators, although there are concerns about the actual strength and long-term sustainability of these organisations (see Mitullah 2010; Muiruri 2010). Participation is also differentiated – for example, women have been found to be part of associations more seldom than men (Muiruri 2010). As will be suggested here, the associational landscape was affected by the relocation.

Several observers have noted how street vendors in Nairobi have lacked recognition from the authorities (Muiruri 2010; Kamunyori 2007; Kimathi 2004; Kinyanjui 2011; Mitullah 2003a). While relations between vendors and governing powers have undergone shifts through time, the attitudes of the urban authorities have been predominantly negative towards vendors, with recurrent incidents of harassment, arrests and confiscation of goods. Women have been particularly vulnerable, something aggravated by the masculinist planning system in place (Kinyanjui 2011). As the number of street vendors grew in central Nairobi, confrontations with the city police became increasingly frequent and violent, resulting sometimes in deaths, as explained by one association representative. Visions of an orderly and modern CBD, capable of attracting investors, in the context of a national vision that seeks to improve the global competitiveness of the country (Republic of Kenya 2007) may have contributed to this escalation.

Relocations have been one of the strategies through which the Nairobi authorities have dealt with hawkers (Mitullah 2003; Kimathi 2004, Kiura 2005). One example was the relocation of the hawkers to the back lanes of the CBD in 2003. One association representative explained that the call for an alternative space for vending came not only from the authorities but also from vendors themselves who were tired of constantly being harassed by the city police. He stated that the leaders of the various vendors associations in the CBD were asking for alternative vending locations. Soon, all vendors were moved from the streets of the CBD to the back lanes. But after a while, he explained, due to a lack of customers, as well as the incapability of the authorities to enforce 'order', vendors abandoned the back lanes and returned to the streets of the CBD (see also Kiura 2005).

By 2007, tensions between the hawkers and the authorities had once again grown to a critical point. One association leader recalls that a hawker was killed by the city police, an event that was followed by demonstrations. In a Cabinet memorandum, the Minister of Local Government (n.d.: 1) described the situation around that time in the following terms: 'The problem of dealing with hawkers has become critical and urgent because of the increasing ferocity of conflict between the Council enforcement structures and the traders. The threat of a general and widespread breakdown in law and order is now very real'. It was therefore urgent to find a durable solution. It was in this context that the idea of a new market for Nairobi CBD hawkers emerged. As noted by D.Gatimu, according to one of the planners involved in the project, the new market would differ from previous relocations as it would take into consideration the livelihood needs of the vendors and would be centrally located – in the area of Muthurwa, located on the south-eastern border of the downtown area, after which the market was named (Gatimu 2008). If successful, the idea of a hawkers market would be implemented across Kenya's urban centres.

As with the above relocation to the back lanes, vendors associations were not passive. Interviewed representatives of one association claimed that it was the leaders of the vendors associations in the CBD that came up with the idea of a new market and presented it to the government. Their association, they stated, actively lobbied for the market. The market would be able to accommodate most of their members and at the time it seemed like a good solution, one of them explained. However, many vendors felt differently, as explained below.

Muthurwa market was designed and planned by a team of urban planners, architects and engineers at the City Council of Nairobi and the Ministry of Local Government. It was to be located near to two major arteries that link central Nairobi to its peripheries and beyond, and was to operate in combination with a new minibus transport terminus adjacent to the market. With the opening of the terminus, the *matatu* traffic (the local communal minibus transportation) in the CBD would be banned. The estimated 20,000 minibuses servicing the Eastern peripheries of Nairobi would cease to drive the whole way into the CBD and would have their last/first stop at Muthurwa. According to the Advisory Plan, when at the terminus, each minibus would be given 20 minutes to offload and pick up new passengers, after which it would have to exit the terminus. The design of the combined market and transport terminus was such that, to take another bus, passengers would have to pass through the market, which was expected to generate a substantial flow of customers for the market traders.

The market was to comprise a number of blocks, each consisting of a concrete floor and a metal roof and was enclosed by a wall, intended to protect the city image, on which the hawkers were perceived to impact negatively (Gatimu 2008). There would be no storage facilities, as this would make it possible to accommodate more hawkers, as explained by a member of the planning team. The market was intended to shelter between 6,500 and 8,000 vendors who would occupy 1.75 square metres each. Each hawker would thus be assigned a certain slot at the market for which they would pay a daily fee but they would not be granted permanent rights to their vending spaces, only temporary user rights (Gatimu 2008: 13). One of the associations later made attempts to advocate for security of tenure at the new market but the City Council denied their request.

The relocation: dis-organising hawkers

The CBD hawkers were given a sudden notice from the City Council that once the market was opened, hawking in the CBD would be strictly forbidden. Hawkers caught in the CBD would face heavy fines or even imprisonment. The interviewed former CBD hawkers recall that this time they knew they would have no other option than to leave the CBD and move to the new market. In contrast to the statements of association leaders who claimed that Muthurwa resulted from the vendors crying for an alternative space, the interviewed hawkers said that they were reluctant to leave the CBD and only moved because they had no other choice. They also reportedly demonstrated against the relocation (*Daily News*, 5 March 2008) but apparently with little success.

The coordination of the move to the market in a fair, organised and peaceful manner turned out to be a major challenge, given the large number of hawkers operating in the CBD area. According to various respondents, the authorities did not make any efforts to organise the move. At least two hawkers associations that organised vendors in the CBD streets appear to have been active in trying to organise the relocation. In fact, interviewed representatives of both associations claimed that their association was the one assigned the main responsibility for coordinating the move into the market. According to its chairman, association A made numerous attempts to call together the hawkers and the leaders of the associations operating in the various streets of the CBD. He recalled that once the meeting gathered, there were so many hawkers that they had to rent the City Hall in order to have enough space. However, the association's attempts to assemble and coordinate the vendors faced considerable interference, sometimes leading to the cancellation of meetings. He explained: 'Every time we held a meeting, hooligans, hired by the politicians, would appear, starting fights and interfering. Even hijackings occurred [...]. That is how much the politicians fear the organisation of the informal sector.' According to him, the politicians feared such organisation because, if organised, they could endanger the positions of some politicians.

Association B was also trying to coordinate the move of the CBD hawkers into the market. One of its leading persons made clear that they sought to do this without involving the leaders of other associations. He explained: 'It was a time of euphoria; we felt like we could do it on our own. We did not need the help of [other associations] and eventually, they were overthrown by us.' According to other respondents, the association was being 'encouraged' by one politician to conduct the move to the market on its own and its leaders were promised the ownership of some of the facilities at Muthurwa such as the food court. The members of that association, the respondents claimed, were then given permission to enter the market before it was formally opened whereby they could occupy the most lucrative locations at the market. In the view of one interviewee, it was necessary for the politicians to create division between the vendors and their associations in order to be able to intervene. He added that hawkers, being poor, are easily manipulated by politicians who have the money and power to make promises.

Muthurwa market thus became a focus of considerable political attention and a highly politicised matter as was demonstrated in interviews with both association leaders and government officials. Muthurwa was at that time perceived as a positive accomplishment by the authorities and, as national elections were coming up, politicians from different political factions competed with each other in taking credit for the achievement. After all, the hawkers constituted a big block of voters and, by being perceived positively by them, politicians could gain a great advantage in rallies, the secretary of one of the associations explained. In this context of heightened political competition, a major split developed between vendor associations which would have significant consequences for the representational structures at the market.

As it turned out, when the market opened in late 2007, the move into the market was highly disorganised and uncoordinated as described by both interviewed vendors and government officials. The number of people that moved in exceeded the amount of hawkers the market was supposed to accommodate. Many shopkeepers and non-CBD traders also joined the battle for market slots. Some described the move as resembling the survival of the fittest: the physically and economically strongest vendors occupied the best slots as weaker and poorer hawkers, especially women, were pushed out. This was the general perception among the interviewed vendors. An elderly female vendor described the events: 'There was a lot of violence as people were fighting for the slots. One person was even killed, women were beaten and raped [...]. So the strongest people got the best slots, and we [old women] just took whatever was left for us.'

Some vendors occupied spaces that were much bigger than the designated 1.75 square metres. Many CBD hawkers did not get a slot at the market. A representative of association A claimed that about 800 members of the association were left without a slot. More generally, it is evident that the 8,000 vending spaces at the market envisaged by the authorities were from the beginning insufficient to accommodate the estimated 15,000–20,000 hawkers operating in the CBD. Many vendors thus occupied the pathways and spaces at the *matatu* terminus from the start.

Muthurwa was built for the City Council to run. The City Council was thus formally in charge of the management of the market, including the daily leasing out of slots, cleaning and maintenance of infrastructure. However, many vendors stated that the only thing that the Council does at the market is collect the daily fees. A market committee was also created, consisting of eleven executive members and some twenty committee members. According to its chairman, its role was to identify problems at the market and present them to the City Council if they were unable to solve them by themselves. The committee is headed by the leader of one of the above-mentioned associations. He explained that the committee is funded through public facilities at the market, such as the restrooms and the restaurants. Vendors in each block have a representative who is supposed to bring the concerns of those vendors to the executive. However, only a few of the interviewed vendors knew the committee existed and they expressed low trust in its representational role. Also, vendors who failed to occupy slots within the blocks were not represented by anyone.

Subverting containment

Within a couple of years following the inauguration, the number of vendors operating in the market declined from an initial estimated 8,000–10,000 to 3,000–4,000, according to estimates from the associations' representatives. The vendors came to be concentrated along the alley within the market that gave access to the transport terminus; large parts of the market had been abandoned by the vendors. Virtually all of the interviewed vendors were disappointed with the volume of their sales at the market compared to what they earned while hawking in the CBD streets. The falling incomes were experienced by the vendors as result of several factors. To begin with, there was a lack of customers. This was partly related to a steady decline in the number of *matatus* offloading at Muthurwa, as explained by an engineer at the Transportation Unit of the City Engineers Department at the City Council of Nairobi. It was evident that the terminus was not functioning in the way it was intended to. According to multiple respondents, the *matatu* operators were not only violating the time limits regulating the duration of off- and on-loading; they were also driving all the way to the CBD instead of coming into Muthurwa, thus ignoring the ban on *matatu* traffic in the CBD. With their powerful organisations and political connections (Rasmussen 2012), they appeared sufficiently confident to do so and to follow their own regulations instead. There was little the vendors could do about it.

Another critical factor behind the declining incomes of the vendors was the loss of their mobility. When operating on the street, hawkers targeted hectic commuters or impulsive buyers. Their mobility brought them close to the customer and gave them some advantage in relation to fixed (and often better-off) vendors. Fixing the hawkers in slots at the market removed this advantage. In addition, they were faced with the same market fees as more affluent traders. Many of the poorer vendors could not cope with the competition. As stated by some of the hawkers who left Muthurwa for the CBD: 'Meeting the daily fee just became impossible. We had no other option but to leave.' In contrast, the better-off traders, usually occupying the few profitable areas of the market, were able to invest in large and diverse stocks of high value goods (such as clothing, shoes or electronics). Many had occupied areas bigger than the designated size and had built walls around them – practices which went against the market regulations.

The more disadvantaged vendors were not passive in the face of the conditions of unequal competition, unequal access to viable locations and an insufficient flow of customers. Many hawkers abandoned the market altogether and returned to the CBD streets in hope of better sales. Others left their slots to go hawking on the pathways of the few viable areas of the market. By doing this, they could avoid payment of the daily market fee for their slots to the City Council of Nairobi, which was unaffordable for many. By going back to hawking, they were also trying to regain some of the comparative advantage they had lost by being forced into fixed slots. In this way, they could come closer to passing customers and eventually undercut the advantage of the larger-scale vendors. Another way of dealing with competition from the larger vendors that was reported by female food vendors was through mutual help and rotating savings groups. As stated by one vendor: 'Joining forces is the only way for us to compete against the stronger men.'

Some of the hawkers walked around selling refreshments, candy, plastic bags or other products to passers-by. Other hawkers sold second-hand clothing, shoes or bags from a fixed spot on the attractive alleys of the market which often required an agreement with the owners of the slots in their immediate proximity. Frequently however, this latter type of hawkers sold the same products as the fixed vendors in these areas and thus posed direct competition to them. Worth mentioning is that an estimated smaller share of the hawkers were employed by larger vendors to attract customers to their slots which suggest that diverse relations between hawkers and with fixed vendors were at work.

Vendors who (re-)turned to hawking in the CBD or in the market area often rented out or sold their slots to other vendors. As mentioned earlier, vendors did not have any juridical right to the slots they occupied. However, this did not prevent the hawkers from selling or renting out their slots informally to other vendors. Informal ownership came to prevail, thereby subverting the initial intention of confinement without tenure. Renting out one's slot was in many cases a last resort for poor vendors whose sales were not enough to make the enterprise go round. But some vendors mentioned that renting out one's slot was also a conscious business strategy by some hawkers, seeking to increase their incomes by hawking in better locations of the market, by collecting a daily rent for their slots, and by avoiding payment of the market fee. However, as more and more vendors left their slots and the market, their negotiation power in relation to vendors interested in buying or renting their slots seemed to decrease. In particular, buying out poor vendors for cheap prices became easy.

Returning to hawking, however, was not without problems. First, hawking on the pathways created animosity in the market between hawkers and fixed vendors, particularly when both were selling identical products. Some of the fixed vendors interviewed claimed that hawkers blocked the entrance to their slots or stole their customers and they were therefore quite negative towards the hawkers. One vendor even said she had called the police to remove the hawkers from the pathways in front of her slot. Hawkers were also perceived to cause crowding which according to some of the interviewed vendors attracts pickpockets and makes consumers reluctant to come to the market.

Second, trading outside one's slot involved the risk of being caught by the city police who occasionally raided Muthurwa. The risk of being arrested was mentioned by the majority of the vendors as one of the reasons why they had not left their slots in order to go hawking in better locations. An interviewed official at the city inspectorate stated that the raids were intended to 'restore order through arresting and fining hawkers who are not in their slots'. He claimed the department was currently lacking the funds for undertaking the necessary measures to ensure the hawkers stayed in their designated slots. But given that hawking on the pathways is prohibited, he continued, the city police would continue to carry out strikes against the hawkers in order to show that the violation of market regulations was not tolerated or accepted by the Council. Two other interviewed senior officials at the City Council of Nairobi were of the opinion that, as revenue was only collected from vendors occupying slots, the failure of keeping vendors in their slots resulted in low revenues for the Council – although one of them also admitted that an important share of what was indeed being collected also disappeared.

By leaving their slots, the hawkers not only became exposed to the wrath of the authorities and to the irritation of fixed vendors but also formally lost the support of the market committee – the only entity in the market that claimed to represent the interests of the market vendors. It became apparent that the market committee only represented vendors who were in their slots and that there was no entity in the market representing the hawkers' concerns in any way. Other former CBD association leaders made attempts to organise the vendors and the hawkers at Muthurwa into one group. However, they reported that they found difficulties in convincing a very diverse vendor population to come together. While in the CBD, one of them explained, the fight against the authorities was a force pulling the different kinds of vendors together. At the market, there was no common enemy. Thus, poorer vendors who had abandoned their slots in order to go hawking seemed to be particularly unprotected as well as vulnerable to 'order-restoring' raids and to hostilities from other vendors.

Disciplining techniques and contradictory agency

The Muthurwa project can be seen as a strategy to contain and remove expanding numbers of informal operators from Nairobi's CBD, a strategy perceived by the city authorities as necessary to modernise the city centre. As has been noted by others, such clearing interventions are not without political consequences as the visibility of marginalised groups in public space is critical for their citizenship (Mitchell 2003). The prohibition of minibus operators in Nairobi's CBD and the relocation of street vendors into a market surrounded by high walls can possibly be interpreted as a strategy for the invisibility and erasure of these actors from public sight.

The displacement and relocation of urban groups dependent upon informality for survival has been identified as part of attempts by governments to regain control over such populations (Kamete 2009; Tranberg-Hansen 2004; Brown 2006). Such interventions are often accompanied by moves to introduce taxation which is often another major reason for the relocation of vendors to designated markets as identified in other urban contexts (Tranberg-Hansen 2004; Brown 2006). Both of these intentions seem to have inspired the Muthurwa project. The project seems to have been conceived in such a way as to allow the introduction of new spatial and temporal disciplining techniques on the targeted informal populations. Minibus operators were to keep out of the CBD and to observe strict directives while at the terminus concerning the time allowed for loading and offloading of passengers. This imposed temporal austerity most probably went against the requirements of their operations which are usually based on fluid timetables and embarking on a fresh journey with a maximum number of passengers instead of a half-empty minibus. The spatial confinement of the vendors into the designated market was intended to make possible the disciplining of large numbers of street vendors, perceived as unruly, into governable subjects. Spatially fixing the hawkers and locating them in specific slots would not only make them traceable and 'legible' but also enable the authorities to more effectively tax an otherwise mobile population, potentially increasing the revenues of the local government. The provision of market slots, however, did not lead to an improved sense of livelihood security or entitlement. Hawkers were only given temporary use rights to the slots, were supposed to display their goods on the pavement, storage facilities were non-existent and only a very minimum of infrastructure facilities was provided. Operating in these camp-like conditions and imprisoned by the market walls, the majority of vendors therefore faced a situation of confinement without security, and a continued existence in uncertainty. The new spatial regime also decimated the incomes of many whose advantage in relation to bigger traders lay in their mobility.

The new forms of spatial and temporal discipline were never internalised in the Foucauldian sense – which posits the internalisation of discipline as critical for subjects' self-regulation and 'the conduct of conduct', under conditions of dispersed government. As the disadvantages of the new spatial and temporal regulations were increasingly felt and the limited capacity of the state and its agents to systematically enforce those regulations became evident – limited to occasional raids in the market – non-compliance became widespread. As explained above, minibus operators ignored the time regulations and the CBD ban. In the market, the vendors began to treat the slots as if they owned them, and circumvented or refused to pay the market fees. They resisted the strictures of confinement and fixity by resuming hawking activities. The vendors not only ignored market regulations but a good number of them also reclaimed the city streets as their space of operation. The political significance of these transgressive spatial practices should not be underestimated. They potentially disrupted and undermined the dominant vision for central Nairobi and laid bare the inadequacy of a national strategy of dealing with street vendors in urban Kenya through the establishment of hawkers markets.

Indeed, these responses to the market project can be understood in terms of insurgent practices through which the vendors sought to regain their mobility, re-occupy the streets, and reinsert themselves in the public spaces of the city centre. These individual and small-scale spatial practices seem to be in line with notions of 'quiet encroachment' and 'familiarisation of space' which are the forms of agency often ascribed to subaltern subjects. However, the case presented here also suggests that a celebratory reading of these practices tells only half of the story and cannot capture some of the complexities involved.

The first important observation that can be made is that the agency of the vendors and their associations was not always politically subversive or autonomous from the state. To begin with, the relocation of the hawkers from the CBD into the market (and before that, to the back lanes of the CBD) was not something that was pushed unilaterally by the authorities on the vendors. As mentioned, and whatever the motivations, associations' representatives were reported to have lobbied for the market, with some even claiming that the idea for a hawkers market came from the vendors associations themselves. Furthermore, the period preceding the move to the market seems to have been characterised by intense political networking which appears to have led to selective deals between some association representatives and sections of the political elite. These interactions were certainly more complex than could be unravelled through this study, but these examples indicate the entangled nature of relations between dominant and informal actors. This entanglement has been emphasised in research that uncovers how the latter actors become part of vertical clientelist networks which facilitate the penetration of the power of the state into the lower echelons of society (see for example Reno 2000 and Bayart *et al.* 1999). Autonomous organising from this viewpoint becomes virtually impossible. But even if that power is not necessarily all-pervasive or inescapable, there are reasons to consider how 'domination' and 'resistance' are seldom clear-cut, but rather entwined. These complexities thus cast a doubt over simplistic ontological conceptions of subaltern political agency that emphasise and assume its distinctive, subversive and autonomous nature. Rather, we ought to consider the ambivalence of relations and the contradictory forms that political struggle can take (Roy 2011).

Understandings of the political location of subalternity that ascribe to the subaltern a coherent and distinct political identity are further disturbed by the developments after the relocation. The vendors at the new market had highly varied experiences of the relocation and of its consequences. The economic effects were experienced very differently by different groups. A select group seemed to have benefited from the relocation; they had gained privileged access to the best located slots and had been able to expand their stocks. A clique also had control over key resource-generating facilities in the market. In contrast, the poorer vendors (many of them being women and the elderly) found themselves in the less viable areas, deprived of customers and suffering the effects of (incarceration and) imposed immobility. While the vending population was diverse already prior to the move, the immobilisation of the poorer hawkers further depleted their incomes and made them more vulnerable to competition from the more affluent vendors. The responses and practices of these differently affected groups were very different. The well-stocked vendors seemed to thrive under conditions of immobility, and further invested in building walls and in consolidating their positions in the market. The poorer vendors on the other hand abandoned their slots and resorted to hawking inside and outside the market. This resonates with Crossa's (2009) findings in her study of displaced vendors in Mexico City and the different spatial practices that differently affected groups deployed.

Crucially, the poorer vendors were not only resisting incarceration and the new regulations imposed by the authorities; they were also resisting the bigger traders, the 'big men', as the vendors themselves explained. They were thus experiencing and resisting several forms of injustice, including income inequalities and gender disadvantages among vendors themselves. Even if there were various forms of collaboration and compromises among different vendors, tensions were also mounting (including animosities against mobile hawkers) and the vendors were sometimes blaming each other. These multiple layers of grievance and divergent experiences among vendors can hardly be reduced to a distinct and coherent identity anchored in an easily identifiable subject position; rather, they indicate that they are bearers of diverse, multiple and fractured identities.

If the economic fates of vendors at Muthurwa were highly diverse, politically too, the vendors were not equally 'marginalised'. In other words, it seems that the political effects of the relocation were not equally distributed. In the first instance, it seems that the relocation did not have a favourable effect on vendors' collective organisation. The period preceding the relocation was marked by heightened competition and antagonisms between different vendor organisations and the 'divide and rule' activities of politicians hampered the organising efforts of some of them. Apparently, one association overpowered the other associations and proclaimed itself as the sole legitimate organisation at the market, the market committee. Although the implications of this change were not fully apprehended, judging from the views of ordinary vendors it is doubtful that this change represented a unifying or upscaling of their collective organising and may even have weakened representation among the vendors, as some association representatives reported loss of membership. Importantly, vendors who left their slots to go hawking could not count on protection from any collective body, and were left without collective representation. Second, vendors at Muthurwa were not equally exposed to the enforcement of market regulations. As mentioned, a better-off group seemed to stand immune to law enforcement, even though they were ignoring certain regulations – for example by occupying bigger areas than they were allocated and by building walls around their slots. They seemed to enjoy a degree of protection from enforcement and to feel secure to make such investments. In contrast, the poorer vendors who were pushed into hawking and thus violated the regulations that prohibited mobility were vulnerable to the wrath of the authorities. They were clearly classified by key city officials as law-breakers and as the main targets of order-restoring raids. Politically disconnected, deserted by the market committee and unable to depend on whatever association they may have belonged to prior to the relocation, the hawkers were left to fend for themselves.

This selective enforcement of regulations is indicative of the flexibility of dominant power to apply or revoke the law and of its ability to differentially deploy its power upon diverse populations (Agamben 1998; Ong 2006) – even if this power is far from unlimited. Such 'ways of governing that differentially value populations', leading to 'different social fates', in combination with the differentiated political outcomes of the relocation in terms of collective representation, could be interpreted as an instance of what Aihwa Ong (2006: 78–9) calls 'graduated citizenship'. Such nuanced notions can help complicate assumptions about a distinct and singular political location of subalternity.

Conclusions

This case study is situated within ongoing debates that connect urban informality to insurgency, citizenship and urban struggles in the global South. The exploratory findings suggest that simplistic understandings that essentialise the forms and nature of subaltern agency and subjectivity are inadequate to capture the diversity of experiences and the complexity of political processes that were at work. The ways in which the relocation and its effects were experienced varied considerably among a differentiated vendor population, which disrupts conceptions of the political location of the urban subaltern as given and of its political identity as coherent. The manifestations of their agency were diverse and contradictory, casting doubts over assumptions that subaltern agency takes a distinct form and is necessarily subversive and autonomous. In this case, it took both the form of small-scale individual acts, public demonstrations and more organised forms where association leaders played a part; it involved resistance and contestation as well as complicity and political alliances. Different groups resisted, negotiated or even appeared to embrace the intervention.

The case study illustrates how the state strikes back and reclaims spaces formerly familiarised by disadvantaged urban groups. This reclaiming required the deployment of several modalities of power. These included the development of new forms of regulatory control and disciplining techniques as well as the exercise of power through informal channels leading to political deals between politicians and some association leaders. These tactics appeared to circumscribe hawkers' insurgent activities at first and to mute or paralyse the resisting capacities of their associations. This suggests that resistance by the subaltern is not unconstrained, contrary to what is sometimes assumed, and may even be incorporated by the political elites. But those tactics of the powerful were only partly successful. The widespread return to hawking exposed the poor capacity of the state to regulate urban space as well as the incompleteness of its power, as hawkers both evaded state regulations and could not be fully controlled through (or incorporated into) the vertical political networks through which political elites apparently sought to extend their influence to the grassroots.

What can then be said of the assumed transformative potential of the agency of the subaltern, in this particular case? Even if dominant power was not complete, the opportunities this incompleteness might have created for the subaltern agency of the hawkers should neither be diminished nor exaggerated. The exercise of their agency was potentially complicated by the alliances between politicians and association leaders, as non-compliant practices may have entailed exclusion from associations, loss of protection and political disconnection. The dis-organising effect that the relocation apparently had on CBD vendor associations potentially further contributed to the hawkers' lack of options. In addition, initiating alternative associations is a considerable challenge in such an environment marked by tangible pressures from political factions and competition between associations. In some cases, traders in fact prefer to collaborate in small-scale groups and networks rather than to scale up into visible and vocal associations, as a way of deflecting political attention and avoiding co-option and the pressure of politicians (M. Kinyanjui, personal communication). Many hawkers may also refuse to join associations altogether due to distrust and earlier disappointments, when their interests have been misrepresented or insufficiently protected in the past.

But one should also consider cases where subaltern groups are able to take advantage of the competition among political factions and to draw considerable benefits for their members from vertical clientelistic relations. In the transport sector in Nairobi, the Mungiki movement has, through political brokering, been able to secure and control *matatu* routes in Nairobi and to actively re-shape the city (Rasmussen 2012). With their organisational strength, they have occasionally been capable of paralysing the city through their strikes. In the trade sector, the umbrella organisation Kenya National Alliance of Street Vendors and Informal Traders (KENASVIT) has, with the support of international partners and networks, been able to achieve recognition and to influence local and national state actors in the past (Mitullah 2010).

While collective organisation is not always possible or even preferred, nor necessarily uncontaminated by dominant power or progressive forces, it can open new political possibilities (Lindell 2010a, 2010b; Pieterse 2008). It may enable marginalised groups to collectively assert themselves as belonging in the city and as legitimate citizens, to claim recognition and substantive rights, to expose and contest the various forms of power that exclude them from opportunities in the city, to collectively challenge hegemonic city visions and articulate alternative ones, and to strategically ally with other subaltern actors and achieve greater influence over processes of city visioning and place-making. This is not to deny the importance of everyday space-making by marginalised groups, but rather to suggest that different forms of political agency *can* coexist and even complement each other (Pieterse 2008; Lindell 2010b). Collective organising may consolidate and expand the gains achieved through daily transgressive practices. For the advances made through the insurgent practices of non-compliant hawkers are reversible and precarious, particularly in the prime spaces of the city centre. The studied situation where no-one seems to be fully in control is marked by a high degree of uncertainty and unpredictability and a heightened sense of risk. This uncertainty works against the weak by keeping them on the move and is particularly harmful for the weakest of the weak, those less able to take risks. Ultimately, it may work in favour of dominant power. Urban 'subaltern spaces', then, are contested, continuously re-made and un-made, from above and from below, through territorial struggles involving both dominant actors and the subaltern. They are, as others have noted, 'emergent spaces'. But this emergence is a more dangerous process than often assumed.

References

Agamben, G. (1998). *Homo sacer: sovereign power and bare life*. Palo Alto, CA: Stanford University Press.

Bayat, A. (2004). Globalization and the politics of the informals in the global South (pp. 79–102). In A. Roy and N. Alsayyad (eds), *Urban informality: transnational perspectives from the Middle East, Latin America and South Asia*. Oxford: Lexington Books.

Bayat, A. (2007). Radical religion and the habitus of the dispossessed: does Islamic militancy have an urban ecology? *International Journal of Urban and Regional Research*, 31(3), 579–90.

Bayart, J.-F., Ellis, S. and Hibou, B. (eds) (1999). *The criminalization of the state in Africa*. Oxford: James Currey.

Bromley, R. and Mackie, P. (2009). Displacement and the new spaces for informal trade in the Latin American city centre. *Urban Studies*, 46(7), 1485–1506.

Brown, A. (ed.) (2006). *Contested space, street trading, public space, and livelihoods in developing cities*. Rugby: ITDG Publishing/Practical Action.

Byerley, A. (2011). Ambivalent inheritance: Jinja town in search of a post-colonial refrain. *Journal of Eastern Africa Studies*, 5(3), 482–504.

Crossa, V. (2009). Resisting the entrepreneurial city: street vendors' struggle in Mexico City's historic center. *International Journal of Urban and Regional Research*, 33(1), 43–63.

Davis, M. (2004). Planet of slums: urban involution and the informal proletariat. *New Left Review*, 26, 5–34.

Gatimu, D. (2008). *Partnerships in empowering informal traders in Nairobi. Role and scope of planning intervention*. Unpublished paper submitted for fulfilment of the requirements of the Kenya Physical Planners Registration Board Professional Examinations.

Holston, J. (2008). *Insurgent citizenship: disjunctions of democracy and modernity in Brazil*. Princeton, NJ: Princeton University Press.

Kamete, A. (2009). In the service of tyranny: debating the role of planning in Zimbabwe's urban 'clean-up' operation. *Urban Studies*, 46(4), 897–922.

Kamunyori, S. (2007). *Growing space for dialogue: the case of street vending in Nairobi's central business district*. Thesis for Award of Master in City Planning. Cambridge, MA: Massachusetts Institute of Technology.

Kimathi, N. K. (2004). *Claims to urban space: a study of hawkers (street vendors) within the central business district of Nairobi – Kenya*. Thesis for Award of Master of Arts Degree. Nairobi: University of Nairobi.

Kinyanjui, M. N. (2011). *Crossing borders: women in the informal economy and urban dynamism*, presentation delivered at the Nordic Africa Institute, Uppsala, November 2011.

Kiura, C. M. (2005). *Integrating street vendors in urban development. A case study of 'hawkers' in Nairobi, Kenya.* Dissertation for Award of the Master of Arts Degree. Nairobi: University of Nairobi.

Lefebvre, H. (1991). *The production of space.* Oxford: Blackwell.

Lindell, I. (ed.) (2010a). *Africa's informal workers: collective agency, alliances and transnational organizing in urban Africa.* London: Zed Books.

Lindell, I. (2010b). Informality and collective organising: identities, alliances and transnational activism in Africa. *Third World Quarterly*, 31(2), 207–22.

Lindell, I. (ed.) (2010c). Between exit and voice: informality and the spaces of popular agency. *African Studies Quarterly*, 11(2–3), 1–10.

Lyons, M. and Snoxell, S. (2005). Creating urban social capital: some evidence from informal traders in Nairobi, *Urban Studies*, 42(7), 1077–97.

Meagher, K. (2010). The politics of vulnerability: exit, voice and capture in three Nigerian informal manufacturing clusters (pp. 46–64). In I. Lindell (ed.), *Africa's informal workers: collective agency,, alliances and transnational organizing.* London: Zed Books.

Minister of Local Government (Kenya) (n.d.). *Cabinet memorandum on the proposed expansion of markets for management of hawking activities in Nairobi City.* Nairobi: Ministry of Local Government.

Mitchell, D. (2003). *The right to the city: social justice and the fight for public space.* New York: Guilford Press.

Mitullah, W. (2003a). *Street trade in Kenya. The contribution of research in policy dialogue and response*, paper prepared for presentation at the Urban Research Symposium on Urban Development for Economic Growth and Poverty Reduction.

Mitullah, W. (2003b). *Street vending in African cities: a synthesis of empirical findings from Kenya, Cote d'Ivoire, Ghana, Zimbabwe, Uganda and South Africa*, background paper for the 2005 World Development Report. University of Nairobi.

Mitullah, W. (2010). Informal workers in Kenya and transnational organizing: networking and leveraging resources (pp. 184–202). In I. Lindell (ed.), *Africa's informal workers: collective agency, alliances and transnational organizing.* London: Zed Books.

Muiruri, P. (2010). *Women street vendors in Nairobi, Kenya: a situational and policy analysis within a human rights framework.* Addis Ababa: OSSREA.

Myers, G. (2011). *African cities: alternative visions of urban theory and practice.* London: Zed Books.

Ong, A. (2006). *Neoliberalism as exception: mutations in citizenship and sovereignty.* Durham, NC: Duke University Press.

Orlale, O. and Mathenge, O. (2008). Hawkers refuse to move out, *Daily Nation*, 5 March 2008, available from: http://allafrica.com/stories/200803041271.html (last accessed: 15 October 2009).

Pereira, N. (2009). People's spaces: familiarization, subject formation and emergent spaces in Colombo. *Planning Theory*, 8(1), 51–75.

Pieterse, E. (2008). *City futures. Confronting the crisis of urban development.* London: Zed Books.

Rasmussen, J. (2012). Inside the system, outside the law: operating the matatu sector in Nairobi. *Urban Forum*, 23(4), 415–32.

Reno, W. (2000). Clandestine economies, violence and states in Africa. *Journal of International Affairs*, 53(2), 433–59.

Republic of Kenya (2007). *Kenya Vision 2030: a globally competitive and prosperous Kenya*. Available from: www.kilimo.go.ke/kilimo_docs/pdf/Kenya_VISION_2030-final.pdf (last accessed: 14 September 2012).

Roy, A. (2011). Slumdog cities: rethinking subaltern urbanism. *International Journal of Urban and Regional Research*, 35(2), 223–38.

Simone, A. M. (2002). *Spectral selves: practices in the making of African cities*. New School University and Wits Institute for Social and Economic Research (WISER).

Tranberg-Hansen, K. (2004). Who rules the streets? The politics of vending space in Lusaka (pp. 62–80). In K. Tranberg-Hansen and M. Vaa (eds), *Reconsidering informality: perspectives from urban Africa*. Uppsala: Nordiska Afrikainstitutet.

5 Overcoming Socio-Economic Marginalisation

Young West African Hustlers & the Reinvention of Global Capitalism

Basile Ndjio

Introduction

In a majority of African countries, urban youths are one of the main 'victims of modernity' (Bauman 2007). Since the late 1980s and early 1990s, they have endured social and economic marginalisation that has frustrated many in their legitimate aspirations of fulfilling their dreams of modernity. In addition, as a result of their disenfranchisement and *de-citizenisation* by corrupt and clientelist African governments, marginalised urban youths have become the 'lost generation'. Some of them have been turned into 'alien citizens' who are treated as foreigners in their own country. But despite their undoubted 'debasement' and 'disconnection' from the mainstream of both the local and global economies, African youths are far from being hapless victims or passive subjects (see Ferguson 1999). As a matter of fact, some recent studies[1] have attested to the extraordinary ability of marginalised urban African youths not only to adapt to modern changes but also to invent new opportunities for enrichment in a context of austerity, drastic structural adjustment measures, and the dwindling of state resources that in the past had enabled postcolonial leaders to maintain the social balance and order (Bayart 1993; Hibou 2004).

This is the case with young successful Nigerian and Cameroonian confidence tricksters generally referred to in Nigeria as '419' conmen and in Cameroon as *feymen*. Most of them are formerly underprivileged urban youths who have managed through sophisticated business frauds, large-scale deceptions, and confidence tricks to gain access to material and financial resources from which they were previously excluded. Success in internet '419' scams[2] or in what has been popularised in Cameroon as *feymania* has enabled some of these young West African hustlers not only to position themselves as the main challengers of the postcolonial bureaucratic and military elites in the moral economy of hedonism and extravagance, but also to become role models for many

[1] See Jua (2003: 12–36) and Trefon (2004).

[2] This refers to a section of the Nigerian criminal code that deals with business malpractices at large and a specific practice of fraud which involves sophisticated bank frauds and financial deceptions (see Apter 2005).

African youngsters who tend more and more to idealise their flamboyant lifestyles (Malaquais 2001: 101–18; Ndjio 2001 and 2002a). More interesting is the fact that these unconventional economic practices embody the ambitions of many young African 'criminal' entrepreneurs to 'reinvent' global capitalism; that is, to remodel its rationality and logics, as well as questioning the ethical codes, principles and laws that govern economic activities and commercial transactions at both local and international levels.

This chapter draws on ethnographic research conducted between 2000 and 2005 in Cameroon, and in some European countries (France, United Kingdom, Germany and the Netherlands). Its main objective is to show through the examples of Nigerian advance fee scammers and Cameroonian international swindlers how confidence tricks and swindle have become for some disenfranchised African youths a prime means of overcoming social and economic marginalisation and claiming access to full citizenship. The chapter also shows how, particularly since the early 1990s, these cunning young African tricksters have been endeavouring not only to make the most of accumulative opportunities provided by the present system of global capitalism, but also to reframe this dominant mode of capitalisation of riches; that is to 'corrupt' its conventional norms and system of values. One of the main schemes developed by many young African 'criminal' entrepreneurs and adventure businessmen consists in converting global capitalism into a global economy of swindle and fraud.

Social profile of young Cameroonian and Nigerian confidence tricksters

Despite the significant differences that exist between Cameroonian *feymen* and Nigerian '419' fraudsters in terms of itineraries of accumulation, social strategies or relationships with the postcolonial state, most of these young professional swindlers and confidence tricksters[3] have something in common: they have in various ways experienced social and economic marginalisation in their home country, either because of their underprivileged social backgrounds or because of their ethnic origins. This is a reality that is often neglected or poorly studied by most students of what is now glossed by Western criminologists as 'West African organised crime' (cf. Apter 1999: 267–307, 2005; Bayart *et al.* 1999; Hibou 1999, 2004). Indeed, the success stories of many of these young, successful hustlers sometimes overshadow the fact that most of them were formerly excluded from clientelist networks of accumulation and (re)distribution of riches centred on the postcolonial state, and were

[3] Although the large majority of those who tend to use either *feymania* or the '419' scam as a strategy of accumulation of riches are young people, it is however less than accurate to consider these different swindling operations as only a youth phenomenon.

marginalised in their societies. Their marginalisation was partly due to the fact that many of these former disenfranchised urban youths originated from underprivileged families living in the slums and fringe settlements of Douala in Cameroon (Malaquais 2001; Ndjio 2001, 2012a and b), and Lagos, Port Harcourt and Enugu in Nigeria (Smith 2007). These are disenfranchised areas characterised by similar ecological and social features: communal ethnic origin of most of the dwellers, chronic unemployment, deteriorating neighbourhoods, illiteracy, criminality, juvenile delinquency, prostitution, and overwhelming and dreadful poverty.

For example, a large number of Cameroonian *feymen* that I interviewed either in Cameroon or in many European countries between 2001 and 2004 grew up in New-Bell, the poorest and the most overpopulated neighbourhood in Douala, which is now reputed across the country for being the cradle of *feymania*. New-Bell is also a place where more than one million urban poor live in insecure conditions. Here, as in many concentric zones of poverty which have been excluded from the modernist project of the Paul Biya regime (in power since 1982), living is, above all, 'being the master of one's own life; it is acting and creating strategies as you are, and as you want to become', as Séraphin (2000: 12) once wrote about the everyday life of residents of Douala.

For many residents who live in affluent and highly secured residential resorts or in less destitute areas in Douala, New-Bell is above all a disreputable area which offers a haven for all marginal figures of society. Yet, if nowadays New-Bell appears as the dominant site of the social and economic exclusion of many poor urban populations, in the past it was a place of hope and possibilities. Indeed, at the time of the economic boom of the late 1970s and early 1980s, a significant number of residents of this destitute neighbourhood could find causal or permanent employment either in the public service or in several private companies based in Douala. But, with the breakdown of the economy in the late 1980s, and the draconian structural adjustment measures imposed by financial institutions, the social and economic conditions of many residents of this disenfranchised neighbourhood had changed dramatically for the worse. Local youths, who were the main victims of the neo-liberal system endorsed willy-nilly by the Cameroon government (as by many African states), saw their chance of finding permanent jobs in the formal sector, and most notably in the public service, narrowed considerably because government was no longer able to provide job opportunities to the growing number of university graduates (see Konings 2011). With creeping poverty, the lives of marginal urban youths were simply downgraded to a relentless effort to fend for themselves. Eventually, many young people from New-Bell were forced to give up their studies and 'manage' on their own.

It was in this context of general suffering that a significant number of young urban tricksters from Douala learned how to make ends meet.

Indeed, when they were younger many prominent *feymen* from Douala earned their living as street vendors, bouncers, car cleaners, small-time criminals and temporary workers. This was the case for Gnacos, a young successful Cameroonian swindler who is now based in London. He was formerly a car cleaner and a tout at the Douala central market before switching to *feymania*-related activities in the late 1990s. I first met Gnacos in November 2002 in the course of my field research in Kassalafam, a poverty-stricken neighbourhood of New-Bell where I spent much of my childhood. He came from an underprivileged Bamileke family who immigrated to Douala in the mid-1950s. Like many youths from this poor neighbourhood, he had only a First School Leaving Certificate since he was forced to give up his studies when he was in *sixième* (first year of secondary school). At that time, Gnacos's father, who was the family's breadwinner, had just been made redundant from a local brewery where he had worked as a driver, and could no longer afford to pay his school fees and those of his eight siblings. Though this moral economy of marginalisation and exclusion turned most underprivileged Cameroonian youths into what Gyanendra Pandey (2006: 133) has referred to as 'hyphenated citizens' – those whose citizens' rights have become a matter of constant negotiations with holders of political and administrative powers – this situation was even more difficult for young people who hailed from the regions generally associated with the opposition movement. This was particularly the case for many underprivileged young Bamileke from the Grassfields region of the country, a long-standing stronghold of the Social Democratic Front, the main opposition party in the country.

Although they play a predominant role in the local economy, whether through the formal or informal sector, the Bamileke at large – and particularly the younger generations – have always felt discriminated against in the allocation of state resources by different regimes that have been governing the country since independence in 1960. For example, since his accession to power in November 1982, President Paul Biya, who originated from the forest region, has been striving to encourage what some local newspapers often call the '*betisation* of the administration'[4]; that is, the positioning of his own Beti kinsmen from the south and central regions in important posts in the state apparatus. This *betisation* of the public service went along with the patronisation of a new class of young Beti businessmen who could counter the Bamileke's alleged predominance in the national economy. When this strategy proved ineffective, the so-called Beti lobby, which presumably wields political and administrative powers in the country (Bayart *et al.* 1999), did not worry about setting the foreign fox to mind the Cameroonian geese. For example, in her study of the privatisation process in Cameroon, Béatrice Hibou argues that Cameroonian officials (predominantly the Beti)

[4] Cf. *Challenge Hebdo*, 167, 24 April 1992: 3 (a Cameroon daily newspaper); see also *Collectif Changer le Cameroun*, 1990.

allowed foreign interests (notably French entrepreneurs) to have control over many privatised public companies. According to her, 'the government's principal aim was to keep these assets out of the hands of Bamileke entrepreneurs often regarded as potential or occult financiers of political parties opposed to the current Cameroon People's Democratic Movement (CPDM) regime' (Hibou 1999: 73). Moreover, the resentment of many young Bamileke was compounded by the politics of belonging endorsed since the early 1990s by the Cameroon government, one that differentiated citizens along regional or ethnic divides (see Socpa 2002). In many respects, such ethno-politics particularly targeted fellows from the Grassfields region, who were often depicted in pro-governmental newspapers or by some extremist members of the ruling CPDM party as 'traitors in the enemy's pay', 'power-mongers', 'exploitative and unscrupulous fellows', 'domineering settlers', 'land-grabbers', and 'deceitful peoples' (see Konings 2001: 169–94).

It was this strong feeling of being marginalised by the so-called Beti regime that partly explains why many destitute young Bamileke from New-Bell and other disenfranchised areas of Douala received the rhetoric of democracy of the early 1990s with an enthusiasm that sometimes bordered on fanaticism. For them, the multi-party system represented an opportunity to get rid of the hated Biya regime. As a result, many played an active role in the civil disobedience movement popularly known in Cameroon as a 'ghost town operation'; a process which itself held out the prospect of the long-awaited *changement* that was expected to improve people's desperate living conditions (Monga 1995: 359–79). Many of the young Bamileke who later became famous as successful *feymen* were among these young people who were fooled into believing that the upsurge of the multi-party system would put an end to their suffering and distress. This was the case with Marcello, a 35-year-old a former pro-democracy activist who switched to *feymania* in 1995 when he realised that he had let himself be manipulated by what he called 'dishonest politicians' and 'ventriloquist political opponents' (*opposants du ventre*) who had betrayed a good cause for personal interests.

Recent studies on the political economy of contemporary Nigeria have also shown that young underprivileged Igbo[5] from the Southeast Region of Nigeria have experienced a similar marginalisation (Smith 2001: 803–26, 2007). Many of these disenfranchised youths have become key players in a growing economy of deception. Their involvement in illicit or criminal economic practices can be viewed as a legitimate desire to overcome economic marginalisation by the Nigerian state which is dominated by the Hausa-Fulani politico-military elites from the

[5] I do not want to be understood as saying that only young Bamileke or Igbo are involved in *feymania* or in '419' scams, or that these unlawful economic practices are another venal sin of the Bamileke or Igbo, as a misreading of Bayart *et al.*'s (1999) *The criminalisation of the state in Africa* might suggest.

Northern region of the country. One can therefore understand why many Nigerian kingpins of '419' fraud and prominent members of the notorious Nigerian transnational crime syndicate reportedly make use of the social capital of ethnicity, kinship lineage and place of origin to prosper in criminal activities originating from Igboland (Bayart *et al.* 1999: 40; Smith 2007). By impersonating Nigerian government officials, top-ranking military officers, bank managers, oil industry executives in their effort to defraud their victims of their assets – as they generally do – these young Igbo fraudsters re-appropriate the insignias and symbols of the Nigerian postcolonial state that has hitherto discriminated fellows from this rich oil region of the country in the share of the national 'cake'. Uche (pseudonym), a 29-year-old Igbo swindler who I befriended[6] at the time I was living in Amsterdam, exemplified the disillusionment of many marginalised Nigerian youths with their rulers, and especially their pessimistic view about their home country. My informant was one of the leaders of a ring of Nigerian and Cameroonian hustlers who generally operated in the city of Rotterdam, and especially also in the popular neighbourhood of Bijlmer, a suburb of Amsterdam. Though the young swindler maintained strong ties with Nigeria, he generally described his homeland as a place of discomfort where the youths could no longer achieve their ambition of securing a sustainable livelihood.

Yet some clarifications need to be made here. The focus on economic marginalisation to explain the involvement of some Cameroonian and Nigerian urban youths in *feymania* or '419'- related activities does not mean that we overlook other pushing factors that can drive these youths to the kind of activities discussed in this chapter.[7] Nor are we suggesting that social marginalisation ineluctably leads to involvement in criminal activities or that any African youth who is economically marginalised would inevitably turn to illicit enterprises as a means of coping with economic marginalisation. In fact, *feymania* and '419' scams are thriving in Cameroon and Nigeria because of a combination of several complex factors which cannot be reduced to the sole economic marginalisation of youth in both countries.

[6] I came across Uche thanks to my good connections with a group of young Cameroonian *feymen* from Amsterdam and Rotterdam with whom I had built solid and trustful relations in the course of my research on West African confidence tricksters.

[7] For example in a recent work on the moral economy of deception and scam in contemporary Cameroon, I relate the propagation of *feymania*-related activities and other business malpractices to the prevalence in the Cameroonian society of what I have referred to as 'sagacity spirit' and 'ghetto ethic'. These two notions account both for a philosophy and a morale that make an apology for the culture of resourcefulness, ingenuity and adaptability. These popular doctrines also exalt attitudes such as unscrupulousness, dishonesty, double-dealing and recklessness. In addition, I argue that the involvement of many urban youths in criminal or illicit activities was the result of their endorsement of this ethos (cf. Ndjio 2012b).

Feymania and '419' as forms of (re-)citizenisation

To begin with, it is useful to stress again that, although the vast majority of confidence tricksters and professional swindlers are young Cameroonians and Nigerians generally aged between 21 and 35, it is however irrelevant to interpret these practices as exclusively a youth activity: both *feymania* and '419' scams no longer attract only marginalised urban Cameroonian or Nigerian youths as several studies have demonstrated (Apter 2005; Konings 2011; Smith 2007; Ndjio 2001, 2012a, 2012b). For example, in the Cameroonian context marked by pervasive economic depression, many people now perceive *feymania*-related activities as the only means for achieving what Séraphin (2000: 117) calls the '*conquête statutaire*' (statutory quest); that is, moving from the disparaging status of social juniors to that of respectable social seniors.[8] By focusing on marginalised Cameroonian and Nigerian youths, this chapter aims to stress their role as key players in the moral economy of swindle and confidence tricks, and especially the instrumentalisation of *feymania* or advance fee fraud as a means of overcoming their social and economic marginalisation.

Since the late 1980s and early 1990s, advance fee fraud and confidence tricks commonly characterised in Nigeria as the '419' scam, and in Cameroon as *feymania*[9], have become for many underprivileged people in both countries a prime means of gaining access to financial and material resources enabling people to enjoy full citizenship. More importantly, many marginalised urban youths from both countries have come to play a crucial role in these new forms of enrichment that somehow by-pass the role of the postcolonial state in both the production and (re-)distribution of wealth. In addition, these unconventional modes of wealth creation reassure many disenfranchised Cameroonian and Nigerian youths that one does not necessarily need to accumulate university diplomas or have good political connections in order to become successful in life. In other respects, success either in *feymania* or '419' scams has even enabled some of these former left-behind youths to move from rags to riches in a short span of time and sometimes against the will of postcolonial power.

One can understand why both *feymania* and advance fee fraud initially

[8] Smith (2007:16) has also noted about Nigeria that the 419 frauds there are perpetrated not only by young amateur criminals who are attracted by the prospect of fast wealth that '419' activities yield, but also by ordinary Nigerians.

[9] Historically, the term *feymania* was popularised in the early 1990s as a result of the emergence of a group of wealthy young conmen and tricky businessmen who came to be known by the public as *feymen*. The concept '*feymania*' derives from the local urban vernacular expression '*fey*' which, according to many informants, is a distortion of the English word 'fool'. Malaquais (2001: 101–18) rather derives the expression *feymania* from the French word *faire*, which retains an additional meaning of 'deceiving someone'. As she explains, the art of *feymania* is the art of *faire* or *feyre* – the skill of cheating someone.

incarnated the spirit of rebellion with regard to the dominant social and economic order that marginalised underprivileged youths (and continues even today to do so). Both practices somehow first appeared as both a 'popular mode of political action' (Bayart *et al.* 1992) and a 'hidden transcript of resistance' (Scott 1990) that were essentially directed against the dominant groups, since most of the victims of the hustlers' dirty tricks were either the politico-bureaucratic elites or wealthy businessmen connected to the ruling CPDM regime as was the case with Cameroon.[10] However, there are critical questions that deserve to be asked here. How do these young conmen manage to extort huge amounts of money from their victims who are often experienced financiers, entrepreneurs or businessmen? What strategies do they use in order to dupe their victims?

In general, a suitcase or trunk allegedly full of genuine money (generally US$100 bills) is shown to the *mougou* (dupe or gullible person) as Nigerians and Cameroonians call them. However, the notes are all black and the prospective victim is told that they have been ostensibly coated with a special substance in order to transport them safely. The blackening of the notes is usually caused by a Vaseline and iodine solution. The con artist will make use of his 'devilish intelligence' (Hibou 2004: 7) to persuade the *mougou* to purchase a special cleaning solution at a cost between US$100,000 and US$500,000. The so-called expensive chemical, which is allegedly necessary to remove the black substance used to disguise the notes as cash from the authorities, is in fact a mixture of washing-up liquid and any other solution with an unusual odour and colour which the victim will not be able to detect easily. To win over the dupe, who is usually a wealthy Arab or Asian businessman or a white-collar Westerner, the confidence trickster will select randomly between two and four notes from the case. In front of the *mougou*, the hustler will wash them in a tiny portion of the solution, which he has brought with him, returning them to their original form as real bank notes. They are given to the dupe who is asked to spend them or get them checked at the bank or any financial institution to confirm their authenticity. In reality, of course, the con artist knows perfectly well which notes he is selecting and takes the only ones that are there, the remainder being cut-to-size paper. A really dexterous trickster will even invite the

[10] However, it is important to nuance this subversive character of '419' scam or *feymania*-related practices. As we have demonstrated elsewhere (Ndjio 2006) about the practice of *feymania*, this activity has also become an integral part of the ruling CPDM regime's policy of plundering the state. This is because, in its attempt to curb the growing influence of independent Bamileke *feymen* who have always tended to bypass its importance, the Cameroon government has encouraged the emergence of compliant *feymen* from the President's own ethnic group, who rather owe their economic success to their ability to take advantage of the patrimonial character of the Biya regime. As regards the 419 scam, some researchers have noted that many Nigerian kingpins of advance fee frauds maintain clientelist relationships with their politico-bureaucratic elites. In addition, some often achieve their fraudulent activities in the nexus of the Nigerian postcolonial state and within the pervasive networks of patronage and reciprocity which, according to Smith (2007: 13), constitute a significant proportion of the everyday political economy in Nigeria (see also Apter 2005).

gullible to choose notes to clean and use a well-practised sleight of hand to trick the fool into selecting the genuine ones. Unfortunately, it is only later that the *mougou* discovers that he/she has been conned.[11]

The strategy of the Nigerian '419' scammer consists of ensnaring their targets into advancing fees and providing information about their bank accounts against the promise of a much larger return. Practically, the confidence tricksters start by sending to their prospective victims faxes or email messages that generally rely on the symbols of Nigeria's petroleum industry or state apparatuses. In these letters, the fraudsters who generally impersonate government officials, top-ranking military officers, bank managers, oil industry executives, high-profile politicians, or even relatives of a deceased African Head of State, claim to be in possession of millions of dollars obtained by fraudulent means, and frozen in an African bank account or a safety deposit location. The recipients of the letters are asked for assistance in transferring the funds out of the continent, and are promised to receive in turn a percentage (between 30 to 50 per cent) of the hidden funds. A positive reply to the scammers' messages is an indication that the recipients are potential *mougous*. Several mail exchanges or phone conversations will help the fraudsters win the dupes' trust who will not hesitate to send them details of their bank accounts. Such information is useful not only because they enable the fraudsters to withdraw money from their victims' bank account but also because they can help them to apply for credit cards, ask for loans from the victims' banks, or forge cheques useful for illegal bank transactions.

According to Smith (2007: 38), Nigerian criminal networks also rely on clientelist relationships that permeate both the government and the private sector, and on the ties that Nigerians at home generally maintain with their fellow compatriots living abroad. These international networks of crime are increasingly involved in money laundering, bank frauds, '419' scams, counterfeiting of foreign currencies and credit cards, etc. Top figures of Nigerian crime syndicates often recruit individuals to infiltrate banks or bribe employees who can provide them with critical information about customers' bank accounts and addresses. Glickman (2005: 471) has revealed that young '419' scammers also use the internet to prey on banks and individuals. Many Western banks have been victims of some Nigerian scammers who set up fake websites resembling their legitimate sites. Citibank of London has become one of the main targets of some young West African fraudsters who regularly impersonate the bank's website to swindle its clients (Catan and Peel 2003). A German industrialist reportedly lost £1 million in such a sophisticated scam crafted by these cunning African hustlers (Glickman 2005: 471–2).

The above examples suggest that both *feymania* and '419'-related

[11] This passage is drawn from Ndjio (2008: 7) with a slight modification.

activities are 'alternative modes of accumulation' (Geschiere and Konings 1993), which challenge the officially sanctioned methods of wealth creation in both Cameroon and Nigeria. More importantly, these business malpractices constitute new forms of re-citizenisation because they offer opportunities to many Cameroonian and Nigerian youths formerly marginalised and excluded from clientelist networks of accumulation and distribution centred on the postcolonial state to gain access to financial and material resources from which they were previously denied by their corrupt political elites. In addition, on the basis of their wealth acquired by means of *feymania* and '419' scams, successful *feymen* and kingpins of '419' scams have managed to move from a former disparaging position of second-class citizens to an enviable status of *nouveaux riches* who can now command deference and respectability from other social groups such as the impoverished middle classes. Some of these new rich even take advantage of their new social promotion to compete with the local politico-bureaucratic elites in terms of display of wealth, lavish lifestyle and ostentatious consumption of Western commodities generally seen in many African countries as a hallmark of first-class citizenship.

Reinventing global capitalism

Bayart (1999: 32–48) is right in his observation that the social capital of African economies is increasingly taking the form of a widespread use of deception and 'dirty tricks', and that in many African countries, crime, corruption, confidence tricks, business frauds and financial deceptions now influence business activities as well as dominate the conduct of economic transactions. He is also right when he points out the fact that many African social actors have managed to re-appropriate to their own advantage the economic reforms imposed upon them by Western institutions, as much as they have succeeded in capturing the contradictory insertion of their countries into the orbits of global capitalism. These social actors do so by developing new modes of acquisition of wealth which no longer follow conventional economic strategies and norms, and by inventing economic practices which can be morally and judicially classified as criminal or illicit. Symptomatic of this African inventive spirit is the emergence since the late 1980s and early 1990s in many African countries of new modes of capitalisation of wealth that today encourage new economic conducts and new ethos of accumulation that end up rendering obsolete the old system of business transactions and economic entrepreneurship. More important is the fact that this new art of making money heralds a shift in common understandings of the nature of capitalism and business activities. It also prepares the ground for what Janet MacGaffey (1994: 189–204) calls 'African capitalism', which has not yet been sufficiently theorised.[12] What particularly marks out this African capitalism is less the fact that it essentially lives on fraud, prevarication and other fraudulent practices, than the fact that it bothers itself very little – if at all – with ethical values and moral principles which, according to Max Weber ([1920] 1958), guided the behaviour of Protestant capitalists of eighteenth and nineteenth centuries. Another distinctive characteristic of this new African economic entrepreneurship is that it dissolves the difference between criminal behaviour and legitimate profit-seeking, between normal economic activities and vulgar criminal practices.

In many respects, Nigerian advance fee fraud and Cameroonian *feymania* are the embodiment of these unconventional business ventures and unorthodox economic practices that undermine the established logic of international financial transactions (Brittan and Hamlin 1995; Reidenbach and Robin 1989; Sen 1987, 1995: 23–34). Both *feymania* and '419' scams appear to herald a Second Coming of capitalism, not in its millennial, neo-liberal and global manifestations, as forecast by Comaroff and Comaroff (2001), but rather in its criminal, felonious and venal expressions. By this, I suggest that we are dealing today with the kind of unlawful business deals and non-standard ways of bargaining and trading exchanges that prefigure a new form of entrepreneurship in which business people are turned into immoral economic agents whose actions are essentially driven by 'ruthless acquisition, bound to no ethical norms whatever' (Weber [1920] 1958: 71). It is hardly surprising therefore that since the mid-1990s, many self-appointed Western criminal 'experts' have been producing both 'grand narratives', and sometimes a phantasmagorical literature, about the expansion of so-called 'global transnational criminality' in general, and 'West African organised crime' in particular, which allegedly threatens the very foundation of both the market economy and liberal democracy (de Maillard 2001; Handelman 1995; Strange 1998). In so doing, they join their governments in both their lamentations and panic about the progressive transformation of global capitalism into a global economy of crime and venality, in which business ventures are assimilated to criminal enterprises.

Recently, this general concern has led in most Western countries to real political, administrative and juridical offensives against the *méchant* young African criminals who have become a nightmare for many Western governments and financial institutions ensnared into the West African economy of fraud. Apter (2005: 228) has revealed for example that financial scams and business frauds perpetrated in many parts of the world by members of West African organised crime have now

[12] Though it would be untrue to reduce this African effort to 're-invent' global capitalism to the sole agency of youths or to youth entrepreneurship, it would be however theoretically faulty and practically inappropriate not to acknowledge, for example, the actions of young Cameroonian and Nigerian transnational swindlers and tricksters in this process.

'engaged the energies of Scotland Yard, the FBI, Interpol, the Royal Canadian Mounted Police, and a variety of private and subsidiary agencies, such as Better Business Bureau and the Financial Crimes Enforcement Network in the US'.

The fact that young African 'criminal' entrepreneurs who are increasingly active in Western Europe and North America have compelled many Western governments to set up anti-fraud units to combat so-called 'West African organised crime' can be cynically interpreted as a revenge of young African *sans culottes* against the global economic system that has marginalised Africans in the world economy. The fact that Congolese *mikilistes* (young immigrants living in Western countries) and young Ivorian fraudsters have forced many French and Belgian banks to invest millions of dollars in tightening their banking security against the theft of identity is also a strong reminder that Africans refuse to play a passive role in the global market or to occupy the position of underdogs in the world economic game.

In fact, the first generation of young Cameroonian *feymen*, for example, generally asserted themselves as *truands* (tricksters, crooks). In the early 1990s, *truands* symbolised the 'figures of ruse and intelligence' (Hibou 1999: 69–114) who slyly challenged the felonious and brutal postcolonial state in Cameroon. They were also people who rejected the social arrangements that kept the youths away from access to financial and material resources, and specially contested both the local and global social order that, as alluded to earlier, made African youths at large the 'pariahs of globalisation'. They did it by inventing their own mode of enrichment. Some achieved their accumulative project by engaging in unlawful activities or tricky businesses which can be described as acts of insubordination against the dominant political and economic system.

Since the mid-1990s, *feymania* and advance fee scams appear to have concentrated on the bamboozling of white middle-class victims. Indeed, there are many examples of Western politicians, professionals, businessmen or entrepreneurs who have fallen prey to some young African hustlers and confidence tricksters who lured them into providing advance fees against the promise of larger payoffs. For example in 2001, the Canadian newspaper *Canada Newswire* reported a story about a fraud ring of Toronto-based Nigerian hustlers who managed to defraud three hundred Canadian citizens in a large, sophisticated scam. Individual losses rolled from US$52,000 to over US$5 million (quoted by Glickman 2005: 479). This large swindling operation was reminiscent of the scam perpetrated a few years earlier by some young cunning Nigerian hustlers against a former American congressman and a Texas oil executive from whom they swindled several millions of US dollars (see Brady 2003; Glickman 2005: 460–89).

The way in which many of my informants talked about their activities, and especially their comments on what they were doing (or had done), explicitly demonstrated that these young professional tricksters perceived their actions as constituting a form of resistance to both global capitalism and the African postcolonial politico-bureaucratic elites. Some called their activities the *frappe* which stands for stroke in French, viewing themselves as *frappeurs* who only deceived exploitative Westerners or corrupt African elites, as a young *feyman* from Douala once explained to me during a discussion that we had in November 1995 in a friend's house in Douala.[13]

Whether one limits the behaviour of these young African con artists to criminal practices (Hibou 1999: 70–113; Malaquais 2001: 101–18), or interprets it as an avatar of neo-liberal capitalism which has always put up with business frauds (Bayart 2004), the truth is that young West African transnational swindlers have nowadays engaged in a process of redefining the rules of the global economic game, which have so far been set by the West. They are especially involved in a symbolic destabilisation of the hegemonic order that Western developed countries have always maintained in their commercial and economic transactions with African countries in particular, and underdeveloped countries at large. Indeed, one of the often-neglected dimensions of the practices of *feymania* and '419' is that since the mid-1990s, both have been embodying what can be provisionally called African modes of capitalism. Though Bayart (1994), following the French historian Fernand Braudel (1985), was one of the first analysts to advance the hypothesis of 'reinvention of capitalism' as a result of its global expansion, my use of this concept is however different from his. In general, by reinvention of (global) capitalism, he means 'the emergence of differentiation in the logics of capitalism, the change in the way of accumulation and consumption, and the method and spirit of industrial management' (Bayart 1994: 15). He especially discusses this *reinvention* with respect to the emergence or exacerbation of culturalist particularisms in business economic activities, the use of identity strategies in the individual or collective attempt to gain access to wealth and material resources. In short, for him, the reinvention of capitalism goes along with the 'reinvention of difference' – a concept borrowed from James Clifford (1988).

In this contribution, I understand the concept of 'reinvention of capitalism' as an African project of reshaping or re-forming both the classical art of enterprising and trading, and the global dominant economic order that has until now profited Western developed countries. By 'reinvention of global capitalism', I especially make reference to an unprecedented and insidious undermining pressure that some cunning young African transnational swindlers have been exerting on the world economy, pressure which is exacerbating the corruption of its conventional norms and systems of values.

[13] A couple of months following our discussion, the young conman had to flee the country in order to escape from the police who were searching him. He reportedly swindled Fr.180 million FCFA from his girlfriend's uncle, who was then a government official in Yaoundé.

One of the most expressive forms of this denaturalisation of the neo-capitalist system is its slow conversion into a transnational economy of swindle and fraud in which deception is no longer a substitute or an 'alternative mode of accumulation' (Geschiere and Konings 1993) but is rather the driving force of economic entrepreneurship and business ventures, and especially the main methods of making money. Indeed, with the practices of *feymania* and the '419' scam, we are no longer dealing with more classical forms of illegal activities, which sometimes straddle the licit and the illicit, combining both legal and illegal enterprises, as the work of Janet MacGaffey (1992: 514–24; 1998: 37–50) has demonstrated.[14] Instead, we see the emergence of unprecedented forms of criminal business practices which not only make the violation of business rules and economic conventions a norm, but also promote the normalisation of the economy of deception and trickery, the aestheticisation of criminality and venality, the routinisation of business frauds, the moralisation and ethicisation of dishonesty and double-dealing and the immoralisation of honesty and rectitude insofar as, in both *feymania* and the '419' scam, righteousness and virtue are viewed as a vice or a luxury that the hustlers cannot afford. This implies that those who are involved in this economy of falsity (*faux*) and forgery that goes along with unethical values and deceptive ethics, reject what McCloskey (2006) calls 'bourgeois virtues', which generally associate economic success with moral codes or behavioural ethics (Beauchamp and Bowie 1992; Reidenbach and Robin 1989; Sen 1987, 1995: 23–34). For example, members of a gang of young *feymen* I followed in Paris between June and September 2002 had a maxim that can be summarised as: 'in business, it is dishonest to be honest because everybody is dishonest' (Ndjio 2006).

Some might contend that fraud, deception, and trickery have always been common practices in capitalist systems (Warnier 1994: 185), and have played a critical role in capital formation in Western economies (Harvey 1989). Others would probably point out that the activities or practices being described here are only some of the most radical expressions of the dynamism of global capitalism so well captured by Braudel (1985).[15] However, both *feymania* and the '419' scam confront us with new forms of entrepreneurship in which the classical principles, 'honesty is the best policy' – so dear to puritan capitalists of the eighteenth and nineteenth centuries – has been replaced by 'dishonesty is the best policy'. In addition, we seem to be witnessing the emergence of a specific economy of duplicity and treachery in which a business 'partner' is seen above all as a dupe to swindle or a *gros pigeon* to fleece. However, what seems most striking in both *feymania* and advance fee fraud is less the fact that 'money changes hands in one direction only,

[14] See also MacGaffey and Bazenguissa-Ganga (2000).

[15] For Braudel (1985: 78), the main characteristics of capitalism are its 'flexibility', 'adaptability' and 'eclecticism'.

despite the expectations of a return', as (Apter 2005: 234) has observed about Nigerian '419' scams, than the fact that the betrayal of one's partner's trust is common practice. At issue here is a kind of business system in which dirty tricks are no longer marginal or trivial practices developed on the margins of normal economic activities, but are rather integral aspects of business transactions and exchanges. Elsewhere (Ndjio 2002b), I referred to these business malpractices as both the 'economy of distrust' (*sans confiance*) and 'breach of trust' (*abus de confiance*). For, if the art of *feymania* and the '419' scam is the art of the con game which entails above all engaging the mark into 'magical deals' that generally lead him/her nicely into magical tricks, it also implies trapping the dupe in a fool's bargain in which he/she gives everything but receives nothing in turn. Moreover, in this kind of trick game, one party strongly believes that to win or achieve his/her objectives, he/she must put all his/her confidence in the other contractor who has all the reasons to be smart, or to take unfair advantage of his/her partner's trust. That is why the art of the confidence trick is generally associated with the regimes both of disloyalty and dishonesty (Ndjio 2002b).

Conclusion

In many respects, both Nigerian advance fee fraud and Cameroonian *feymania* are examples of the new types of business malpractices, an economy of illusion and trick that emerged in the late 1980s and early 1990s in contexts of disappointed expectations, broken contracts and unfulfilled national development plans (Apter 1999: 267–307, 2005: 226). More important, both are radical expressions of a particular tenacity which enables Africans to adapt to modern changes, but also to invent new opportunities for enrichment in a context marked by economic decline, austerity and drastic structural adjustment measures imposed by international financial institutions. Unfortunately, mainstream academic literature on the topic has so far limited the understanding of these business malpractices and economic malfeasances either to the growing process of criminalisation of the state in Africa (Bayart 1999: 114–16, 2004; Hibou 1999: 70–113, 2004; Malaquais 2001: 101–18) or to the rampant political culture of fraud, corruption and deception in postcolonial Africa (Glickman 2005: 460–89; Smith 2007). In other words, ordinary Nigerians and Cameroonians who try their hands at advance fee fraud and *feymania* are seen as mimicking the criminal and venal attitude of their state-based elites who are notorious for siphoning the state resources into private pockets. This literature fails to grasp the relation between the growth in the economy of swindle and confidence tricks, and the emergence of immoral business practices and felonious capitalism that aggravate the erosion of ethics and morality in international business and economic activities. It also overlooks the dramatisation of alternative modes of accumulation that sometimes downplay the importance of the African postcolonial state as the major centre of production and redistribution of wealth. All these processes are accompanied by the effort of some cunning young African business adventurers to transform the mode of doing business at both national and international levels as is the case with many prominent Cameroonian *feymen* and Nigerian conmen. On the whole, academics and experts have paid insufficient attention to the strategies of malfeasance of these young African fraudsters, their subversive play on the logics of neo-liberal capitalism, and their audacious challenge to the ethical and judicial codes that inform the global economy. I have argued here that one of the remarkable effects of young West African entrepreneurs on global capitalism is its mischievous transformation by young African business adventurers and transnational confidence tricksters into a global economy of magic trick and dissimulation. In this moral economy of dishonesty in which traditional ethics no longer make sense, business transactions are turned into a fool's bargain: one business partner acting as the *truant* (trickster) and another playing the naive role of the *bon* (dupe or mark) who invests everything for receiving nothing. This mimic of global economy, as Homi Bhabha (1994) has argued, embodies not only African *bricolages* (patched-up jobs) of capitalism but also the effort of some Africans to 'reinvent' the global capitalist system. Though critics might disagree with my interpretations of *feymania* and the '419' scam, I insist that a radical form of entrepreneurship is emerging, not only in Africa, but across the world, especially now that young Cameroonian and Nigerian international swindlers and confidence tricksters have started exporting their expertise to places such as the Caribbean, the Philippines, Russia, China, Hong Kong and Singapore (Perry 2003).

References

Apter, A. (1999). IBB=419: Nigerian democracy and the politics of illusion (pp. 267–307). In J. L. Comaroff and J. Comaroff (eds), *Civil society and the political imagination in Africa: critical perspectives*. Chicago, IL: University of Chicago Press.

Apter, A. (2005). *The pan-African nation: oil and the spectacle of culture in Nigeria*. Chicago, IL: University of Chicago Press.

Bauman, Z. (1997). *Postmodernity and its discontents*. Cambridge: Polity Press.

Bayart, J.-F. (1993). *The state in Africa: the politics of the belly*. London and New York: Longman.

Bayart, J.-F. (1994) (ed.). *La réinvention du capitalisme*. Paris: Karthala.

Bayart, J.-F. (1996). *L'illusion identitaire*. Paris: Fayard.

Bayart J.-F.(1999) . The social capital of the felonious state or the ruses of political intelligence (pp. 32–48). In J-F. Bayart, S. Ellis, and B. Hibou, *The criminalization of the state in Africa*. Oxford: James Currey.

Bayart, J.-F. (2004). Le crime transnational et la formation de l'état. *Politique Africaine*, 93, 93–104.
Bayart J.-F., Ellis, S. and Hibou, B. (1999). *The criminalization of the state in Africa*. Oxford: James Currey.
Bayart, J.-F., Mbembe, A., and Toulabor, C. (1992). *Le politique par le bas en Afrique noire: contributions à une problématique de la démocratie*. Paris: Karthala.
Beauchamp, T. and Bowie, N. (eds) (1992). *Ethical theory and business*. Englewood Cliffs, NJ: Prentice Hall.
Bhabha, H. (1994). *The location of culture*. London: Routledge.
Brady, B. (2003). Crackdown on £8.4m African sting. *The Scotsman*, Sunday, 2 March 2003, p. 13. Available from: www.scotsman.com/news/uk/crack-down-on-163-8-4m-african-sting-1-1382507 (last accessed: 15 September 2012).
Braudel, F. (1985). *La dynamique du capitalisme*. Paris: Arthaud.
Brittan, S. (1995). Economics and ethics (pp. 1–23). In S. Brittan and A. Hamlin (eds), *Market capitalism and moral values*. Aldershot: Edward Elgar.
Brittan, S. and Hamlin, A. (eds) (1995). *Market capitalism and moral values*. Aldershot: Edward Elgar.
Catan, T. and Peel, M. (2003). Bogus websites, stolen corporate identities. *Financial Times*, 3 March, 21.
Clifford, J. (1988). *The predicament of culture: twentieth century ethnography, literature and art*. Cambridge: Harvard University Press.
Collectif Changer le Cameroun (1990). *Changer le Cameroun: pourquoi pas?* Yaounde: Edition c3.
Comaroff, J. and Comaroff, J. L. (eds) (2001). *Millennial capitalism and the culture of neoliberalism*. Durham, NC: Duke University Press.
Ferguson, J. (1999). *Expectations of modernity: myths and meanings of urban life on the Zambian Copperbelt*. Berkeley, CA: University of California Press.
Geschiere, P. and Konings, P. (eds) (1993). *Les itinéraires d'accumulation au Cameroun*. Paris: Karthala.
Glickman, H. (2005). The Nigerian '419' advance fee scams: prank or peril? *Canadian Journal of African Studies/Revue Canadienne d'Etudes Africaines*, 39(3), 460–89.
Handelman, S. (1995). *Comrade criminal: Russia's new mafiya*. New Haven, CT: Yale University Press.
Harvey, D. (1989). *The condition of postmodernity: an enquiry into the origins of cultural change*. Oxford: Blackwell.
Hibou, B. (1999). The 'social capital' of the state as an agent of deception, or the ruse of economy intelligence (pp. 69–113). In J.-F. Bayart, S. Ellis and B. Hibou (eds), *The criminalization of the state in Africa*. James Currey: Oxford.
Hibou, B. (ed.) (2004). *Privatising the state*. London: Hurst & Co.
Jua, N. B. (2003). Differential responses to disappearing pathways: redefining possibility among Cameroon youths. *African Studies Review*, 46(2), 12–36.
Konings, P. (2001). Mobility and exclusion: conflicts between autochthons and allochthons during the political liberalization in Cameroon (pp. 169–94). In M. de Bruijn, R. van Dijk and D. Foeken (eds), *Mobile Africa: changing patterns of movements in Africa and beyond*. Leiden: Brill.
Konings, P. (2011). *The politics of neoliberal reforms in Africa: state and civil society in Cameroon*. Bamenda and Leiden: Lagaa/African Studies Centre.
MacGaffey, J. (1992). Solving the problems of urban living: opportunities for

youth in the second economy (pp. 514–24). In H. d'Almeida-Topor *et al.* (eds), *Les jeunes en Afrique.volume 1: Évolution et rôle (XIXe–XXe siècles)*. Paris: L'Harmattan.

MacGaffey, J. (1994). State deterioration and capitalist development: the case of Zaire (pp. 189–204). In B. J. Berman and C. Leys (eds), *African capitalists in African development*. Boulder, CO: Lynne Rienner.

MacGaffey, J. (1998). Creatively coping with crisis: entrepreneurs in the second economy of Zaire (the Democratic Republic of the Congo) (pp. 37–50). In A. Spring and B. E. McDade (eds), *African entrepreneurship: theory and reality*. Gainesville, FL: University Press of Florida.

MacGaffey, J. and Bazenguissa-Ganga, R. (2000). *Congo-Paris: transnational traders on the margins of the law*. Oxford: James Currey.

Maillard, J. de (2001). *Le marché fait sa loi. De l'usage du crime par la mondialisation*. Paris: Foundation du 2 Mars, Mille et Une Nuits.

Malaquais, D. (2001). Arts de feyre au Cameroun. *Politique Africaine*, 82, 101–18.

McCloskey, D. N. (2006). *The bourgeois virtues: ethics for an age of economics*. Chicago, IL: The University of Chicago Press.

Monga, C. (1995). Civil society and democratisation in Francophone Africa. *The Journal of Modern African Studies*, 33(3), 359–79.

Ndjio, B. (2001). Feymania in Cameroon: hidden ways of enrichment and alternative visions modernity. Paper presented during the International Conference on the 'Genealogies of Modernity' organised by ASSR/University of Amsterdam, 27–30 August.

Ndjio, B. (2002a). Feymania: a new way of imagining modernity in the contemporary Cameroon. Paper presented during the Seminar on Africa, Leiden, 15 March.

Ndjio, B. (2002b). Feymania in Cameroon: the politics of (dis)trust. Paper presented during the International Conference on 'Terms of Trust in Africa', organised by CNWS, Ethnology Museum and ASSR, Leiden, 18–20 September 2002.

Ndjio, B. (2006). Feymania: new wealth, magic money and power in contemporary Cameroon. PhD dissertation, University of Amsterdam.

Ndjio, B. (2008). Cameroonian feymen and Nigerian '419' scammers: Two examples of Africa's 'reinvention' of the global capitalism. ASC Working Paper 81.

Ndjio, B. (2012a). *Magie et enrichissement illicite. La feymania au Cameroun*. Paris: Karthala.

Ndjio, B. (2012b). Sagacity spirit and ghetto ethic: Feymania and new African entrepreneurship (pp. 56–89). In J. Abbink (ed.), *Fractures and reconnections: civic action and the redefinition of African political and economic space: Studies in honour of Piet JJ Konings*. Leiden: African Studies Centre.

Pandey, G. (2005). *Routine violence. Nations, fragments, histories*. Stanford, CA: Stanford University Press.

Perry, J. (2003). Ripped off the headlines, *US News & World Report*, 16 June 2003, pp. 54–9. Available from: www.usnews.com/usnews/biztech/articles/030616/16dujour.htm (last accessed: 16 September 2012).

Reidenbach, R. and Robin, D. (1989). *Ethics and profits: a convergence of corporate America's economic and social responsibilities*. Englewood Cliffs, NJ: Prentice Hall.

Scott, J. (1990). *Domination and the arts of resistance: hidden transcripts.* New Haven, CT: Yale University Press.

Sen, A. (1987). *On ethics and economics.* Oxford: Blackwell.

Sen, A. (1995). Moral codes and economic success (pp. 23–34). In S. Brittan and A. Hamlin (eds), *Market capitalism and moral values.* Aldershot: Edward Elgar.

Séraphin, G. (2000). *Vivre à Douala: L'imaginaire et l'action dans une ville africaine en crise.* Paris: Karthala.

Smith, D. J. (2001). Ritual killing, 419, and fast wealth: inequality and the popular imagination in south-eastern Nigeria. *American Ethnologist,* 28(4), 803–26.

Smith, D. J. (2007). *A culture of corruption: everyday deception and popular discontent in Nigeria.* Princeton, NJ: Princeton University Press.

Socpa, A. (2002). *Démocratisation et autochtonie au Cameroun: tragectoires régionales divergentes.* PhD dissertation. Leiden: CNWS/University of Leiden.

Strange, S. (1998). *Mad money: when markets outgrow governments.* Ann Arbor, MI: University of Michigan Press.

Trefon, T. (ed.) (2004). *Reinventing order in the Congo: how people respond to state failure in Kinshasa.* London: Zed Books.

Warnier, J. P. (1994). La bigarrure des patrons camerounais (pp. 175–201). In J.-F. Bayart (ed.), *La réinvention du capitalisme.* Paris: Karthala.

Weber, M. ([1920] 1958). *The Protestant ethic and the spirit of capitalism.* New York: Scribner.

6 Accepting Authoritarianism?
Everyday Resistance as Political Consciousness in Post-Genocide Rwanda

Susan Thomson

Background and introduction: state and society in Rwanda after 1994

In April 2013, Rwanda commemorated the nineteenth anniversary of the genocide that engulfed the country for 100 days in 1994, during which more than half a million people were killed, most of them from the Tutsi ethnic group, at the hands of their ethnic Hutu ncighbours. The post-genocide government of Rwanda, led by the Rwandan Patriotic Front (RPF), has received international acclaim for its efforts to rebuild the country. According to the United Nations, Rwanda's post-genocide reconstruction and reconciliation policies deserve to be emulated in other post-conflict societies in Africa and elsewhere (UN-OHRLLS/UNDP 2006). An important cornerstone of these efforts has been the national unity and reconciliation programme, the neo-traditional *gacaca* local-level courts, and the country's agricultural policy. The RPF claims that these initiatives have been successful and that they enjoy wide popular support from rural Rwandans, some 85 per cent of the population. President Paul Kagame stresses to both domestic and international audiences that he enjoys broad-based, popular support, evidenced by his 2010 electoral victory with 93 per cent of the vote (Kagame 2011). Indeed, this electoral legitimacy is part of a broader narrative of Rwanda's successful reconstruction since 1994. Under the leadership of President Kagame and his RPF, the country has achieved rapid reconstruction of state institutions and its infrastructure, including new roads, bridges, airports and Wi-Fi internet hotspots as well as new and improved service delivery in education, justice and health. Donor representatives praise the government for its low levels of corruption and high institutional accountability and transparency as well as its impressive economic growth, averaging six per cent a year since 1998 (Economist Intelligence Unit 2011; World Bank 2012).

Rwanda's rapid socio-economic reconstruction is rooted in the government's near total control of the political landscape, including repression of individual human rights and control of political opponents (HRW 2012; Reyntjens 2011). Under the leadership of the RPF, the post-genocide state is strong and centralised as the government is able to exercise territorial and bureaucratic control exceedingly well (Longman 1998). Like the regimes that have preceded it, the RPF controls the state apparatus from 'on-high' in Kigali, the capital city (Desrosiers and Thomson 2011; Newbury 1992). This means that state power is exercised at the local level in the form of directives from the central government and through the strict monitoring of the ability and willingness of local leaders to implement government orders effectively and efficiently. Local leaders are empowered to keep a watchful eye on the activities and speeches of individuals within their bailiwick, accountable to the central government through *imihigo* (performance) contracts, not to the rural residents they are meant to serve (Ingelaere 2010: 288; Thomson 2011b: 369).

Compliance with the dictates of government policy for all citizens is paramount. Rural Rwandans are subject to the exercise of the power granted to local leaders and must conform to the government's authoritarian directives in the name of national unity and reconciliation. Rwandan elites – educated, gainfully employed (many as state *fonctionnaires*) and resident in urban areas – tend to benefit from the post-genocide policies of the RPF (Howe and Mackay 2007). Those who benefit least are the rural poor – some 85 per cent of the population – who are subject to RPF-empowered local leaders and who must adhere to agricultural and land policies that negatively impact their livelihoods (Huggins 2011; Newbury 2011). Many rural Rwandans complain that they have been left out of Rwanda's economic gains since the 1994 genocide. Income inequality has increased from a Gini co-efficient of 0.47 in 2001 to 0.51 in 2006 (GoR 2007). Central to the exercise of oppressive state power at the level of the Rwandan rural resident are the government's ambitions to transform a predominantly subsistence agricultural sector into a large-scale engine for economic growth. In rejecting subsistence farming – the primary source of income for most rural Rwandans – the government forcibly imposes commercial farming on its rural residents. As Ansoms (2009: 299) notes, 'Rwandan policy makers see very little role for small-scale peasants in economic development'.

This gap between the government's claims of broad-based support for its post-genocide policies and increasing rural poverty and hardship raises questions about why rural actors have not agitated for a more equitable distribution of Rwanda's economic gains. Part of the explanation can be found in Rwanda's tightly controlled administrative structure that I outlined above. Another factor is Rwanda's rigid social hierarchy that limits economic mobility for many Rwandans – one's social status is directly related to one's relation to state power, which in Rwanda's authoritarian system also controls the economy (Ansoms 2009; Ingelaere 2010). This means that many rural Rwandans do not expect their lot in life to improve, so they do not collectively organise to demand that government changes its rural policies (Gravel 1968;

Newbury 1992). Taken together, these explanations only tell part of the story of why rural Rwandans might appear to accept the authoritarian practices of the ruling RPF that go against their interests as peasants.[1]

The purpose of this chapter is go behind the usual analysis of peasant 'obedience' to Rwandan political elites as explained by both their docility and lack of political consciousness as explanations for their compliance to government elites (Mamdani 2001: 41; Prunier 1995: 141). Instead, I argue that peasants exercise tactical forms of compliance to give the appearance of obedience to elite policy directives in ways that have yet to translate into collective political consciousness. Indeed, following the Arab Spring uprisings in 2011, the Rwandan government tightened its grip on society in deploying additional military personnel at the local level and rounding up members of the political opposition to remind them of the government's desire to continue to violently control the political realm.[2] Despite a lack of opportunity for imminent collective action, my research finds that Rwandans at the lower rungs of the social hierarchy are becoming aware of their personal ability to challenge government through their everyday acts of resistance to its many demands. While participants are cognisant of the many risks involved, my findings point to a nascent political activism, organising to demand a more equitable distribution of wealth. The Rwandans I consulted are loath to challenge government for systemic change because they understand that calls for political change are likely to result in mass political violence – something they wish to avoid after the horrors of the 1994 genocide. Still, socio-economic conditions in rural southern Rwanda, where I conducted life-history interviews and participation observation in 2006, are sufficiently dire for peasants I spoke with to consider rising up against the government. For example, peasant men, particularly released prisoners, shared with me how they used the market-place as a domain where they could whisper news of political developments. They shared information with each other: who had been arrested, denounced, or put in prison since the last market day. Tutsi survivors who are forced to attend the return ceremony of a Hutu individual who they believe should not have been released from prison will laugh outlandishly at the remarks of local authorities during their 'welcome home' speeches. In this way they practise everyday resistance: they attend the mandatory meetings but let officials know in subtle ways their contempt or disrespect. Such secretive ingenuity facilitates the flow of political information between rural Rwandans.

[1] By 'peasants', I do not mean those who hold formal political power as members of the political elite, nor those individuals engaged as agents of the state (police and military personnel, civil servants, local authorities, and others). I use the term to refer broadly to the non-elite and largely peasant citizenry resident in rural Rwanda.

[2] According to Clark (2012), President Kagame expressed concern about the role of social media in fomenting the Arab Spring uprisings. In reaction, he appointed a team of special media advisors, and 'at the annual government retreat, instructed all cabinet ministers to use Facebook, Twitter and other online tools to respond directly to the government's critics at home and abroad'.

To make my case, I focus on the everyday acts of resistance of two of the 37 rural Rwandans I consulted. An analysis of the everyday acts of resistance of peasant Rwandans to the oppressive policies of the ruling RPF illustrates the dissatisfaction, frustration, and distrust of political elites felt by the rural Rwandans with whom I had direct contact. It also reveals that their most pressing issues are poverty, lack of land and jobs, and a desire to be able to express their views and have a voice in policies that affect them. Far from being apolitical, passive and ignorant individuals who need government officials to teach them how to behave in the 'new' Rwanda, the Rwandans I consulted practised everyday resistance to make their lives more sustainable in the face of oppressive rural policies.[3] Analysis of their everyday acts of resistance, meaning the subtle, indirect and non-confrontational acts that make daily life more bearable under an authoritarian government, demonstrates that in discussing their means of resisting with me, they became aware of the politicised nature of their actions.

In the first section of my chapter, I sketch out my research methodology, since identifying both forms of resistance and political consciousness could yield unreliable results. Criticism of government policy is not only taboo; it subjects Rwandans – elites and non-elites alike – to considerable sanction, including harassment, intimidation, fines, imprisonment and, in extreme cases, disappearance and even death. Thus the question of gaining access to rural Rwandans in their home communities to discuss politically sensitive topics matters greatly. Also important here is the process through which peasant Rwandans at the lowest rungs of the social hierarchy begin to experience themselves as stronger, more insightful and capable of acting and organising politically. In the second section, I describe Rwanda's socio-economic hierarchy to illustrate the challenges and obstacles it creates for those at the lower rungs of society. I also set out my theoretical framework for understanding and explaining everyday acts of resistance. This approach illustrates the connections between individual acts of everyday resistance and political consciousness.

In the third section, I compile ethnographic vignettes from Jeanne and Jean-Bosco, two of the rural Rwandans that participated in my 2006 research to illustrate how they realised that they resisted government demands while expressing their frustration with local officials who show no concern for their needs, and under an authoritarian system that allows little space for their views and concerns. Jeanne recounts how she was sad and worried about her inability to feed her family as she

[3] International journalists coined the phrase the 'new' Rwanda in July 1994 to explain the monumental changes in Rwandan society envisaged by the RPF-led government of national unity and reconciliation (Pottier 2002). The RPF leadership then picked up the phrase in some of its policy documents, and the speeches of senior government officials, notably President Kagame, to justify its policy choices. For example, 'In the "new" Rwanda, we do not tolerate ethnic divisionism of any kind. Those who preach it will suffer the consequences [...]' (executive secretary of the National Unity and Reconciliation Commission, speaking on Contact FM, Kigali, April 2006).

negotiated for social support from her local government officials. Jean-Bosco narrates the hopelessness he feels of being wrongfully accused of acts of genocide by the new regime, and his role in not resisting the pre-genocide actions of 'Hutu Power' government officials in his community. In sharing these experiences with me Jeanne and Jean-Bosco detail the personal power they felt in resisting what they considered to be unjust intrusions of the government into their daily lives. I focus on the stories of Jeanne and Jean-Bosco out of the dozens of examples I could have drawn upon from my fieldwork because of the ways in which both stories explore both everyday resistance and political consciousness in the broader context of Rwanda's centralised political structure and top-down post-genocide reconstruction and reconciliation policies (for more examples, see Thomson 2011a, 2013). I use ethnographic vignettes to allow the reader to experience the process in which Jeanne and Jean-Bosco gain political consciousness through their acts of everyday resistance in their own words as much as possible. Finally, I conclude with an analysis of what the combination of continued oppression and individual consciousness of rural Rwandans means for the country's present and future peace and security.

How does everyday resistance become political consciousness?

This chapter draws on participant observation, semi-structured interviews with Rwandan government officials, and life-history interviews conducted over a seven-month period in 2006 with 37 ordinary Rwandans resident in the south of the country.[4] In addition, I consulted approximately 400 Rwandans from across the country through participant observation – meaning spontaneous, casual conversation in the course of everyday life. In order to identify and situate the everyday acts of resistance of typical Rwandan citizens in their broader context, I administered interviews with state authorities, from members of the Senate and the Office of the President down to local government officials, resulting in 79 hours of recorded material. The primary sample comprised three ethnic Twa, twenty ethnic Hutu and fourteen ethnic Tutsi – all of whom lived through the 1994 genocide. The majority of the sample were subsistence farmers or day labourers; only two of the participants held formal employment. The sample is representative of Rwandans on the lowest rungs of society, as it solely comprises individuals who live on less than US$1 a day, similar to approximately 66 per cent of the country's population (Howe and Mackay 2007: 200).

Since open criticism of authority is taboo for most people in Rwanda, simply asking ordinary Rwandans about their lives since the 1994 genocide is difficult. Researchers cannot reasonably expect frank and forth-

[4] Nowhere in the chapter do I use specific place or community names. Names used throughout the chapter are pseudonyms.

coming answers from the individuals they consult, since asking and answering too many probing questions about socio-political realities since 1994 can draw the unwanted attention of the Rwandan authorities (Ingelaere 2010: esp. 49–50; Purdeková 2011; Thomson 2010). Two key factors explain the willingness of ordinary Rwandans to speak openly with me. The first was that I let trust and emotional engagement drive the research relationships I developed with each of the individuals who participated in my project. I thus spent most of my time building human relationships, meaning that I listened more than I spoke (sometimes through a translator, but usually not), and met people where they lived as early as 4 a.m. to avoid the watchful eye of local officials. Second, the emotional relationships I was able to establish with ordinary Rwandans helped to create a safe space in which they were willing to share their secrets with a foreigner who had no formal ties to the country.

Two categories of 'speaking up' shape individual relations with government officials. Those who belong to the first category are known among their peers as *abasazi* (plural, meaning foolish). *Abasazi* use their 'madness' to give the impression that they are mentally unstable to justify their willingness to say what others will not or cannot attempt for fear of government penalties. In the second category are those known as *ibyihebe* (plural, meaning fearless). The individuals who fall into this group understood the risks of sharing their experiences and no longer feared speaking out because of the hardships they had endured. This is true mainly of Tutsi survivors of the genocide, many of whom consider themselves to be 'walking dead' because of their experience of being targeted for death during the genocide, and subsequent post-traumatic stress diagnoses. By necessity, Rwandans' everyday acts of resistance are tactical since government officials and other agents of the state suppress any perceived challenge to their many demands, sometimes with a ferocity that dramatically exceeds the original violation. Individual acts of resistance are not tied to the overthrow of the Rwandan state. Instead, they are acts of individual subversion that make daily life more dignified and sustainable. As such, acts of everyday resistance are more than signs of individual agency – they also allow for an analysis of the forms of power that ordinary Rwandans are caught up in and of the complex processes of the policy of national unity and reconciliation from their perspective, not that of government elites.

The process of individual empowerment to challenge or resist government policy is rooted in one's willingness and ability to speak out against government policy or openly defy the directives of government officials. It is this process of becoming self-aware of the individual capacity to defy government that I identify as 'political consciousness'. This minimalist definition differs from Marx's (1976) classic statements on political consciousness as the process of individuals claiming their own historical path, rather than adopting the ideology of the ruling class as in their best interest. Instead, I situate the individual political consciousness of the peasant Rwandans I consulted within the framework of the oppression they have experienced in their daily lives since the 1994 genocide, rooting their consciousness in the observation that when people are treated poorly, they resist (Scott 1990). Among these Rwandans, the realisation of their ability to speak out in ways that allowed them to critique government policy without immediate penalty is at the root of their political consciousness. This recognition of pre-existing ability to speak up and subtly critique government is both an act of resistance and a moment of consciousness. In these moments, many of them imagined a life based on respect and equality, including efforts to stand up to government officials in ways that avoid sanction while enlarging their ability to do so. Central to this awakening of political consciousness was an individual recognition that one could speak out in strategic ways through cultural mechanisms that have traditionally been reserved for 'important people', meaning Rwandans who are higher in the socio-economic hierarchy than are the peasants I consulted.

Close examination of the everyday acts of resistance that peasant Rwandans employ in their interactions with government officials and local authorities reveals that these are more than signs of individual agency, rather than simply compliance or obedience. It also demonstrates that peasant Rwandans utilise creative ways to negotiate, manoeuvre and muddle their way through the various demands of the post-genocide government. As Scott (1985: 1–27) notes, if the outcome of the exercise of power is to serve the interests of the power holders, then everyday resistance, when effectively executed, is intended to serve the interests of the powerless. My use of the concept of 'everyday resistance' differs from that put forth by James Scott. He argues that peasant politics is generally concerned with 'bread-and-butter' issues and he uses 'everyday resistance' to understand and explain confrontational forms of class struggle, not the various forms of state power that peasants confront in their daily lives (Scott 1985: 296). Instead, I use the concept of everyday resistance to 'bring to light power relations, to locate their positions, find out their application and the methods used' (Foucault 1980: 209). This agent-centred approach to understanding the power relations in which individuals are enmeshed differs from traditional approaches to studying resistance. The resistance literature in Africa focuses largely on organised and national-level resistance to colonialism in the 1960s and 1970s. Analysis of individual acts of resistance is instead trumped by an analytical focus on organised and group action. This focus on national-level outbreaks of revolutionary protest mutes our ability to understand and explain the 'constant strategic alertness' that some peasant Rwandans practise in their daily lives (Sivaramakrishnan 2005: 350).

Everyday resistance as political consciousness: socio-economic context

The 37 ordinary Rwandans I consulted hardly lack political consciousness; on the contrary, they are very much aware of their subjugated position within society and understand their presumed powerlessness to mean that they must take orders from 'important people' like local government officials and other state officials, even when those orders go against their interests. It is this moment, when they take official orders that work against them, that these Rwandans become aware of their oppression, and act to enlarge their position vis-à-vis the state. Thus, everyday resistance is an important analytical concept because it highlights the scope and nature of power in most forms of relationships (Abu-Lughod 1990). I define 'everyday acts of resistance' as any subtle, indirect, and non-confrontational act that makes daily life more sustainable under a strong and centralised state power (Thomson 2011a, 2013). They include some combination of persistence, prudence, and individual effort to accomplish a specific goal vis-à-vis the government. Everyday resistance, in contrast to open resistance, reflects a degree of oppression in which the latter is not deemed possible by the resister. This does not mean that open resistance is held to be impossible because there is a law against the act in question but more simply that individuals are taking a calculated risk to maintain or enlarge their position in relation to the state or representatives of its power. It is also the moment when rural Rwandans at the lower rungs of the socio-economic hierarchy realise that they have the personal attributes and abilities to express their dissatisfaction with the government in efforts to subvert the expectations of local government officials, and begin to modify the conditions of their daily lives.

Crushing poverty shapes the everyday lives of most Rwandans. An estimated 87 per cent of Rwandans are subsistence farmers (National Institute of Statistics 2006: 27). The official poverty line is a daily cash income per adult of 250 Rwandan Francs (Frw.) (US$0.54)[5] while the extreme poverty line is a daily income per adult of 175 Frw (or US$0.38) (MINICOFIN 2001: 9). Among the ordinary Rwandans who participated in my research, the average income per household was 50 Frw (US$0.11) per day or 20,000 Frw per year (US$43). Only three of my 37 participants said that they had ever seen paper money, even though the lowest available denomination is 100 Frw (US$0.21). With rare exception, the ordinary Rwandans I met were thin, barefoot and dressed in ragged clothes, which in many cases is the extent of their full wardrobe. Their hands and faces were weathered and gave the appearance of an

[5] The exchange rate at the time of the research in 2006 is used in all equivalents here and below. The rate at end of August 2013 was USD$1: Frw 639.

older age than their biological years. People's eyes were lacklustre from continued hunger; some had orange hair, a tell-tale sign of malnutrition. In 2009, the FAO (2010: 2) estimated that the per capita consumption of calories in Rwanda was 2,070 kcal, of which a mere 54 calories are protein. I regularly saw evidence of starvation; several of my research participants as well as their children exhibited symptoms of kwashiorkor and marasmus (forms of malnutrition caused by lack of protein in the diet). Women like Jeanne who participated in my research told me that they sometimes eat dirt or swallow pebbles to ward off hunger pangs; two women lost children to starvation. Men like Jean-Bosco told me that they drank banana beer to fill the void of days without food.

Women suffer the additional indignity of struggling with the men in their lives for resources and personal power at the household level. The legacy of the genocide means that women head more than a third of Rwandan households, and 56 per cent of them are widows of the genocide (UNDP Rwanda 2007: 33). Female-headed households have a 'higher and deeper incidence of poverty' than other households (UNDP Rwanda 2007: 3). The average life expectancy for Rwandans is 45.2 years; half of the children born in Rwanda since the genocide will not live past their fortieth birthday (UNDP 2008). For all of the 37 ordinary Rwandans who participated in my research, the lack of food, clean water as well as affordable and proximate health services was a constant lament as were the difficulties of living with post-traumatic stress disorder (PTSD). Psychosocial trauma is widespread in Rwandan society; some studies suggest as many as 95 per cent of Rwandans witnessed or participated in 'extreme acts of violence' (Ndayambajwe 2001: 46). Many of the women who participated in my research had the additional burden of child-care, including the care of orphaned relatives whose parents died before, during or after the genocide.

Compounding the challenges faced by ordinary Rwandan men and women is the perception on the part of government officials, at both the local level and in Kigali that peasants are but a homogeneous mass to be governed. Within this 'mass' of poor peasant Rwandans are the socio-economic categories and the inequalities these engender that in turn shape individual life chances as well as opportunities for moving up or falling down the social ladder. All of the ordinary Rwandans that participated in my research understand that only elites can hold political power (i.e. it is both acknowledged and accepted that politics is the domain of the elite, whether political, business or religious). Social mobility, or moving up to the ranks of the powerful is rare, and is not something that peasant Rwandans expect to happen.

This lack of opportunity for social mobility exists where hierarchy is the societal standard, inequality is anticipated, less powerful people expect to be dependent on more powerful people, centralisation of state institutions is popular and unquestioned, subordinates envision being told what to do, and privileges and social status are expected for elite members of society (Archer 2003: 136–137). In a resource-poor environment like post-genocide Rwanda, where the social structure is firmly entrenched and where individual options and opportunities are structured by one's location in the social hierarchy, it is important to understand where individuals are situated economically. This matters because one's socio-economic class shapes one's life chances as well as determining how and when other Rwandans, notably elites, will engage and interact with the vulnerable, poor and salaried poor individuals that participated in my research, as well as how they interact with others in their socio-economic class and each another. An appreciation of the socio-economic categories that stratify Rwandan society is also important because it shapes individuals' options to practice everyday resistance and move on to enacting consciousness.

The boundaries of the six socio-economic categories that stratify Rwandan society are relatively fixed (MINECOFIN 2001). There are differences between Rwandans who occupy the three lowest categories – the most vulnerable, the vulnerable, and the poor – which are muted by the fact that many of these peasants have little or no access to cash, leaving them most susceptible to climatic shock. Members of these socio-economic categories also have little formal education. In the lowest category are the *abatindi nyakujya* (the most vulnerable; *umutindi nyakujya*, sing.); these are individuals who have no social standing whatsoever. Most beg to survive; some resort to prostitution or theft, which in turn isolates them from other categories of peasants as these individuals are considered by many, including other most vulnerable individuals, as 'without hope'. The individuals who participated in my research occupy the *abatindi* (vulnerable) and *abakene* (poor) categories. *Abatindi* (*umutindi*, sing.) sometimes own land but are unable to work it successfully, either through personal inability or because the field is fallow. They eat only when they are able to share in the harvest of others. They often have some form of makeshift shelter.

The next category up the socio-economic ladder is the *abakene* (poor; *umukene*, sing.), all of whom hold land which is rarely sufficiently productive. They own small livestock such as chickens, goats or sheep. *Abakene* are most likely to be called upon by members of higher socio-economic classes to work their fields in exchange for cash. Some have excess harvest that they take to the market to sell. Access to micro-credit is also a possibility but this is through alliances within their social network of relatives and friends, not through formal credit facilities. The *abakene bifashije* (the poor with means) constitute the last, and highest, category of the peasantry. These individuals usually have a one-room house and some land. They often own more than one cow along with several goats, sheep and chickens. Some own motorcycles; most own bicycles. It can be a great shame if an *umukene wifashije* has to work for others as he can usually sell some livestock to weather climatic or economic downturns. These families usually live off the means of production which can include ownership of a kiosk shop or a taxi-moto (motor-cycle taxi).

Abakene bifashije often act as appointed local officials within communities, even though they receive no salary for their work. Many are also elected *gacaca* judges. The prestige of being asked to serve can open up opportunities to become an *umukungu* (rich without money), the socio-economic category of many salaried local officials. *Abakungu* have more than one plot of land, and often own several heads of cattle. They often have development-related jobs and can gain a small salary whether as salaried local officials, or as project officers or managers of civil society organisations. Many have servants from among the poor and vulnerable categories. *Abakungu* are without money because there is little left over for productive means once school fees and health costs have been paid. They often have access to a vehicle and housing through employment, with their yearly salary averaging 350,000 Frw (US$780). The highest socio-economic category is that of the *abakire* (the rich), being the category of most political and economic elites, the majority of whom live in Kigali. They have land, excess production, several heads of cattle and other livestock as well as paid employment, either as civil servants or in private business. Ordinary Rwandans told me that *abakire* are easy to identify 'because they are always dressed up, and they never walk anywhere'. They own at least one car and always have servants to prepare their meals and keep their homes presentable for entertaining and other social festivities, notably weddings.

It is within this stratified socio-economic hierarchy that ordinary Rwandans battle daily to ensure their own and their family's survival; to do so they must continually protect themselves against the apparatus of the state, the RPF and its agents who vigorously promote top-down development policies. Central to the awakening of political consciousness that my Rwandan participants felt was the individual realisation of their pre-existing ability to challenge government without necessarily compromising their personal safety or the well-being of their family. A majority of them acknowledged that their recognition of their own pre-existing ability to resist shaped individual capacity and willingness to resist government authority and other forms of oppression – the two are intertwined in a reciprocal relationship where the ability to resist shapes political consciousness and vice versa. This realisation in the course of formal interviews and casual conversations with rural Rwandans was rooted in cultural meanings of resistance. Most people assumed that because their resistance was neither obvious, nor collective, that they did not practice some form of resistance.[6] Conceptually, it is best to think

[6] I acknowledge that a focus on the everyday acts of resistance of peasant Rwandans runs the risk of exaggerating their ability to make choices and act upon them. It also runs the risk of over-emphasising individual ability to counter or mitigate the socio-political structures of domination they confront in their daily lives. Rather than reading 'all forms of resistance as signs of the

of everyday resistance as a mechanism with which to think about how individuals subject to authoritarian oppression respond to it rather than how they are affected by it.

Responding to authoritarian oppression through everyday acts of resistance

Rural Rwandans' awareness of their everyday resistance to authoritarian oppression resulted in their ability to see themselves as stronger, more insightful and more capable of responding to the demands of government officials in ways that made their everyday lives more dignified and sustainable. Indeed, all of the people I consulted had been subjected to some form of physical and emotional violence, both during and after the 1994 genocide. The violence they experienced took many forms, including physical and sexual assault and battery, as well as more structural forms of violence like humiliation and socio-economic exclusion based on perceived behaviour during the genocide. Two ethnographic vignettes highlight the relationship between the subtle acts of everyday resistance rural Rwandans practised, and their political consciousness.

Jeanne, widow of the genocide, four of her seven children surviving, subsistence farmer

When I first met Jeanne in the spring of 2006, she confided that she had been sad and worried ever since the genocide officially ended in the summer of 1994. She had been diagnosed with PTSD by a foreign psychiatrist who worked in Rwanda for a local civil society organisation. Jeanne rejected the diagnosis, stating: 'those with PTSD are ruined on many levels. No-one, not family, not friends, not even the government, will support you [financially and emotionally] if you have PTSD because they think you'll always need more support than they can provide.' In our conversations, Jeanne's primary worry was her ability to 'get on with her life' since the genocide, citing depression and a generalised fear about her future, and that of her children in the 'new' Rwanda. Since the genocide, Jeanne has had 'the same fears about feeding my children, and sending them to school, but now I am alone' (i.e. without a husband to support her financially or emotionally). In the course of our interviews, Jeanne reported that she had been repeatedly raped during the genocide by a man that lived in her community, and who was unlikely to go to

(cont) ineffectiveness of systems of power and of the resilience and creativity of the human spirit' (Abu-Lughod 1990: 42), my emphasis is on individual agency to understand the power hierarchies they produce (Emirbayer and Mische 1998). This approach allows for analysis of how individual actors, however marginal they might be, are able to critically evaluate the conditions of their lives to identify the power relations in which they are enmeshed, and how they are positioned differently in relation to the mechanisms and practices of state power. For specific reference to local agency in Rwanda, see Newbury and Newbury (2000).

prison for his crime because 'he is politically connected. He has contacts in Kigali, and I am a poor widow. He has the power, and I have nothing but a broken heart. In Rwanda, everyone is broken so no-one pays attention to people like me. I have nowhere to go for support.' She then said that she missed her deceased sister, Sophie, because 'she could really fight back. She had always been *abasazi* (foolish) so she had the space to do what she wanted. She could really handle government officials in a way that let her live her life without interference.' Jeanne did not tell me what Sophie did to enlarge her personal space vis-à-vis government but it was clear that she admired her sister for her ability to do so, and lamented her own inability to 'stand up' for herself when government officials demanded she plant coffee instead of a crop that could actually feed her family (like sweet potatoes or beans), or participate in a government-led mandatory community service called *umuganda*.

Jeanne's admiration for Sophie's ability to handle all that the government threw her way shaped much of our time together. She described how Sophie responded mentally and physically to official attacks as they occurred, and at different points in her life. Jeanne told me that she was often with Sophie when her sister stood up for her rights, and that one time she even prevented the *nyumbakumi* (a community-level government administrator) from putting her in prison for 'no good reason!' Jeanne also told me about the hiding place that she and Sophie built together to hide the crops they had grown without government permission, and how she once distracted the *nyumbakumi* when he came to confront Sophie about her coffee yields so he would not find their supply of potatoes and beans. According to Jeanne, she became openly defiant of government directives about what crops to grow, and when to attend reconciliation activities 'that the government cooks up to make us [peasants] believe we Tutsi and Hutu are reconciled when there is still much hatred in our hearts because of being forced to forgive and forget!' Jeanne also admitted that she had little respect for government authorities, and found ways to subtly resist her *nyumbakumi*'s treatment of her as a person who was 'problematic' because she stood up for Sophie when he used her as an example of a 'bad Rwandan' in his monthly speeches to residents of her commune.[7]

Jeanne went on to articulate her beliefs about what living with dignity meant to her. She told me, 'it is important for survivors of the genocide like me to be treated with respect', and went on to share examples of how she treated her *nyumbakumi* with respect 'even when he did not deserve it!' Jeanne told me of how her *nyumbakumi* would disrespect survivors by 'telling us when to forgive, and how to forget what

[7] The sanctions and consequences of being a 'bad citizen' are analysed in Purdeková (2012). She notes that individuals are monitored by a dense administrative and military apparatus to ensure that they both respect the authority of the state while sacrificing individual preferences and sublimating private realities to work for the greater goal of unity and reconciliation. 'Good citizens' are docile and compliant ones who follow the orders of the government and its local officials.

happened to us during the genocide. I pay him different courtesies by listening, respectfully telling him he is wrong about reconciliation, and saying that I will pray for him to have a change of heart.' I suggested to Jeanne that her behaviour towards her *nyumbakumi* marked her as fearless (*ibyihebe*) because as she made efforts to stand up to his demands, she was actually practising everyday resistance in ways that protected her dignity, and helped her take care of her family. In our subsequent discussion about how Jeanne resisted, she admitted that she 'felt a lot stronger' and was eating and sleeping better, and feeling less fearful in her everyday life, and even more optimistic for her children because she felt well enough to negotiate with her *nyumbakumi* to sign the required paperwork to receive school fee and health care benefits from the government. Jeanne continued:

> I went into his office, and I felt capable of asking for what we need. It is true I lost many people during the genocide, but I am also responsible for many who survived. If I cannot take care of myself, how can my remaining children count on me to take care of them? So, I went in to see him, and asked for my rights, and he signed, he signed the paper in front of me, and now I have new resources for my children! Can you believe it?! I am getting on with my life because I now know that I know how to stand up for myself.

When I asked Jeanne how she felt about being able to accomplish these things, Jeanne beamed as she recounted the ways she had handled her local government official, and how she felt that she could probably handle just about any situation. Jeanne was 'getting on with her life'.

Her actions not only exhibit the non-confrontational, prudent, determined and individual dimension of everyday resistance but also demonstrate an awakening of her political consciousness. Jeanne became acutely aware that government is not to be feared but rather that its officials can be engaged, and that she has power to challenge their control and authority over her life, and that of her children. It is important to note here that Jeanne's political consciousness is nascent, and is not yet something that she is prepared to bring into the public sphere. Because she lives her life under the close surveillance of government officials, Jeanne knows that she cannot openly protest her living conditions or any government directive because these efforts are likely to be met with threats, imprisonment or loss of hard-won school fees and health care privileges. At the same time, Jeanne's sense of self-empowerment through her acts of everyday resistance illustrates her individual agency, directly challenging academic and policy analyses that situate peasants at the lower levels of the socio-economic hierarchy as 'obedient' without understanding the forms of close surveillance that make open, collective protest unlikely. Yet, Jeanne's everyday resistance, and resultant political consciousness, signals more than the strategic nature of her compliance to government directives. Her actions are more than indicators of her personal dissatisfaction with the current Rwandan regime but also provide an analytic entry point for identifying the potential for, if, and when individual acts will cascade into a collective movement for systemic political change. At the moment, collective action like that witnessed during the Arab Spring is unlikely but does put government elites and local officials in a quandary as so many rural Rwandans have been left out of the economic gains the country has experienced since the genocide (Crisafulli and Redmond 2012). Since Rwanda's impressive annual economic growth requires that agricultural land be developed, subsistence farmers like Jeanne will have to be displaced. Yet, the regime offers few employment opportunities for unskilled labour. The RPF will need to address this trend if it wishes to contain the potential for collective action.

Jean-Bosco, former medical doctor, two of his nine children surviving, imprisoned on allegations of committing acts of genocide in 1994

During our third interview in Butare prison in 2006, Jean-Bosco told me that his wife had left him just before the 1994 genocide because 'she thought I was too close to the [genocidal former] regime. I begged her to stay with me for the sake of our children. I heard in July 1996 [two years after the genocide officially ended] that she was living with a senior military officer of the new regime!' Jean-Bosco confided that as a medical doctor, he stayed behind in Butare town to save lives but that the new government decided he was guilty of genocide for 'not saving enough Tutsi lives!' He continued, 'I mean, I am a Hutu so anything I say or do links me to the genocide in the "new" Rwanda. I am not a killer but I have no-one to listen to me!' Jean-Bosco related feelings of hopelessness, sleeplessness and fears that his children had a new father. 'I mean, I never have any visitors, and don't even know where my children are or who is their other parent!' He also said that his fall from the status of a medical doctor under the Hutu-led regime of the former government to a 'mere prisoner with no rights or privilege' gave him some insight into and sympathy for 'the plight of unimportant people like the peasants I now call my family [his fellow prisoners]'.

Over the course of our next few interviews in the prison, Jean-Bosco opened up about his own passive behaviour during the genocide, and his lack of assertiveness to stand up and advocate for his wife and his freedom from prison. I did not ask Jean-Bosco about what he did during the genocide as I had learned in the course of my fieldwork that the question was too upsetting for nearly all Rwandans. Instead, I asked if he thought he was too close to the former regime as his wife alleged. Jean-Bosco admitted that he was spending a lot of time with senior government officials in their community, and that he thought being close to these men would protect his family from the violence he 'knew Rwandans were capable of'. He also acknowledged that being close to government brought his family many new privileges, including free housing and a car. He admitted that he never gave any thought to the emotional well-being of others of lesser socio-economic standing in the tumultuous and heady days of the pre-genocide period. 'There was never any idea that Hutu Power might lose to the [then rebel, now government] Rwandan Patriotic Front.' Jean-Bosco told me that he felt that his wife spent less time with him as his relationship with senior government officials solidified, and that their children stopped calling him 'Papa'. In addition, his two teenage sons began to refuse to cooperate with him, or go to church or any public outing with Jean-Bosco. In the course of our conversations, Jean-Bosco became aware of the ways in which his wife and sons may have felt vulnerable and unsafe as he pursued personal relationships with high-ranking government officials. He also admitted that when his authority as head of the household was challenged, as his wife regularly did, fearing that his relationships with government were a liability to the family, he would hit her 'as a way to regain his manhood'. Jean-Bosco continued:

> When I hit my wife, my sons hid, and I forced them to come out and watch me hurt her. I thought I was being a good husband and provider because Rwanda was at war at that time, and I had no way to assure the protection of my family except to join up with Hutu Power government. A plan for genocide was never discussed, and it is true that I did nothing [meaning he did not kill anyone]. I didn't try to protect anyone but my family, and they rejected that support because of the change in my character. I realise now that I lacked any sense of self – I lost my dignity in behaving like the Hutu Power officials wanted me to behave. I behaved like a coward to protect my family, and they rejected that support. Am I in prison for standing by when I should have stood up? If I had been stronger, perhaps my wife and sons would respect me for being *ibyihebe* (fearless). Instead, I have the character of a fool (*abasazi*). I sold my soul for a few possessions [car, housing] and I lost everything. And in the new Rwanda, I am labelled a killer, so rebuilding my life from prison is impossible. I was part of the problem before the genocide [as a member of Hutu Power] and I am part of the problem since the genocide [as an accused prisoner]. Part of my suffering is that I realise my family is right to reject me. I abused them, and I did not respect their feelings.

Jean-Bosco's narrative is illustrative of the pressures of individuals who remained complacent in the face of the dominant social forces that created the conditions for the 1994 genocide to occur. As a medical doctor, he had access to the resources of the government, and was himself an important person (compared to 'lowly peasants who work with their bodies, not their minds'). In recognising his abuse of power before the genocide, Jean-Bosco begins to understand and appreciate his role in losing his wife and family, and of being imprisoned. Had he stood up to Hutu Power officials, rather than allowing himself to be co-opted into their promises of economic and social gains 'when our side wins the war', perhaps 'things would be different' for him. This realisation marks Jean-Bosco's moment of political consciousness. In not resisting the invitations to stand with Hutu Power officials in Butare town, and in suppressing his wife's questioning of his motives, Jean-Bosco reveals his passive behaviour to government, and opens up discussion of how his present condition is a result of actions he did not take before the genocide. In the course of our subsequent conversations, Jean-Bosco demonstrated how he lost his privileges to speak up since the genocide:

> Prisoners have no rights because we are considered violent killers. I did not kill. But I did not speak up. I had a voice and I did not use it, and now I have little voice, and no role in the new Rwanda. I abused the authority and privilege I had. It is up to me to try to fix my situation.

There is something quite powerful in Jean-Bosco's realisation from his current position of marginality that is, he feels, partly responsible for his current detention. He feels the sting of not resisting when he had a chance, of going along when he could and should have stood up against Hutu Power, and finds it difficult to live with himself in his current condition as a prisoner accused of genocide. Still, Jean-Bosco's experiences as someone who stood by stripped him of more than his family; he also lost his sense of self-worth and personal dignity. His fall from someone with social standing to someone without marks a profound moment in Jean-Bosco's imprisonment as he also realised that he was largely powerless against the forces of Hutu Power in much the same way that his fellow prisoners are powerless against allegations of committing acts of genocide when many did not.[8] At this moment of self-awareness, Jean-Bosco stood up from the table where we were seated outside the office of the director of the Butare prison, and said, to no-one in particular, 'I am no longer resigned to my fate; I will no longer sit around unhappy, not participating [in prison work assignments]. If I am to prove my innocence, I must do so myself, and as a prisoner. I am no longer a doctor. This is my life now!' This critical consciousness has a double implication for Jean-Bosco. He understands and appreciates the difficulty of resistance in a context of strong state power, and that in accepting the status quo offered by Hutu Power officials he treated himself, and those around him disrespectfully. Jean-Bosco also realises the difficulties of everyday life in systems of violence and oppression, and articulates a nascent sense of political consciousness that all Rwandans, not just those like him with social standing and prestige, practice. The last time I saw him in August 2006, Jean-Bosco reported a stronger sense of self, and of actually working with his fellow prisoners 'as equals' as a way to strategise his release from prison. He was aware of his position of marginality in the new Rwanda but was resolved to address his needs, and those of his fellow prisoners. I learned in 2010 that Jean-Bosco was released from prison as scheduled for time served in November 2009, and that he had

[8] The current government estimates that some one million Rwandans participated in the genocide and it has adopted a strategy of 'maximal prosecution', meaning that adult Hutu men are presumed guilty of genocide. Careful research by Straus suggests that between 175,000 and 225,000 individuals participated in the 1994 genocide (Straus 2006: 117).

taken up work with his local church group to advocate for 'his former comrades [prisoners]'.

Conclusion

Any act of everyday resistance in contexts like post-genocide Rwanda, where state power is oppressive and violent, illustrates that the individuals I consulted understood well the risks of speaking out against the government and this awareness on their part imbues their actions with added weight. Combining analysis of everyday acts of resistance with the moment of political consciousness, being the moment when the individual recognises his or her individual capacity to push back against the power of the state, provides insight into the ways in which individuals maintain their personal dignity in coercive contexts. It also highlights the difficulty for peasants and other marginal actors to organise politically without stripping these individuals of their potential as political actors. I must caution however that this combination also runs the risk of over-emphasising individual ability to counter or mitigate socio-political structures of oppression. Engaging in acts of resistance provides the necessary foundation for the transformative political process that consciousness provides. The peasant Rwandans I consulted are well aware of their marginal socio-economic position, and of the limited opportunities to improve their lot in life. In the moment of recounting their acts of everyday resistance to me, they also realised ways in which they could redress the emotional and physical harm caused by their marginal socio-economic position as well as their experiences of living through the physical violence of the 1994 genocide.

A focus on the everyday acts of resistance as political consciousness of those individuals at the lower rungs of Rwanda's socio-economic hierarchy also illuminates how the post-genocide state seeks to depoliticise peasant people while seeking to close off the possibility for them to join together to organise politically. It also highlights that peasants have little opportunity to publicly express their politics. Their everyday acts of resistance 'show how Rwanda's new leadership opted for a strategy of repression and control that will at best delay national recovery and at worst rekindle intercommunal tensions and violence' (Habimana 2011: 354). Their individual political consciousness illustrates that peasant Rwandans understand that the practices of the post-genocide government go against their interests as peasants and are an affront to their everyday life since the genocide.

Analysis of everyday resistance as political consciousness is useful in understanding the myriad ways in which peasants appear to accept the forms of authoritarian oppression they are subject to in their daily lives. Owing to Rwanda's stratified social hierarchy, the opportunities for upward mobility are near nil and the peasant Rwandans I spoke to understand that their prospects for economic gain and political inclusion are also limited. Rwandan peasants, because of their disadvantaged socio-political position have less reason to support the existing political system, meaning that there is no feasible outlet for their political consciousness. My chapter demonstrates that, as a group, peasants are incapable of significantly altering the post-genocide order. Still, their practices of resistance are indicators of more than individual dissatisfaction with a particular regime; they do provide the foundation for creating alternative spaces for political ideas and action. It is difficult to predict if and when these individual acts of resistance and consciousness by the peasantry will cascade into a collective movement that may lead to peaceful contestation of power or culminate in riot or rebellion. They do, however, demonstrate the potential for such upheaval.

Acts of everyday resistance and the resultant political consciousness are indicators of new forms of confrontation with government officials and local authorities. As the largest socio-economic sector in Rwanda, peasants have potential political influence. Historically, their political attitudes and proclivities have been influenced by their perceptions of socio-economic mobility, relative socio-economic status and rural development policies (Newbury 1992). In turn, state-led development policies, market forces and individual experiences of violence during the 1994 genocide shape peasant perceptions of the post-genocide political order (Newbury 2011). These factors, taken together, have led Rwandan peasants to be restless, less tolerant of the political status quo, and dissatisfied with the local government officials, making an upheaval such as those of the Arab Spring a possibility.

References

Abu-Lughod, L. (1990). The romance of resistance: tracing transformations of power through Bedouin women. *American Ethnologist*, 17(1), 41–55.

Ansoms, A. (2009). Re-engineering rural society: the visions and ambitions of the Rwandan elite. *African Affairs*, 108(431), 289–309.

Archer, M. (2003). *Structure, agency and the internal conversation.* Cambridge: Cambridge University Press.

Clark, P. (2012) Arab Spring south of the Sahara? 24 May. Available from: www.opendemocracy.net/phil-clark/arab-spring-south-of-sahara (last accessed: 31 May 2013).

Crisafulli, P. and Redmond, A. (2012). *Rwanda, Inc.: how a devastated nation became an economic model for the developing world.* New York: Palgrave Macmillan.

Desrosiers, M-E. and Thomson, S. (2011). Rhetorical legacies of leadership: projections of 'benevolent leadership' in pre- and post-genocide Rwanda. *Journal of Modern African Studies*, 49(3), 431–55.

Economist Intelligence Unit (2011). *Country report: Rwanda, November 2011.* London: The Economist Intelligence Unit.

Emirbayer, M. and Mische, A. (1998). What is agency? *American Journal of Sociology*, 103(4), 962–1023.

Food and Agriculture Organization – FAO (2010). *FAO statistical yearbook: Rwanda*. Available from: www.fao.org/docrep/015/am081m/am081m00.htm (last accessed: 20 June 2012).

Foucault, M. (1980). *Power/knowledge*. Worchester, MA: Harvester Press.

Government of Rwanda – GoR (2007). *Economic development and poverty reduction strategy 2008–2012*. Kigali: Ministry of Finance and Economic Planning.

Gravel, P. (1968). Diffuse power as a commodity: a case study from Gisaka (Eastern Rwanda). *International Journal of Comparative Sociology*, 9(3–4), 163–76.

Habimana, A. (2011). The dancing is still the same (pp. 354–56). In S. Straus and L. Waldorf (eds), *Remaking Rwanda: state building and human rights after mass violence*. Madison, WI: University of Wisconsin Press.

Howe, G. and McKay, A. (2007). Combining quantitative and qualitative methods in assessing chronic poverty: the case of Rwanda. *World Development*, 35(2), 197–211.

Huggins, C. (2011). The Presidential Land Commission: undermining land law reform (pp. 252–265). In S. Straus and L. Waldorf (eds), *Remaking Rwanda: state building and human rights after mass violence*. Madison, WI: University of Wisconsin Press.

Human Rights Watch – HRW (2012). *World report – Rwanda*. Available from: www.hrw.org/world-report-2012/world-report-2012-rwanda (last accessed: 24 January 2012).

Ingelaere, B. (2010). Peasants, power and ethnicity: a bottom-up perspective on Rwanda's political transition. *African Affairs*, 109(435), 273–92.

Kagame, P. (2011). *Opening address by H.E. Paul Kagame, President of the Republic of Rwanda at the 9th National Dialogue Council, 15 December 2011*. Available from: www.paulkagame.com (last accessed: 17 January 2012).

Longman, T. (1998). Rwanda: chaos from above (pp. 75–91). In L. A. Villalón and P. A. Huxtable (eds), *The African state at a critical juncture: between disintegration and reconfiguration*. Boulder, CO: Lynne Rienner.

Mamdani, M. (2001). *When victims become killers: colonialism, nativism and the genocide in Rwanda*. Kampala: Fountain Publishers.

Marx, K. (1976[1867]) (Trans. B. Fowkes). *Capital: Volume 1: A critique of political economy*. Harmondsworth: Penguin.

Ministry of Finance and Economic Planning (Rwanda) – MINECOFIN (2001). *Participatory poverty assessment*. Kigali: National Poverty Reduction Programme, MINECOFIN.

National Institute of Statistics (2006). *Preliminary poverty update. Integrated living conditions survey 2005/6*. Kigali: National Institute of Statistics.

Ndayambajwe, J.-D. (2001). *Le génocide au Rwanda: un analyse psychologique*. Butare: Université Nationale du Rwanda, Centre Universitaire de Santé Mentale.

Newbury, C. (1992). Rwanda: recent debates over governance and rural development (pp. 193–219). In G. Hyden and M. Bratton (eds), *Governance and politics in Africa*. Boulder, CO: Lynne Rienner.

Newbury, C. (2011). High modernism at the ground level: the *Imidugudu* policy in Rwanda (pp. 223–39). In S. Straus and L. Waldorf (eds), *Remaking Rwanda: state building and human rights after mass violence*. Madison, WI: University of

Wisconsin Press.
Newbury, D. and Newbury, C. (2000). Bringing the peasants back in: agrarian themes in the construction and corrosion of statist historiography in Rwanda. *American Historical Review*, 105(3), 832–78.
Pottier, J. (2002). *Reimagining Rwanda: conflict, survival and disinformation in the late twentieth century*. Cambridge: Cambridge University Press.
Prunier, G. (1995). *The Rwanda crisis, 1959–1994: a history of a genocide*. Kampala: Fountain Publishers.
Purdeková, A. (2011). 'Even if I am not here, there are so many eyes': surveillance and state reach in Rwanda. *Journal of Modern African Studies*, 49(3), 475–97.
Purdeková, A. (2012). Civic education and social transformation in post-genocide Rwanda: forging the perfect development subjects (pp. 192–209). In M. Campioni and P. Noack (eds), *Rwanda fast forward: social, economic, military and reconciliation prospects*. London: Palgrave Macmillan.
Reyntjens, F. (2011). Constructing the truth, dealing with dissent, domesticating the world: governance in post-genocide Rwanda. *African Affairs*, 110(438), 1–34.
Scott, J. (1985). *Weapons of the weak: everyday forms of peasant resistance*. New Haven, CT: Yale University Press.
Scott, J. (1990). *Domination and the arts of resistance: hidden transcripts*. New Haven, CT: Yale University Press.
Sivaramakrishnan, K. (2005). Some intellectual genealogies for the concept of everyday resistance. *American Anthropologist*, 107(3), 346–55.
Straus, S. (2006). *The order of genocide: race, power and war in Rwanda*. Ithaca, NY: Cornell University Press.
Thomson, S. (2011a). Whispering truth to power: the everyday resistance of peasant Rwandans to post-genocide reconciliation. *African Affairs*, 100(440), 439–56.
Thomson, S. (2011b). Rwanda (pp. 359–70). In A. Mehler, H. Melber and K. van Walraven (eds), *Africa yearbook 7: politics, economy and society south of the Sahara 2010*. Leiden: Brill.
Thomson, S. (2010). Getting close to Rwandans since the genocide: studying everyday life in highly politicized research settings. *African Studies Review*, 53(3), 19–34.
Thomson, S. (2013). *Whispering truth to power: everyday resistance to reconciliation in post-genocide Rwanda*. Madison, WI: University of Wisconsin Press.
UNDP (United Nations Development Programme) (2007). Turning vision 20/20 into reality: from recovery to sustainable human development. Available from http://hdr.undp.org/en/reports/national/africa/rwanda/name, 3322,en.html. Accessed August 20, 2013.
United Nations Office of the High Representative for Least Developed Countries, Landlocked Developing Countries and the Small Island Developing States (UN-OHRLLS) and UN Development Programme (2006). *Governance for the future: democracy and development in the least developed countries*, UN-OHRLLS/UNDP report. Available from: www.unohrlls.org/UserFiles/File/Publications/Governancereport.pdf (last accessed: 15 September 2012).
World Bank (2012). *Worldwide governance indicators: country data report for Rwanda, 1996–2011*. Available from: http://info.worldbank.org/governance/wgi/pdf/c188.pdf (last accessed: 19 January 2012).

Part III

POPULAR CULTURE AS DISCURSIVE FORMS OF RESISTANCE

7 Participatory Politics in South Africa
Social Commentary from Above & Resistance from Below

Innocentia J. Mhlambi

Introduction

The political and economic compromises to which the African National Congress (ANC) agreed during the settlement negotiations had an effect that saw enormous marginalisation of the poor majority of Africans in South Africa. This state of massive marginalisation presented a scenario which suggested that the excluded constituencies have been deprived of a critical vocabulary with which to challenge the new ANC-led government, save for the independent activism of new social movements such as the Anti-Privatisation Forum, the Treatment Action Campaign, the Soweto Electricity Crisis Committee and other social movements that have been active during the mid-1990s (Rosenthal 2010; Dawson 2010). During this period, the absence of criticism from the masses conveniently made invisible, temporarily, historical contingencies which have been masked by the ANC-led alliance government's endeavour to create an amorphous race-less state, and its push for a host of hegemonic policies that lobbied for the new rainbow nationalism. Since the nationalist agenda of the ruling party has subsumed most voices of dissent and stripped the subaltern and the non-aligned groups of their vocality, popular cultural terrains emerged as sites where everyday struggles between dominant and subordinate groups were to be played out.

This chapter considers two such popular sites of post-1994 politics: political laughter by South African comedians and serious political commentary by intellectual political analysts. In particular, the chapter will interrogate, compare and contrast Eugene Khoza's political laughter and Andile Mngxitama's political commentary. These two distinctive cultural sites of opinion-making will be explored as lenses through which to investigate the ANC's depoliticisation strategies which in this chapter are viewed as increasingly being embraced by the comedians, a move seen contrary to those of leftist political analysts, especially of Mngxitama's calibre who, it is argued, re-inscribe grammars of resistance into such politics. I argue in this chapter that the commercialisation of the comedians' craft to be in line with government's neo-liberal policies has resulted in stunted political satire, which explained away political fallouts rather than arming the marginalised polity with critical vocabulary with which to demand accountability and responsibility from the ruling elite. I will also demonstrate that the political commentary offered by leftist intellectuals such as Mngxitama, strikes more on (un-)resolved historical anxieties than the liberal political analysts are shown to be articulating. In most instances, the latter group has been shown in state media as intermediaries between the state and the citizens. Perhaps the guiding questions to some of the issues to be raised by these forms of opinion-making in South Africa have to do with the nature of the hegemonic bloc that the new ANC-led government has created and the popular contestations to it. Paramount in this line of argument is questioning how such hegemony functions – is it working through negotiation, incorporation or concession? Which sectors are articulating hegemonic views, and how? What historical relational issues are at stake in the government's desire to create rainbow nationalism with the kind of economic structure for which it has opted? Are such endeavours for a national identity and economic development successful and what happens to unresolved historical anxieties that resurface now and again and remind the new society of its racial chequered and unequal past? How are the rejoinders to memories represented by historical anxieties such as these handled by the governments' information technocrats?

The post-1994 dispensation has seen a number of protests by civil society, particularly from the doubly disenfranchised African majority. Scholarly findings from social movement circles postulate that the ANC's macroeconomic policy shifts in 1996 from redistributive ideals to a neoliberal agenda created a fertile ground for the re-emergence of collective action against the government by certain sectors of civil society. This economic restructuring of the economy saw the replacement of the Reconstruction and Development Programme (RDP), an agenda that was aimed at redressing the inequities created by apartheid, with Growth, Employment and Redistribution (GEAR), a programme that initiated waves of structural adjustments in the government sectors and corporate South Africa that led to job losses, mostly among the working and lower middle classes. The failure of President Zuma's administration to influence a return to 1994's RDP agenda since having been voted into office in 2009, with an understanding that he would be sympathetic to redistribution of income, was attended by an escalation of civil protests, with many being framed as violent and criminal which would then justify the brutality with which the South African Police Service (SAPS) reacted, just as in the apartheid past. Rosenthal (2010: 230), drawing from Tilly (1986), points out that collective action by social movements has established resistance actions, which Tilly termed 'repertoires of contention'. These movement repertoires range from peaceful demonstrations to more violent forms of protest. It then becomes a reflection of state bias in South African resistance politics when the mainstream media draw on long-standing partisan conventions established during apartheid years of representing these protests to a post-apartheid media audience. More often than not, the focus in these media representations is away from the contentious issues at stake that justified the protest action in the first place, while emphasis is on framing these protests as criminal, thereby downplaying their effectiveness. The escalation of violent retaliation and retribution against these citizens by the police, whose orders are issued from the office of the National Commissioner of Police, also elicit a barrage of conflicting responses from different quarters of the public, with the government side citing political conspiracy by the many African National Congress detractors (hence the heavy-handedness), and with the other side pointing to corruption, social instability, economic uncertainties and failure to deliver on 1994 election promises as justification for social mobilisation and collective action. For the latter quarter, the fermenting restlessness was a just reaction to neo-liberal policies, social disintegration and endemic maladministration running through the fibres of the ANC-led administration. The severity of these accusations prompted the Zuma administration to institute the Office of the Public Protector, whose role was to investigate improper conduct, maladministration and the abuse of power in state affairs (Public Protector 2009).

Political analysts – mainly intellectuals from universities across South Africa and non-governmental organisations – offered informed interpretations and predictions of these activities as they assessed the impact of these fallouts on South Africa's fledgling democracy. For many other middle-class South African citizens, these commentaries, broadcast 'live' in mainstream media, particularly on South African Broadcasting Corporation (SABC) news bulletins and current affairs programmes, offered a neutral layer of political interpretations that seemed autonomous enough and not government-controlled. Through these 'live' broadcasts, citizens were led to believe that they are given alternative or balanced analyses as these opinions were articulated mainly by academics or social scientists. However, the intensification of service delivery strikes was accompanied by the sudden rise of a new generation of African commentators who because of a shared political history with the subaltern seemed to be offering 'insider' knowledge and an understanding of their frustrations. This shift created the impression that there was no gap between these new intellectuals and ordinary African citizens. The language factor came to play a significant role in these commentaries, as the African-language mediums used in these broadcasts seemed to create affinities that the use of English by academics and social scientists for commentary could not achieve. However, the proliferation of African commentators in traditional and new mainstream media outlets, who used African languages, primarily dominated during social collective action, or a race toward elections, or when there were ANC policy and elective conferences. Their commentaries were missing when ANC's contentious policies or bills were introduced or when issues of corruption by high-profile government officials were circulating in the media. It seems that the new generation of African political analysts was deemed effective only when the state technocrats needed them.

The government-controlled media, such as the SABC in particular, came to feature this new class of emerging local African analysts and commentators, who offered their commentaries and analyses in African languages, mainly in isiXhosa and isiZulu as in the case of Dr Somadoda Fikeni, Dr Mncedisi Mdletyana, Dr Nkondlo, Professor Binza and others. The fact that some of these political commentators also featured prominently in a popular South African broadcaster's current affairs programme, *Asikhulume*, broadcast on Sundays evenings (with Xolani Gwala, also a political reporter, as anchor), created an impression with mainly African citizens that these analysts' critical responses to societal issues were part of the broader discourses of ordinary citizens. Furthermore, the fact that these African political analysts and commentators were drawn from and shared the racialised history and struggle of the African majority, blurred to some extent the distinctive class alliances that emerged after 1994, and hid from view the inherent class interests and their ideological positions (Gramsci 1971; Arnold 2000). These major shifts in the ANC hegemony, and the emergent forms through which political opinion makers reacted to these, recast a number of aspects relating to the notion of participatory politics as conceptualised and carried out in South Africa. The fact that a combination of serious and popular platforms are used to articulate these responses highlights Hall's (1981: 235) arguments that popular culture is a site of negotiation, incorporation and concession and, most significantly, that popular forms do not carry self-enclosed, fixed, unchanging values but hold constantly mutating values that traverse the whole spectrum between resistance and conformity.

The trend towards the blurring of distinctions became progressively problematic in post-1994 South Africa as the adopted neo-liberal policies had faltering outcomes that recreated classic polarities between the different classes, racial categories and political outlooks of these different social groups, with the intellectual class forming a buffer between the rulers and the subject people, in a manner that Gramsci (1971) illustrates. The stand-up comedians' take on the betrayal of South Africa's national consciousness was simultaneously sharpened through accurate observations but dampened through humour, pain, angst, outrage and shock at the unfolding political realities. The position of stand-up comedians added to the conflicting ways through which to view them, as their trade in many instances depended on commercial networking and dissemination outlets which the majority could not access and which were intricately connected to state bureaucrats. Some of these outlets are corporate and state functions, top notch jazz bars and lounges, television shows on the SABC and the private channel eTV, performances at live or road shows and high-profile casinos such as Carnival City, Emperors Palace Hotel and the Sibaya Hotel and Casino, as well as in international arenas like Toronto, New York and London. Although their audiences are drawn from South Africa's different sections of society, it is evident from the billings of the events and the venues at which the comedians perform, that their target audience is the burgeoning African middle class and the African aristocratic elite. In many instances the language used is accessible, as township English, *tsotsitaal*, and a variety of African languages are used for the jokes, anecdotes, rumours and gossip. The content and fodder for their trade is drawn from ordinary citizens and mainstream media outlets. However, the comedians' association with the high end of the country's economic divide and their connections with the corporate and the state bureaucrats casts doubt on their political satire.

It would seem that in essence a number of intellectual political analysts and comedians took on roles of articulating on behalf of South African citizens without having clarified first their ideological positions after 1994 and more significantly without having problematised the media outlets and the social spaces through which they normalised the anomalies characterising South African politics. Basically they act as opinion makers, adding new layers of delusion to notions of a participatory and democratic South Africa. In the process of their delivery and performances, they appropriate quotidian repertoires and registers of resistance on the one hand, and public spaces of the state or of the affluent and famous on the other, to communicate carefully thought-out satires or comments that create false consciousness and confuse the body politic instead of offering a critical voice to the masses.

On the surface, the question of language as employed by both these types of opinion makers seems to work as follows as pointed out by Spivak (cited in Morton 2007: 163) when she talks about the languages of the global South as subaltern languages, 'presumably because the official languages of national and global political institutions tend to privilege elite national or European languages, and in so doing effectively marginalise the languages of the Southern Hemisphere and restrict the expansion of their literacy'. The language issue in South Africa has remained a thorny one. Nine indigenous African languages have been declared official languages but South Africa's two former official languages, English and Afrikaans, remain the languages of vertical and horizontal communication used by the government. With regards to politics, indigenous languages – together with an array of popular cultural metaphors as accompaniment – get to be used during political rallies, especially around the voting season. In this way language use by political leaders and officials as key to participatory democracy should rather be considered as a ploy to get more votes than as a means to allow citizens to have a stake in South Africa's political processes. The challenges presented by the status and attitudes toward African languages demonstrate how complex South Africa's political performances are, invariably rippling into broader public domains including that of political commentators and comedians. As this chapter reveals, this goes against the grain of what most scholarship on subalterns and their everyday struggles indicates (Bahl 2001; Sarkar 2001; Masselos 2001), and instead illuminates complex political formations that continually divide the public and dissipate any chances of a collective voice that will cut across all sections of South Africa's population. The following section will interrogate subaltern paradigms as set against the South African post-1994 political scenario. This discussion will be followed by explorations of theoretical underpinnings of satire, and an analysis of Khoza's political laughter and Mngxitama's politics.

Unique quagmires: contained radicalism

Ludden's (2001) theorising on the subaltern would appeal to states where the subaltern form a distinctive class with a discourse that remains outside mainstream praxis. In South Africa, a large section of the population that would have represented this category has been subsumed into mainstream political thinking through concession and other modes of ideological control that have brought them into a conspicuous consumerist culture. The ruling technocrats' re-strategising entails that conventional wisdom on the politics of resistance will find it hard to interpret South African post-1994 politics from the same prism of refraction as from elsewhere. For instance, Chatterjee (2000), Arnold (2000), O'Hanlon and Washbrook (2000), Bayly (2000), Haynes and Prakash (1991) and other subaltern studies scholars have stressed the role of the underclass in bringing about a change in power. In South Africa, however, the post-1994 quasi-socialist and neo-liberal nationalist agenda has organised these categories in ways that their radical discursive practices are channelled and handled by different organisations which also act as representatives of particular constituencies. For example, in 1994, the Congress of South African Trade Unions (COSATU) formed an alliance with the ruling party ANC and the South African Communist Party. COSATU has in many instances acted as a representative of this constituency during collective action. This alliance makes it a referee and a player at the same time. Although its Secretary General, Zwelinzima Vavi, has been the most critical of Zuma's administration, there is an instance during the civil service strike of 2007 where he, together with COSATU, were accused of negotiating in bad faith as the strike was called off before the workers' demands were met. This action generated perceptions that COSATU's role in the alliance is that of containing any untoward praxis that might jeopardise national interests.

In addition, subaltern agency evident during the period of the struggle against apartheid has been urged by the newly formed tripartite alliance to fold up and join mainstream organisations such as the National Civics Organisation (NCO), the National Economic Development and Labour Council (NEDLAC) and others. Furthermore, in terms of post-1994 historiography, there has been an unopposed trend in mainstream politics to foreground the ruling elite as key historical actors with little or no regard given to the heroic roles played by subaltern groups or township communities. This trend, because left unchallenged in the mainstream, has instead been appropriated by different ideological apparatuses, and has since created impressions that, post-1994, the subaltern voice had no or little contribution to the struggle and therefore is non-existent. Physical forms of resistance, as expressed through protest actions that are currently marking South Africa's political and labour landscapes, are attempts by subalterns to regain their autonomy – an autonomy that is being suppressed through other channels as they can only engage the 'officialese' through their elected representatives, who have become spokespersons and key negotiators during these outbreaks. The added role of political analysts and comedians in normalising scenarios such as these because of their shared history and shared languages with the subalterns, accentuate matters, and are thus rightfully viewed ambivalently. As Spivak (cited in Morton 2007: 161) has pointed out, were political analysts and comedians to have sought to educate the subalterns to be able to 'identify and question the dominant systems of political representation, which silence and exclude them because of their class position', then their intellectual roles in directing opinions would have been viewed differently. Although what is painted above is a general view, there are a few exceptions.

As for the comedians, almost all have been organised in ways that reflect that they have been appropriated into the mainstream. None whatsoever offers an untainted alternative discourse that can be associated with forms of resistance. Bucciferro (2009) discusses how in post-dictatorship Chile, the mainstream media set the agenda for public debate. It would seem that the South African mediascape is fully implicated in this practice as well. In many instances the comedians' witty observations are usually made up of currently circulating news stories; the comedians appropriate these stories and put them humorously. The current comedians' satires are non-investigative, unlike the satires of Pieter-Dirk Uys (stage name Evita Bezuidenhout, aka Tannie Evita) during the time of apartheid. Evita Bezuidenhout would reveal deeply embedded dark secrets of the private lives of the Nationalist Party 'morally upright' oligarchs, sending embarrassing shock waves through the corridors of power, the South African public spheres and international business sympathetic to apartheid's racial capitalism. The self-proclaimed social and political activist also used humorous satire to criticise and expose the ridiculousness of apartheid's racial policies. As pointed out by his critics though, much of his work was uncensored, a very troubling aspect in view of the strict government censorship routine to which all other expressive forms by artists of different races were subjected around the same time. Pieter-Dirk Uys' exemption from censorship points to 'a closet approval of his views by many members of the ruling party, who were not so bold as to openly admit mistakes and criticise the policies themselves' (Wikipedia n.d.). The latter revelation regarding Uys' satire is troubling because it laid down a template of complicity between this form of trade and the officialese, and this association has become even more pronounced with some post-1994 comedians when the corporate interest also came into play. The corporate logic further clouded the otherwise cryptic observations that post-1994 comedians make, particularly with regards to political scandals. In instances where political and corporate interests are apparent, there are many unanswered troubling questions.

Existing scholarship on humour exalts the role of jokes in challenging a dominant repressive government (Willems 2010; Clark and Holquist 1984, 1977; Prakash and Haynes 1991). Willems (2010: 12), whose study on popular humour and rumour in Zimbabwe helps in foregrounding the very same concepts in the South African context in this discussion, concludes that for the Zimbabwean case, these practices should be considered as forms of everyday resistance that contributed to some very subtle changes in the relation between the Zimbabwean government and its citizens. On some occasions the Zimbabwean government was forced to counter these rumours by making public announcements through the Zimbabwean Broadcasting Corporation (ZBC), thus exemplifying Prakash and Haynes' (1991) arguments about how forms such as these continuously provoke power to respond. Clark and Holquist (1984: 301), whose study is an interpretation of Bakhtin's carnivalesque laughter, conclude that 'festive laughter engendered by the carnival keeps alive a sense of variety and change [...] [S]uch an emphasis on change and becoming is directly opposed to the official emphasis on the past, to a stasis so complete that it becomes eternity'. Views such as those advanced above are applicable in societies where there is a neat polarisation between the ruling elite and the subordinated citizenry, and significantly where the subordinated group is directly opposed to the ruling elites' imperatives.

However, the South African case, as far as these popular oral forms are concerned, reflects a different interpretation altogether. In South Africa, post-1994 neo-liberal policies had far-reaching repercussions in all spheres of life, to such an extent that the disaffected group's attempts to find a common voice by reverting to known forms of rallying consciousness around common aspirations have been difficult because of rampant expansion of commercialism, consumerism and commodification. Popular South African comedians, who play crucial roles as opinion makers, primarily consider their art as an industry (Unknown 2009). Eugene Khoza, together with Loyiso Gola, Trevor

Noah, David Kibuuka, David Kau, Riaad Moosa and Kagiso Lediga, are all organised under the Podium Comedy Merchants, a commercial entity which had a turnover of R3 million per annum in 2010 (Unknown 2009). The Podium Comedy Merchant was established in 2005 as a specialist comedy-specific agency. Its aim has always been to take advantage of the opportunities that could be found in the corporate industry and the local and international comedy fraternity. According to the Podium Comedy Merchants' website, the company has a broader business agenda and has interlinked with the entire South African commercial market in its attempt to transform comedians into strong local and international comedy brands that are national assets for tourism and export markets (Podium n.d.). As can be noted, these comedians are not aligned with the power plays between the ruled and the rulers. Instead, theirs is a professional approach to business that aims to exploit the lucrative black urban consumer market, the very sector that leftist politics depend upon for heightened senses of political conscientisation.

Insightful views of Spanish satirists are illuminating for understanding South African comedians. Brandes (1977) postulates that Spanish satirists do not have any positive effect on actual political life in the country, but instead operate as a safety valve for anti-government sentiments and therefore only have a conservative influence. Brandes (1977: 345–6) further points out: 'Laughter creates at least a temporary sense of well-being and satisfaction, and to this extent political jokes may be perceived as a means by which Spaniards trick themselves into acceptance of unpleasant realities.' To a large extent, the effect of South African comedians' performances work within the broader frameworks of depoliticising politics, neutralising the public sphere through laughter and contributing to the disappearance of a critical discourse in the popular imagination. According to Bucciferro, such depoliticisation strategies have an important impact on social consciousness and organisation because social discourses are 'generated' by a select group, 'received' and 'approved' by official agencies and circulated through carefully channelled communication ecologies.[1] She goes on to postulate that by controlling the official discourses that circulate in society and by creating conditions under which no alternative narratives could emerge and be spread, political technocrats aim at controlling the way in which people make sense of the events and the light in which they remember them (Bucciferro 2009: 96).

[1] It is fascinating to note that the comedians organised under the aegis of Podium Comedy Merchants perform for corporate functions, appear on broadcast media, oversee events and travel abroad for their gigs. All these are high socialite spaces that allow for the communication of conspicuous consumer culture embraced by the new 'black diamonds'.

Khoza and the office of the Police Commissioner

Khoza's laughter captures in acute ways Bucciferro's sentiments. The Podium website describes him as a new age comedian who breaks down boundaries, builds bridges, challenges prejudices and inverts stereotypes. He works in English as a second language. His performances are spruced with African vernaculars, oral references and vivid characterisation with witty dialogues. He has a large ethnic fan base which he reaches through his multilingual delivery, his understanding of South Africa's different cultures and his ability to engage them all on a humorous level. Probably it is for this reason that he has been contracted by Kaya FM radio station. His slot on the station has the backing of NedBank, a conglomerate banking entity in South Africa. Kaya FM is owned by Primedia, a post-1994 media company that has a Black Economic Empowerment (BEE) component (Primedia n.d.). This company has extensive links with the commercial market. The fact that the Podium Comedy Merchants, to which Khoza belongs, intend to exploit these already existing business connections for their own profit means that political laughter embodied by comedians of Khoza's calibre, then, is far from the traditional conception offered by scholars such as Mbembe (2001), Sekoni (1992), Oring (2004) and others. Khoza's laughter is not aimed at any 'tiny revolution' or mass conscientisation. Instead, what is interpreted from the association of the Podium Comedy Merchants with Kaya FM is what Hall (1986) views as mediation for consensus making.

In this chapter Khoza's laughter is viewed as part of the broader schemes as per ANC's hegemonic shifting strategies to negotiate explanations for its political fallouts by inducing laughter from the public. This discussion will illuminate this perception through extrapolating interpretations from Khoza's take on the Office of the National Police Commissioner. Between 1994 and 2012, there have been five National Commissioners, two of whom left office under acrimonious conditions. Jackie Selebi was accused and convicted of corruption, and Bheki Cele of corruption and maladministration of taxpayers' money. During their leadership, both drew negative publicity. Jackie Selebi not only incurred the wrath of society by downplaying the disconcertingly high levels of crime but he also unabashedly publicly acknowledged his close acquaintance with Glen Agglioti, a drug lord known for international drug dealing. Bheki Cele, his successor, also drew attention when he advocated brutality in reacting to crime and proposed suppression of legitimate collective action. Bheki Cele's successor, Riah Phiyega, the first woman Commissioner, was appointed amid controversy, owing to her lack of experience of the police force, as well as accusations of political manoeuvring by the Zuma administration.

When Cele's lease saga[2] surfaced for the first time in 2011, Khoza's reactions to Cele's corruption charges parodied not only Cele's ethnic take on his Zulu manhood (where being reproached by a woman is unheard off) and the corruption charges levelled at him, but also took swipes at the Public Protector, Thuli Madonsela, whose taste in hair fashion was always presented by the mainstream media as dishevelled and in disarray, a composition which goes contrary to the 'weave hair culture' where each and every strand of fake hair should be in its proper place. Khoza's drawing attention to Madonsela's weave projected a woman hard at labour trying to tame a shrewish Zulu man who had earlier vowed never to leave his top cop post until he had finished his job. Through his laughter, Khoza lightens the seriousness of Cele's offence and draws attention to non-imperative issues such as the hairstyle and the sweaty countenance of the Public Protector, Thuli Madonsela. It seems Khoza's satire always functions in this way, further demonstrated by his take on the subsequent Police Commissioner, Riah Phiyega:

> Radio announcer: Eugene, the new Police Commissioner is a woman.
> Khoza: I love her surname more than anything. If you say it without a pause, it sounds very wrong, Ria mrhmmm (makes farting sounds).
> Voice 1: *Go tlo nkga go sa bola mo!* (There'll be stench without anything rotting here).
> *Kgale le ye tirela, le etsa di up and down.* (You have done as you will for far too long).
> *Le etsa di tshwitshwi'tshwir'tshwir'!* (Making all these funny noises).
> *Go tlo nkga mo!* (There'll be stench in here).
> Voice 2: *Jwale berete oa e enyaka?* (Now, did you need a beret?).
> Voice 1: *Ke ea peri already, ke ka ye nyakang?* (I am wearing it already! Why will I need it?).
> *Leng nnyakang mara he?* (But what do you want from me, he?).
> *Hona hotle mona go tloba ele di phepher' phepher'!* (Everywhere, there'll be farting sounds).
> *Batho, di khriminali di se ke de re...hey!* (People, criminals will not say...hey!).

It should be noted that Commissioner Phiyega, except for initial public reactions to her posting, has not been accused of being on the wrong side of the law. However, what is interesting is that Khoza creates the impressions that hair fashion tastes of women leaders are somehow related to their job performance. Commissioner Phiyega's hairline has receded so much that it is as if she wears a beret, a flat-crown hat very fashionable with African working class women. This beret-like shape of her head gives her a very pedestrian, (un-)sophisticated look which veers towards a masculine countenance. Khoza's drawing attention to Phiyega's hairline invites attention, a negative kind, as it elicits doubt

[2] Bheki Cele was National Commissioner of South African Police from 2009–11. He was accused of corruption in two cases of police offices lease deals. The bone of contention regarding this lease saga concerned his undeclared interests in the deal he struck with a business tycoon, Roux Shabangu, alleged to be his friend. The Public Protector found Bheki Cele to have acted inappropriately, and found him to be unfit for the office, and he was dismissed as national police chief.

on Phiyega's suitability for the post, especially in view of the complex nature of the Office of the National Police Commissioner, which within a period of three years has seen two male commissioners leave in disgrace. His condescension to women leaders constitutes his laughter, demonstrated also by another joke about the Minister of Basic Education, Angie Motshekga, where he drew attention to her hairdo also and linked it to the scandal around delays in delivery of textbooks to schools in Limpopo Province. Hence, Khoza's jokes can be viewed as redirecting listeners' criticism away from contentious issues as it feeds on already dominant sentiments and perceptions circulating in the public domain.

Before Cele's suspension earlier in 2011, perceptions were already circulating in the public domain that he would not be charged for improper behaviour and maladministration due to his control of the support base of the ANC in the province of Kwa-Zulu Natal (KZN), which President Zuma also depends on as his key power base. In view of his high-profile position in the ANC politics of KZN, general views created the impression that Thuli Madonsela would fail to charge him successfully. Contrary to these views, she was able to get him convicted on corruption charges and has since had him dismissed. Despite this, her success in this case and in many others where she challenged corruption in state institutions has not made Khoza desist from satirising her. Lately, he joked that Thuli Madonsela's weave is fake Ethiopian human hair.[3]

The above case is one of the examples where perceptions created are subjected to the uncertainty of rapid changes within political manoeuvrings, as demonstrated when the perception that Cele would not be charged changed when political bickering from national politics spilled over to the police bureaucracy and led to his firing. There are instances where such perception-generating ploys do achieve the intended effect as in the case of the Minister of Basic Education, Angie Motshekga, who, despite calls for her sacking by opposition parties and interests groups, still remained in office. Perhaps what further exemplifies the effects of paddling political perceptions that are recirculated in media and have the desired effect relates to Jackie Selebi's case as taken on by Khoza:

> Eugene Khoza: [Jacky Selebi mustn't go to jail. He is old. I don't see him going to jail benefiting me anyhow. What they must do, they must make him do all the work adverts they think off. Like he must sing that one].
> '*Uthini nge-Ace?*' (What do you have to say about Ace?).
> '*EkaS'lebi, iyantshontsha, ayibanjwa*' (It is S'lebi's, it steals, it does not get arrested).
> [We must make him do].
> '*Uthini ngoS'lebi?*' (What do have to say about S'lebi?).
> '*Iyashelela, igugile, futhi iyondile*' (It is smooth, it is old and it is emaciated).
> *Uthini nge-Ace?* (What have you to say about Ace?).
> Mmmm... I like it (an overlain sound image).

[3] *180 with Eugene*, on Friday 3 August 2012, 8.30–9.00 a.m.

Narrativised escapades about Jackie Selebi already abounded in the public domain when Khoza reframed them as a political joke. Khoza's drawing from dominant perceptions about Jackie Selebi reinforced certain perceptions already circulating in the public domain and locked them within that perceptual framework. In other words, Khoza's construction of political views of the officialese, and of Selebi, in this case does not add to or subtract from what is already known, except that these perceptions are illuminated or amplified by being given a humorous dialogue and personality. After drawn-out court battles and a failed attempt at appealing his case, it became apparent that Jackie Selebi would be convicted and have to serve time in jail. Ideas immediately began to circulate that Jackie Selebi was too old and frail to go to prison. On the first day of his term for his jail sentence, reports of his poor and rapidly degenerating health surfaced. Since then, he has spent most of his sentence in hospital and has been granted amnesty by President Zuma. Some quarters of the population were outraged as his release was a rerun of the case of Shabir Schaik, who was also pardoned on condition of ill-health, but was later reported fighting reporters and seen in high-profile social clubs. Khoza's joke had already alluded to a potentially mild treatment and in a way this has helped contain public outrage when eventually he was released. Selebi's joke is derived from a very popular Ace Mealie Meal advert in which children's voices are captured saying 'mmm... I like it'. This infantilisation discourse is a general indictment directed to the public for their divided view on Selebi's misdemeanours. Although the media followed up on Selebi's case ferociously immediately after the judgement, this coverage receded from the public sphere and propped up again when news of his parole circulated. The question is: was Khoza's laughter prefiguring this possibility or was his laughter preparing the different publics, soliciting their understanding for his eventual release? Jackie Selebi's case actually buttressed processes of how cases of top political brass are handled by post-1994 South African law.

'Vuka darkie cuz' 94 changed fokol': Andile Mngxitama's politics[4]

Andile Mngxitama's political commentary, unlike that of Khoza, illustrates how his ideological positioning resonates with subalterns' discourse (Haynes and Prakash 1991; Scott 1985; Morton 2007; Ludden 2001; Chaturvedi 2000), thereby accentuating the politics of resistance rarely noticed in the accounts of other political analysts. Mngxitama is a Black Consciousness thinker involved with activities of

4 This is the Blackwash slogan for awakening the consciousness of the youth, available from: www.nl/africa/article/black-movement-aims-dictatorship-masses (last accessed: 29 March 2012).

a number of new social movements. His critical columns are given space in the new social movement website of *Abahlali baseMjondolo*. Mngxitama's radical opinions, which he considers as offshoots of Steve Biko's version of the Black Consciousness Movement, have elicited varying responses from different sectors of the community. Most of these responses are from the vast array of South Africa's citizens and therefore engage the citizen not only to give surface reactions to political mismanagement of the country by the ANC, but also go beyond and dig out silenced topics that are crucial in beginning to engage post-1994 realities. Mngxitama's ability – through his blogs, talks, lectures and publications – to incite impassionate, radicalised and openly anti-depoliticisation resistance politics, forces different races to deeply reflect on how each racial category continues – through complacency, self-entitling and self-privileging tendencies, and self-proclaimed rights to supremacy – to recreate inequalities and disparities between South Africa's citizens and perpetuate endemic socio-political and economic ills that directly or indirectly affect all citizens. Perhaps what accentuates Mngxitama's politics is his active involvement with the disenfranchised groups through structures that they have established such as the Landless People's Movement and Blackwash.

Andile Mngxitama, just like the majority of his generation, comes from a very humble background and has undergone Bantu Education[5] just like the forgotten masses for whom he agitates. His tertiary education and his engaged activist life have made him to become one of the most outspoken analysts and a leading Black Consciousness thinker and organiser in South Africa. He co-edited, *Biko Lives! Contesting the legacies of Steve Biko* (2008), a collection of essays on the philosophical writings of Steve Biko's version of the Black Consciousness ideology. The collection examines the relevance of the ideologies of Black Consciousness. These ideologies are situated within a global framework as well as within a specific context which is the legacy of Steve Biko. Mngxitama's work further recasts post-1994 politics against the culture and history of anti-apartheid movements. In 2009, Mngxitama published the first four essays in the New Frank Talk series, a journal of critical essays in which he uses his extensive political knowledge, incisive intelligence and powerful rhetoric skills to examine the African condition. Mngxitama is also a columnist for *The Sowetan* and *City Press* newspapers.

Hall (1978), in his public talk 'Racism and reaction', used the metaphor of the tea leaves of the British cup of tea and its sweet tooth in order to situate and map out its racial moral panics that reacted to race and class-related resistance that surfaced as mostly crime in Britain at that moment. Perhaps the South African case also needs a similar

[5] The Bantu Education Act of 1953 created an inferior education system that the Nationalist Party instituted for Africans. It was intended to curtail African intellectual growth and career opportunities, mainly channelling Africans to achieving those educational standards that would make them better serve their white employers in domestic service.

metaphor which will help explain the current crises which the government attempts to cover up in ways that will point to historical contingencies which have been made conveniently invisible. Post-1994 political crises to which comedians and political analysts react in South Africa are not only the making of a post-1994 scenario but are constitutive of 'South African-ness' with its histories of racial capitalism, land theft and dispossession, racial exclusion and division (Gordon 2006), the results of which have come to replay themselves anew despite the new government's attempts to conceal them.

Mngxitama has been able in the past few years to rise to prominence because of the critical stance he has taken against the ANC's post-1994 agenda. His politics begin with a demand for justice that will begin to address past legacies of racial exclusion, dehumanisation and deprivation. Through his essays, columns, lectures, radio interviews and letters-to-the-editor, he has been able to get his racially differentiated audience to reflect beyond the boundaries that the post-1994 government has set for its citizens (see Pillay 2010). Because of their provocative content, essays like *Blacks Can't Be Racist* (2009) and *Why Biko Wouldn't Vote* (2009) have equally triggered a critical response from audiences. He engages people of all walks of life to begin to open up, though some are outraged by his ideological leanings. The essence of his commentaries is that South Africans should be engaged in frank dialogues about issues affecting them as post-1994 citizens as is demonstrated in the following extract from one of his essays:

> At the beginning we argued that Biko's vision of liberation was fundamentally anti-racist as opposed to anti-racialist [...]. [T]he fact that anti-racialism or non-racialism inevitably leads to accommodation with white supremacy, whilst anti-racism seeks to end the world as we know it [...]. The 1994 watershed inaugurated the realisation in a formal sense of anti-racialism in South Africa. A moment best described as the birth of 'born again racism' [...]. This is achieved at the point of abandoning the promises of liberation as a matter of structural transformation into a matter of inclusion [...]. In the South African context this meant the sedimentation of reconciliation without justice into the DNA of our law and constitution. From this perspective, blacks can't claim reparations, can't ask for justice for past transgressions; blacks cant [*sic*] even simply speak the specificity of their black suffering. The black grammar of being, which is in essence a grammar of suffering, is actually not only socially frowned upon, it's outlawed [...]. Anti-racialism, or in our case non-racialism, erases the category of race but not racism. It disables those marked out for racism by the colour of their skin to claim redress or name the crime (Mngxitama 2009c).

It can be deduced from the above that Mngxitama appeals to people who perceive themselves as marginalised, post-1994. Currently, his ideologues have found a home with *Abahlali baseMjondolo* and the Landless People's Movement, social movement groups that are forcing the government through their protests to respond to the needs of the poor in South Africa. His views are widely disseminated through the websites of these social movement groups that go to the heart of South Africa's post-1994's failure to deliver. His activism with these groups aims to foster a collective voice between the poorest and the elite in the society.

Mngxitama's politics do not normalise South Africa's post-1994 scenario. His ideologues elicit mixed reactions; those that divert attention from engagement with the government have posted extremely defensive comments that fail to see beyond the social and economic engineering of racial hierarchies from the legacies of colonialism and apartheid:

> We are all inherrently [sic]'racist' if we like it or not, what ever racism means. [...] [W]hy then do we insist on multi-culturism. Or why if Blacks feel so intimidated and hated by whites, would they then want to share the Boardroom or workplace with whites [...]. I certainly don't feel the Love in all these Blogs and comments about racism and brotherhood of man. If we are all honest, maybe it's apples for apples and just maybe we can tolerate each other, as long as we live (and dare I say it) APART (Cobus de Wet 23 March 2010).[6]

Some refer to the very abysmal state of post-1994 intransigence in order to dismiss his opinions. The depth of criticism of his audience suggests that he engages educated and well- informed audiences whose take on post-1994 politics is critical, as can be noted from the excerpt below:

> 'Andile reckons the definition of "racism" must include the ability of one group to subjugate another, and since black people have never had the social, economic or political power to subjugate white people, they cannot be racist, by definition.' I became confused and would like to ask a few questions: Surely 'racism' is not a convent [sic] that exists only between 'black' and 'white' alone? Weren't similar theories of 'racism' applied by the Great European Empires to the natives of India, China, Mexico, Brazil and Australia? Also does such a definition of 'whiteness' then not include Jews who suffered subjugation and discrimination for thousands of years? By 'black' do we mean all peoples who are not 'white'? If so then when 'black' people subjugate others based on perceived generic difference (such as with the Tutsi and the Hutu) then we cannot call this racism? ...Thus all races are equal but 'whites' just had the proverbial gems, guns and steel and therefore had more opportunity to be racist than 'blacks'? Are 'blacks' 'saved' from becoming racists by a mere accident of geography? (John Everyman 24 March 2010)

There are also those who agree with his take on the current political problems whose roots lie in the social engineering of the past:

> Please do not lie to us and take us for one. Racism is the progressive subjugation of one race by another through economic, political and social means and was taught from infancy. Who taught Blacks to be racist? Who came with colonialism and apartheid? If you can answer only these two basic questions, I may reconsider my opinion which suggests Blacks cannot be racist. For now politics are in Black hands in our country

[6] Names of commenters occur in the References alphabetically by first name/nickname.

> but the economy is in White hands through all the political, economic and social engineering of 350 years (Phemelo 24 March 2010).

Conclusion

This chapter has examined two popular sites of post-1994 politics: political laughter by South African comedians and serious political commentary by intellectual political analysts. Comparing and contrasting Eugene Khoza's political laughter and Andile Mngxitama's political commentary has indicated that Khoza represents a whole class of comedians who emerged as not only embracing commercial imperatives embodied in the national agenda, but also actively depoliticising, neutralising and containing public opinion, while Mngxitama on the other hand, a leftist, represents a category of new African political analysts. Alongside this, it has been argued that, owing to their standing in South African society, some political analysts – either as scholars or as emerging from a common past with the African majority – were only being approached by mainstream South African news agencies, such as the South African Broadcasting Corporation, to comment on carefully selected political debates and events. Their role significantly emerged during heightened political situations where African languages play a crucial role in helping the state win the hearts and minds of the African masses. However, Mngxitama's radical political views place him in a position opposing that of the government. This position allows him to re-inscribe grammars of resistance into post-1994 politics. His activism in a range of social movements helps in the dissemination of his political views particularly in the underclasses. In this way, he is seen as arming the marginalised polity with critical vocabulary with which to challenge the ruling elite. Outside this realm, his comments usually expose those historical contingencies that have been unresolved and which continually resurface as 'national anxieties' which the present government would rather have the citizens forget about. The responses to his comments from a cross-section of the South African society have revealed that the 'band-aid' that the post-1994 government put on South Africa's chequered past is unsuccessful in healing the divisions that still exist owing to lack of collective moral understanding of crucial issues that originally brought about the kinds of divisions that are besieging South African society today.

The post-1994 proliferation of neo-liberal policies allowed for commercialism to dilute South Africa's political imperatives to such an extent that effective, appropriate vocabularies of resistance cutting across South Africa's diverse citizens are yet to emerge. Furthermore, the government's depoliticisation programme which had been effective in the first decade seems to be failing during the second one, as there is once more a heightened consciousness experienced by the masses. But historical contingencies, such as continuities of past legacies of entitlement, privilege and racial hierarchies, undermine what constitutes South African-ness now. Ongoing racial and class divisions in post-1994 South Africa demonstrate that rainbow nationalism has never been defined equally by all South Africa's citizens. As a result, South African citizens fail to demonstrate a united front in their responses to commonly shared social experiences. There is no lack of resistance to the power abuses of the post-1994 ANC-led government but the major divisive factor is the manner in which this resistance degenerates into historical politics and class interests that prevent citizens from sharing a collective vision of the future.

References

Alexander, J. (2004). Toward a theory of cultural trauma (pp. 1–30). In J. Alexander, R. Eyerman, B. Giesen, N. J. Smelser and P. Sztompka (eds), *Cultural trauma and collective identity*. Berkeley, CA: University of California Press.

Appiah, K. A. (1991). Is the post- in postmodernism the post- in postcolonial? *Critical Inquiry*, 17(2), 336–57.

Arnold, D. (2000). Gramsci and peasant subalternity in India (pp. 24–49). In V. Chaturvedi (ed.), *Mapping subaltern studies and the postcolonial*. London: Verso.

Bahl, V. (2001). Relevance (or irrelevance) of subaltern studies (pp. 358–99). In D. Ludden (ed.), *Reading subaltern studies: critical history, contested meaning, and the globalization of South Asia*. Delhi: Permanent Black.

Bayly, C. A. (2000). Rallying around the subaltern (pp. 116–26). In V. Chaturvedi (ed.), *Mapping subaltern studies and the postcolonial*. London: Verso.

Brandes, S. H. (1977). Peaceful protests: Spanish political humor in a time of crisis. *Western Folklore*, 36(4), 331–46.

Bucciferro, C. (2009). In Pinochet's shadow: social memory and national narratives in Chile. *Journal of Global Mass Communication*, 2(1–2), 87–107.

Chatterjee, P. (2000). The nation and its peasants (pp. 8–23). In V. Chaturvedi (ed.), *Mapping subaltern studies and the postcolonial*. London: Verso.

Chaturvedi, V. (2000). Introduction (pp. vii–xix). In V. Chaturvedi (ed.), *Mapping subaltern studies and the postcolonial*. London: Verso.

Clark, K. and Holquist, M. (1984). *Mikhail Bakhtin*. Cambridge, MA: Harvard University Press.

Cobus de Wet, comment in Diakanyo, S. (2010). Can blacks be racist?

Connerton, P.(1989). *How societies remember*. Cambridge: Cambridge University Press.

Eyerman, R. (2004). Cultural trauma: slavery and the formation of African-American identity (pp. 60–111). In J. Alexander *et al.* (eds), *Cultural trauma and collective identity*. Berkeley, CA: University of California Press.

Gordon, D. (2006). *Transformation and trouble: crime, justice and participation in a democratic South Africa*. Ann Arbor, MI: University of Michigan Press.

Gramsci, A. (1971) (Q. Hoare & G. Nowell Smith trans. & eds). *Selections from the prison notebooks of Antonio Gramsci*. London: Lawrence & Wishart.

Dawson, M. C. (2010). 'Phansi Privatisation! Phansi!': The Anti-Privatisation Forum and ideology in social movements (pp. 266–85). In W. Beinart and M. C. Dawson (eds), *Popular politics and resistance movements in South Africa*. Johannesburg: Witwatersrand University Press.

Diakanyo, S. (2010). Can blacks be racist? *Mail & Guardian* Thought Leader column, 18 March. Available from www.thoughtleader.co.za/sentletsedi-akanyo/2010/03/18/can-blacks-be-racist (last accessed: 14 August 2013).

Hall, S. (1978). Pluralism, race and class in Caribbean society (pp. 150–82). In UNESCO (ed.), *Race and class in post-colonial society*. Paris: UNESCO.

Hall, S. (1981). Notes on deconstructing the 'popular' (pp. 227–40). In R. Samuel (ed.), *People's History and socialist theory*. London: Routledge and Kegan Paul.

Hall, S. (1986). Popular culture and the state (pp. 22–49). In T. Bennett, C. Mercer and J. Woollacott (eds), *Popular culture and social relations*. Milton Keynes: Open University Press.

Haynes, D. and Prakash, G. (1991). *Contesting power: resistance and everyday social relations in South Asia*. Oxford: Oxford University Press.

John Everyman, comment in Pillay (2010), One simple reason why blacks can't be racist.

Ludden, D. (2001). *Reading subaltern studies: critical history, contested meaning, and the globalization of South Asia*. Delhi: Permanent Black.

Masselos, J. (2001). The dis/appearance of subalterns: a reading of a decade of subaltern studies (pp. 187–211). In D. Ludden (ed.), *Reading subaltern studies: critical history, contested meaning, and the globalization of South Asia*. Delhi: Permanent Black.

Mbembe, A. (2001). *On the postcolony*. Berkeley, CA: University of California Press.

Mngxitama, A. (2009a). Blacks can't be racist. *New Frank Talk*, 3, 1–32.

Mngxitama, A. (2009b). Why Biko would not vote? *New Frank Talk*.

Mngxitama, A. (2009c) Why Steve Biko wouldn't vote: continuity in the post-1994 era. *Pambazuka News*, 428, 16 April. Available from: http://pambazuka.org/en/category/comment/55639 (last accessed: 29 September 2012).

Mngxitama, A., Alexander, A. and Gibson, N. C. (2008) (eds). *Biko lives! Contesting the legacies of Steve Biko*. New York: Palgrave Macmillan.

Morton, S. (2007). *Gayatri Spivak: ethics, subalternity and the critique of post-colonial reason*. Cambridge: Polity Press.

O'Hanlon, R. and Washbrook, D. (2000). After orientalism: culture, criticism and politics in the Third World (pp. 191–219). In V. Chaturvedi (ed.), *Mapping subaltern studies and the postcolonial*. London: Verso.

Oring, E. (2004). Risky business: political jokes under repressive regimes. *Western Folklore*, 63(3), 209–36.

Phemelo, comment in Diakanyo, S. (2010). Can blacks be racist?

Pillay, S. (2010). One simple reason why blacks can't be racist. *Mail & Guardian* Thought Leader column, 23 March. Available from www.thoughtleader.co.za/mandelarhodesscholars/2010/03/23/one-simple-reason-why-blacks-cant-be-racist (last accessed: 29 March 2012).

Podium Comedy (n.d.). Website. www.podiumentertainment.co.za/about.pho?keepThis=true&TB_iframe=true&height=450& (last accessed: 24

March 2012).
Primedia (n.d.). About us. www.primedia.co.za/about_us (last accessed: 28 March 2012).
Procter, J. (2004). *Stuart Hall.* London: Routledge.
Public Protector South Africa (2009). Website. www.publicprotector.org/about_us/Vision_mission.asp (last accessed: 3 August 2012).
Rosenthal, K. (2010). New social movements as civil society: the case of past and present Soweto (pp. 243–65). In W. Beinart and M. C. Dawson (eds), *Popular politics and resistance movements in South Africa*. Johannesburg: Witwatersrand University Press.
Sarkar, S. (2001). The decline of the subaltern in subaltern studies (pp. 400–429). In D. Ludden (ed.), *Reading subaltern studies: critical history, contested meaning, and the globalization of South Asia*. Delhi: Permanent Black.
Scott, J. (1985). *Weapons of the weak: everyday forms of resistance.* New Haven, CT: Yale University Press.
Sekoni, R. 1997. 'Politics and urban folklore in Nigeria'. In K. Barber (ed.) *Readings in African popular culture*. Bloomington, IN and Indianapolis, IN: Indiana University Press.
Smelser, N. (2004). Psychological trauma and cultural trauma (pp. 31–59). In J. Alexander *et al.* (eds), *Cultural trauma and collective identity*. Berkeley, CA: University of California Press.
Tilly, C. (1986). *The contentious French*. Cambridge, MA: Harvard University.
Unknown (2009, July 13). The serious business of the comedy merchants. Business Day Live. www.businessday.co.za/article/content.aspx?id=75565 (last accessed: 24 March 2012).
Wikipedia (n.d.). Pieter-Dirk Uys (last accessed: 19 March 2012).
Willems, W. (2010). Beyond dramatic revolutions and grand rebellions: everyday forms of resistance in the Zimbabwe crisis. *Communicare*, 29, 1–17.

8 Laughing at the Rainbow's Cracks?

Blackness, Whiteness & the Ambivalences of South African Stand-Up Comedy

Grace A. Musila

> The emptiness behind the binary opposition is the emptiness behind the equation 0=0. One thing is opposed to another thing in a two-fold opposition incapable of accommodating marginalities, third forces, or synthesis (Brockman 1986: 160).

Introduction: 'Don't touch me on my studio'

On 6 April 2011, South African television audiences watched an unscripted flare-up between e.tv anchor Chris Maroleng, *Afrikaner Weerstandsbeweging*[1] (AWB) Secretary General Andre Visagie, and political analyst Lebohang Pheko during a live current affairs programme on race relations in South Africa, following the brutal murder of outspoken right-wing AWB leader Eugene Terreblanche. Terreblanche – a familiar figure in South African politics with strong views on race – was allegedly bludgeoned to death by his black farm workers.[2] What stood out about the episode was not that Visagie and Maroleng almost came to blows on live television; nor that Visagie walked off the set in anger as the cameras rolled and the nation watched. The incident was unique in terms of the subsequent humour the South African public inscribed into Maroleng's agitated statement to Visagie: 'Don't touch me *on* my studio!' to which Visagie repeatedly shouted: 'I will touch you *on* your studio!' The grammatical error in the preposition 'on' had the country in stitches, with spoofs of the incident mushrooming across social media networks.

A few years earlier, an advert for Channel 1 of the national broadcaster, South African Broadcasting Corporation (SABC1), had provoked a similar mixture of heated debate, laughter, and anger across South African publics because it was variously deemed funny, offensive and racist. The advert showed an 'ordinary' day in a township dweller's life: a young man waking up in a shack in a township, dressing up in what has come to be seen as township style, walking to the road, catching a taxi to the city, walking into a shop, and having the police call on him because he looks like a wanted criminal. This advert's humour lay not so much in its content and the accompanying stereotypes – a pretty recognisable, everyday reality of millions of black people across the country's

1 Afrikaans for Afrikaner Resistance Movement.
2 See Staff Reporter (2010) for a detailed description of the case.

townships – but in its imagined racial inversion: the young man is white, and white people live in the townships – with all their inconveniences – while black people live in the better-resourced suburbs, roll up their car windows at the sight of young white men (coded as potential criminals) and shrug stereotypically – 'they all look alike'– when it turns out the young man is not the wanted criminal.

That the question of race relations is an unfinished business in South African public life is an obvious, albeit under-acknowledged truism. While the ways in which racial tensions (as opposed to racism *per se*) are a manifestation of particular hegemonies of power may not be obvious at first glance, the question of race and its complex intersections with class in post-apartheid South Africa continues to manifest itself as a particular power dynamic, perhaps not articulated in the outright state-backed repressive patterns of apartheid South Africa, but certainly retaining influential imprints on the socio-economic and material realities of South Africans, with implicit state endorsement. Further complicating the picture is the unstated tabooing of robust debates on the question of race, and its complicity in particular forms of dominance and the retention of a structural racism that colludes with crude capitalism to sustain a problematic status quo in which black people remain the poor majority in the country. Indeed, close to two decades into democracy, the rainbow project remains fractured along racial fault lines by contestations over the social, cultural, economic and political landscape of the country. These contestations unfold in numerous institutions, platforms and media. Among the important media that engage with what I term 'the cracks in the rainbow' is comedy. As Ebenezer Obadare (2009: 244) reminds us, 'humour is [...] vital to the ways in which ordinary people endure social asperities, as we negotiate, shape and contest the public domain of critical deliberation'. Elsewhere, in an essay provocatively titled *Laughing all the way to freedom? Contemporary stand-up comedy and democracy in South Africa*, Julia Seirlis (2011: 514) notes that 'comedy's relationship with power and the social order is always precarious, slippery and complicated, but it provides a compelling means to understand the workings of power and the nuances of the social order'. While more scholarly attention on humour as a form of resistance has been paid to satirical forms of humour that parody state power, I am interested in comedy's confrontation of hegemonic socio-cultural patterns of power as manifested along racialised cleavages in contemporary South Africa. Taking its cue from what Seirlis describes as 'the nuances of social order', this chapter examines South African stand-up comedy's engagement with the thorny question of race relations in South African public life. I am interested in the interface between laughter and the cracks in the rainbow project, as signalled by the two incidents outlined above. Although South African stand-up comedy forms the core focus of analysis for this chapter, I see the two incidents outlined above as rich entry-points into this discussion, flagging up both the difficulty of conversations about race relations in South Africa, and the ambivalent role of comedy in addressing the race question. Though different in content and context, the two scenarios have two things in common: both underscore the 'taboo' status of the race question in South Africa, as well as the centrality of humour in initiating conversations about race in South African public life. A third, less obvious dimension which equally interests me is the ambivalence of humour as a vehicle of engagement with the difficult question of race. This begs the question: what are the possibilities of humour as a vehicle of transgressive engagement with a problematic racial status quo in South Africa? What do we make of the public laughter that turned Eugene Terreblanche's violent death, and the equally brutal problem of farm labourers' working conditions, into a laughing matter, on the basis of a simple grammatical slip of the tongue? How do we interpret the controversial responses to the SABC1 advert, and the very logics of the advert – the inversion of the socio-economic landscape of the country – as a source of humour? I see these questions as inviting us to not only rethink the possibilities of humour as a vehicle of resistance but to revisit the very question of resistance, and particularly hegemonic understandings of resistance in Africa.

In recent years, many scholars have questioned the conceptual reach of the idea of resistance in making sense of African realities. For Achille Mbembe (1992: 3), to understand postcolonial power relations, 'we need to go beyond the binary categories used in standard interpretations of domination, such as resistance v. passivity, autonomy v. subjection, state v. civil society, hegemony v. counter-hegemony, totalisation v. detotalisation [which] cloud our understanding of postcolonial relations'. Mbembe (1992: 4) argues that these binary frames fall short of making sense of postcolonial realities, primarily because the shared living space between the so-called dominant and the so-called subordinate results in a certain form of domesticity and familiarity which he terms 'illicit cohabitation'. Similarly, Anne McClintock (1995: 15) remains 'unconvinced that the sanctioned binaries – coloniser-colonised, self-other, dominance-resistance, metropolis-colony, colonial-postcolonial – are adequate to the task of accounting for, let alone strategically opposing, the tenacious legacies of imperialism'. In his reading of the stereotype as an instrumental tool in colonial discourse, Homi Bhabha (1983: 18) proposes that the stereotype is 'a form of knowledge and identification that vacillates between what is always "in place", already known, and something that must be anxiously repeated', resulting in what he terms 'the productive ambivalence of the object of colonial discourse – that Otherness which is at once an object of desire and derision'. Similarly, in his chapter 'Of mimicry and man: the ambivalence of colonial discourse'[3], discussing the ambivalence of mimicry – as 'almost the

[3] I am grateful to Sharlene Khan for drawing my attention to the links between this chapter and my interest here.

same but not quite' – Bhabha (1994) emphasises the slippages and forms of excess produced by this ambivalence.

I use Mbembe's notion of illicit cohabitation and Bhabha's idea of the productive ambivalence of the stereotype in a different sense, as a springboard into thinking through both the complex ambivalences of resistance as a conceptual category in African popular culture – in this case stand-up comedy – and the possibilities and limitations of the stereotype as one of the core staples in South African stand-up comedy's engagement with the question of race relations. Despite their different contexts – the workings of power in the postcolony and the role of stereotypes in colonial discourse respectively – Mbembe's and Bhabha's works resonate with my interest in making sense of the layered contradictions that haunt South African comedy's transgressive possibilities, as signalled in the two scenarios cited above. If, as Obadare (2009: 245) reminds us, jokes 'constitute a powerful metaphor for understanding the distribution of power and the nature and dynamics of social relationships within any given configuration', then it is important to reflect on the ways in which the contradictions embedded in South African comedy complicate our assumptions about resistance, and indeed invite us to embrace contradiction as a potentially transgressive force. Through a critical reading of the work of comedians Conrad Koch, Krijay Govender, Trevor Noah and Loyiso Gola among others, I suggest that beneath the seemingly clichéd deployment of racial stereotypes, elements of popular lore and fragments of the South African every day, these comedians use ambivalence as a strategic self-location that facilitates the breaking of the various silences around 'taboo' questions of race relations, while allowing them to articulate alternative readings that challenge hegemonic 'common senses' at the core of South African public life. In this context, I suggest, the combination of stereotypes and ambivalence enables stand-up comedians to convene conversations about elements of race relations in South Africa, which are often wrapped up in the thick silence of political correctness and implicit forms of censorship which police the boundaries of the 'speakable'. As such, I argue, stand-up comedy surfaces the cracks that fracture the rainbow nation project by using laughter to ease these 'taboo' issues into the terrain of 'the speakable', precisely because the comedian's podium enjoys a certain 'taboo-breaking moratorium' that makes this possible. But my reading further suggests that, ironically, it is precisely in its deployment of stereotype and ambivalence at the moment of 'speaking the unspeakable' that much South African comedy paradoxically opens up the 'unspeakable' to the risk of secondary silencing in form of discursive containment and co-option.

This chapter is structured into three sections. In the first section, I explore stand-up comedy's commentary on South Africa's racial histories and the shadows they continue to cast over the post-apartheid present. Building on this, the second section identifies sex/uality as an important trope in South African comic discourse on race which in many ways harks back to a particular colonial archive of racial anxieties about sex/uality. The concluding section reflects on the 'black accent' as a core component in South African stand-up comedy's commentary on blackness, whiteness and the hegemony of English/ness in South African public life.

Chronicles of the present or the burdens of 'raced' histories

The contested nature of public memory in most societies is a well-acknowledged truism. In South Africa – as in most societies – the question of public memory is subject to much contestation, debate and critique from many different quarters.[4] While most of these debates are directed at the master-narratives of history, and often unfold in such conventional institutions and platforms as academia, media and mainstream arts, little attention has been paid to the role of stand-up comedy as a site of memory and its contestation. In the earlier cited essay, Julia Seirlis (2011: 515) notes that comedy can 'map out the lay of the land, providing a very fast compressed physical and symbolic topography [of] what, where and who have been left behind or left over in the new dispensation of a democratic South Africa'. Seirlis' thinking here pre-empts my reading of comedy as a living archive that simultaneously chronicles contemporary realities and spotlights the gaps and silences in these realities. Comedian Loyiso Gola's work is particularly instructive in this regard. Gola – a black comedian, born in 1983 in Cape Town and brought up there – has been in the industry since 2002, and is one of the best-known comedians in the South African comic scene. In one of his jokes, Gola uses the long incarceration of former President Nelson Mandela under the apartheid regime to offer a double-edged critique of both Mandela and the then African National Congress Youth League President Julius Malema:

> Nelson Mandela is the first and last. There's no black man you can lock up for over 25 years and he comes out and doesn't kick your a**.[5] Never! You try and lock up Julius [Malema] for just 25 days. Tjo! (Loyiso Gola, *The Life and Times*).[6]

Gola here picks up on recent critiques of the Mandela legacy and the popular iconisation of Mandela as the most celebrated statesman in South African public memory; an iconicity that in recent re-readings of post-apartheid South Africa, jars against the sense of frustration, disillusionment, and rage at post-apartheid South Africa's failure to deliver

4 See Hamilton *et al.* (2002).

5 The work of most of the comedians studied here features expletives and swear-words neatly woven into the jokes.

6 All the examples cited in this chapter are drawn from DVD recordings of comedians' live performances.

on the promise of social justice and economic freedom for the majority of the citizenry. It is this latter gap that Julius Malema is known to be most vocal about; and which Gola signals here. Gola's joke is framed as a subtle double-critique which is simultaneously approving and critical of both Mandela and Malema.

Elsewhere, Gola picks up on this theme of frustration with the miscarriage of social justice in post-apartheid South Africa; a phenomenon most visibly expressed through regular service delivery protests, marches and strikes. Gola uses the phenomenon to offer an implicit comment on the racialised socio-economic landscape.

> White people don't march for sh*t. You guys just send an email. (*Mimes typing*) 'I am upset', enter; cc. Mary. And when you do march, you march over the dumbest sh*t. (*Mimes a march*) 'Don't cut the trees', 'Don't cut the trees!', 'Save the panda bear!' I'll tell you now, there's no black person in this room that will march for a f*ck'n panda bear. Imagine Julius [Malema] trying to mobilize the youth for a f*ck'n panda bear. (*Mimics Malema*) 'But comrades we must be sure that we are only marching for the black part of the panda bear. The white part of the panda bear cannot be trusted' (Loyiso Gola, *The Life and Times*).

Gola's joke offers an example of Bhabha's notion of the ambivalence of stereotypes, in this case within the context of stand-up comedy. On the surface of it, the joke delivers a double punch at white people, for activism against what Gola considers to be irrelevant issues; and at Julius Malema, as embodying an unrealistic race politics which would go to the extremes of expecting to march for the black part of the panda bear in isolation. The joke taps into stereotypical coordinates of whiteness and blackness, alluding to the popular perception that black South Africans favour demonstrations as a form of protest; while white South Africans do not take an active interest in such demonstrations. Using these stereotypes, Gola embeds a critique of race relations in South Africa as haunted by a combination of a difference of priorities – implicit politics of disengagement which sees his stereotypical white people marching to protect the panda bear, when there are seemingly 'more urgent' social-economic concerns; and an ongoing culture of racial suspicion best embodied by Julius Malema's absurd desire to protect only the black part of the panda bear. The twin metaphors here – protest marches and the panda bear – form the pivot of Gola's critique, in so far as they reference both a history of apartheid-era (predominantly black) protest culture and an entangled future respectively. Put differently, while signalling a racialised history of distrust and social injustice, the joke is a reminder of a shared fate of South Africans as a nation, where it is in everyone's interests, across the races, to invest in everyone's dignity. From a different perspective though, Gola's panda bear uncannily evokes apartheid-era South African President P.W. Botha's oft-cited zebra metaphor. Botha is said to have responded to economic sanctions against apartheid South Africa by reminding the international community that imposing sanctions on apartheid South Africa is like shooting a zebra: whether one shoots a black stripe or a white stripe, the entire zebra would still die when shot.[7] The echoes between Botha's zebra and Gola's panda bear underscore the imprint of racial boundaries that continue to fracture the rainbow nation and the broader frustrations with the failure of the state to fully dismantle the racialised status quo by delivering social and economic justice to the poor.

The shadow of social injustices that continues to manifest itself in contemporary South Africa is further signalled by another of Gola's jokes:

> I grew up in a township called Gugulethu. White people, do you know where that is? [*silence*]. You should know; you put us there you f**k'*s (Loyiso Gola, *The Life and Times*).

Though performed in 2011, Gola's joke glances back at apartheid-era socio-economic policies, while implicitly drawing attention to present-day economic apartheid along racial lines, not only in the idea that white people seemingly remain unfamiliar with Gugulethu township (still a poorly-resourced black space close to two decades into democracy); but also in the reality of cross-generational economic injustices, where black people remain the face of poverty. Here, we are reminded of the SABC1 advert cited above, whose humour lies in the imagined racial inversion of the township space. The punch of this joke is not so much that white South Africans should know the country well enough to know where Gugulethu is, but that they have never needed to, thanks to a combination of cross-generational economic privilege – which locates a majority of white South Africans in better-resourced suburbia – and the limited inter-racial, inter-class interaction in contemporary South Africa. Gola uses an autobiographical fact – that he was born in Gugulethu – to traverse history and summon a fragment of South African history: apartheid era's 'legal' marginalisation of people of colour, through the Group Areas Act which created congested, under-resourced townships on the edges of most cities to fuel the labour needs of the city. Gola's joke further remembers an important element of South African race relations: like many colonial and white supremacist societies, apartheid's power relations made it unnecessary for white people to know black people's lives. One is reminded here of Cameroonian novelist Ferdinand Oyono's observations about colonial Cameroon when his character, Toundi, a houseboy in a French colonial household observes as follows:

> In Dangan, the European quarter and the African quarter are quite separate. But what goes on underneath those corrugated iron roofs is known down to the smallest

[7] I am grateful to Lynda Spencer for drawing my attention to this aspect of South African history.

> detail inside the mud-walled huts. The eyes that live in the native location strip the whites naked. The whites on the other hand go about blind (Oyono 1966: 71).

Elsewhere though, Gola reads the contemporary cultural blind-spots that mark the rainbow project as a bifocal problem that features across race lines. In a joke about horses, Gola notes:

> Black people don't know how much horses cost. If black people knew how much horses cost, *lobola* (bridewealth) would be a whole different game. You would be there with your cows and they're like, '*hayi* no, in this house we deal with horses, exclusively. Just *amahashe*, don't come here with cows' (Loyiso Gola, *The Life and Times*).

Another prominent South African comedian, whose work comments on the country's racialised histories, is Trevor Noah. Born in 1984 Noah, a biracial comedian – with a white Swiss father and a black South African mother – uses his family background to comment on the country's race politics through a description of his childhood in apartheid Soweto where he playfully claims he masqueraded as an albino. In one joke, Noah claims that in light of apartheid-era criminalisation of inter-racial relations, his mother could not tell anyone that his father was a white man so she 'chose to leave everyone to their own assumptions'; as a result of which people assumed that he was in fact an albino. Noah talks about spending a lot of time with his 'fellow' albinos, who give him the nickname 'Daywalker' as his high tolerance for direct sunlight puzzled them.

If there are two men who are the subject of laughter, parody and critique across the South African socio-political landscape, they are President Jacob Zuma and former African National Congress's Youth League President, Julius Malema. This pair is often read in juxtaposition with the popular icon, former President Nelson Mandela, and has attracted extensive satirical representation in the work of South African newspaper cartoonists and artists.[8] The multitude of jokes mirrors a general consensus that the two men's intellectual acumen leaves a lot to be desired. In his one-man comedy collection, playfully titled *The Daywalker*, Trevor Noah quips: 'It's been a crazy year you know. With America getting their first black president. And South Africa getting *our* black president' (Trevor Noah, *Daywalker*). Noah's emphasis on 'our' black president leaves it to his audience to decide on the semantic associations of blackness evoked by President Zuma, as contrasted with Obama's dignified, inspiring 'blackness'. In another joke Noah makes further commentary on predominant attitudes towards black leadership in South Africa:

[8] One such cartoon – by popular cartoonist, Jonathan Shapiro – resulted in President Zuma suing Shapiro for defamation. A similar case sparked mixed reactions across the country in 2012, when South African artist Brett Murray exhibited a painting featuring President Zuma with his genitals exposed; in a satirical critique of the president's controversy-prone sexual conduct, which has been the subject of much public attention during his presidency.

> There's always a panic around election time in South Africa. You heard them in 1994: (*Mimics*) 'I'm leaving, I'm leaving, I'm going to Australia, Mary. It's been fun, but it's time to go. I'm leaving. You know now they're going to take over'. Then Nelson Mandela became president. And they all stayed. (*Mimics*) 'He's a wonderful man, a wonderful man, hey. I love him, he's amazing. If it wasn't for him I'd have left' [...]. Then it was Jacob Zuma, and people panicked again. But then it was different. For the first time in South African history you had black people going like (*scratches his head*) '*Eish*! How much is that ticket to Australia again?' (Trevor Noah, *Daywalker*).

Noah's joke chronicles historical anxieties about black leadership in South African politics, which in turn highlight some of the cracks of racial complexes that continue to shadow the rainbow project. Interestingly, in this joke, Noah references race-specific responses to the various moments in black government. The punch of this joke is that, for Noah, when President Jacob Zuma ascended to power, even black people started contemplating emigration to Australia.

Elsewhere, Trevor Noah comments on Julius Malema's views on race politics in South Africa, signalled above by Gola's joke about the panda bear. Here, Noah parodies Malema's response to South African athlete Caster Semenya's case, where the gold-medal winning athlete was subjected to 'gender testing' following her dramatically improved performance in the 2009 World Athletics Championships in Berlin. Semenya was subjected to widely publicised investigations to determine whether she enjoyed an unfair advantage over other women athletes; provoking extensive international media attention and equally vocal outrage from local politicians, among them Julius Malema:

> Then Julius [Malema] jumped up: (*Mimics* Malema) 'That's racist! How can you ask a question like that? It's racist. Gender what? Gender what? It's obvious. You're coming here with your hermaphrodite, there's no such thing in my culture. Can't you see? It is obvious, can't you see man? *He* is a woman' (Trevor Noah, *Daywalker*).

In a related joke on Malema, similarly anchored in the popular perception of Malema as an under-educated buffoon, Noah says:

> I feel sorry for the older guys in the ANC. They're always having to put Julius back in his box. (*Mimics*) 'Julius, calm down, calm down'. He always says these outlandish things. Always about racism. The other day he came out and said: (*Mimics Malema*) 'In fact, I'm sick and tired of all these white people in South Africa. They're racist. All of them. They must go. Ja, they must all just go. Ja'. Then the older ANC guys came, you know, and said (*whispers*) 'Julius! Julius! You can't just say that. They're the ones with money, man. Say you're sorry, say you're sorry man'. To his credit though, he apologized. He came out and said (*mimics Malema*): 'Ok, I'm sorry, I'm sorry. White people musn't go. They must LEAVE!' (Trevor Noah, *Daywalker*).

The twin gag points in this joke – Malema's ostensible semi-literacy which renders him unable to recognise the synonymous meaning of 'go' and 'leave'; and the older ANC leaders' chastisement – 'they are the ones with the money'– are insightful; commenting both on Malema's controversial views on race in South Africa and the racially skewed economic landscape.[9]

Sex and the rainbow

Gender, race, religion and sex/ual stereotypes are a widely acknowledged staple in comedy, which have been read variously by different scholars in different contexts[10] and South African stand-up comedy is no exception. Many scholars have observed that the colonial experience was grounded in a sexualised discourse, not only in its grammar of rape, penetration, and the feminisation of the new frontiers[11], but also in what David Attwell (2005: 3) has described as its preoccupation with 'policing intimacy' which in apartheid South Africa became institutionalised through the Immorality Act that forbad sexual contact across race lines. While the rest of the colonial administrations across Africa did not formalise this policing of cross-racial intimacy through laws, their control of native populations was nonetheless equally shot through with sexual anxieties which traced their roots back to an older archive of myths about Africa(ns). Among these were myths of black sexuality – male and female – which was believed to be aberrant and uncontrolled.[12] Against this background, I am interested in the interface between gender, sexuality and race in the work of South African comedians. On the surface of it, the laughter in the comedy under discussion is primarily anchored in a range of sexual and gender stereotypes. However, a closer reading of the jokes in question offers interesting insights into the ways in which sex and gender function as coded shorthand for the articulation of a range of thoughts on racial identities.

A wide range of the comedians' jokes make some reference to sex. In the first joke, Loyiso Gola parodies President Jacob Zuma's goodwill message during the 2010 World Cup tournament hosted in South Africa:

> (*Mimicking Jacob Zuma*): 'We would like to urge all South Africans to behave', and people are like, no man, we're worried about you, mother****r. People are coming here and that guy doesn't f**k around, he will impregnate you. That guy will shake your hand, and bam! pregnant (Loyiso Gola, *The Life and Times*).

[9] Noah's comment is borne out by the 2011 Johannesburg Stock Exchange Ownership Survey, which found that only 17 per cent of the JSE-listed companies were owned by black South Africans.
[10] See for instance Bhabha (1994), Yancy and Ryser (2008) and Weaver (2010).
[11] See for instance Ashcroft *et al.* (1998) and McClintock (1995).
[12] Perhaps the most iconic figure with regard to this is the figure of the Khoi woman, Sarah Baartman, whose body was exhibited across Europe as epitomising this aberrant African sexuality.

Gola's joke here pokes fun at the President's afore-mentioned publicised sex life, which has variously come up in public debates, ranging from a highly publicised legal battle in 2006 in which he was accused of raping a family friend[13] to a sex scandal in which he allegedly engaged in an extra-marital affair with the daughter of South African Football Association (SAFA) Chairman Irvin Khoza and subsequently had a child with her. Zuma's highly publicised sex life was later to inspire a controversial satirical painting by artist Brett Murray.[14]

In another joke, Gola comments on a case in which a female fan allegedly stripped naked and ran into the pitch during an English Premier League soccer game:

> That chick must never try that sh*t in a [South African] Premier Soccer League game. [Kaizer] Chiefs against [Orlando] Pirates[15] (*mimics a player*) *Mbambe, mbambe, yiza naye* (isiXhosa for 'hold her, hold her, bring her here') (Loyiso Gola, *The Life and Times*).

A third example of jokes on sex and rape is offered by comedian Conrad Koch, whose performance features a puppet, Chester. In a joke about the late pop star Michael Jackson's trial for child molestation, Koch and Chester joke about a fictitious case of a puppet that was molested by the pop star:

> Chester: Don't talk about it. I was the puppet (Conrad Koch, *Just Because*).

On the surface of it, the three jokes are seemingly unrelated: the first joke comments on President Zuma's well-publicised sexual indiscretions; the second one comments on the apparent rowdiness of black South African football players; while Koch's joke references claims of pop star Michael Jackson's alleged paedophilia. But the sexual allusions in the three jokes speak to a broader stereotype of black hyper-sexuality and the black man as a rapist. In light of the Jacob Zuma rape trial, the three jokes variously zoom in on the question of rape and ideas of women 'inviting' sexual violation, as was argued in the Zuma rape trial. These jokes represent an example of the entangled, contradictory nature of South African stand-up comedy. Here, the jokes are contextually anchored on a particular South African context with the alarming reality of high sexual violence statistics. Yet instead of offering a critique of this culture of sexual violence, all three jokes appear to signal an implicit celebration of a particular, mythologised virulent black

[13] See Matshilo Motsei's book *The kanga and the kangaroo court: reflections on the rape trial of Jacob Zuma* (2007) and Pumla Dineo Gqola's essay *After Zuma: gender violence and the Constitution* (2006) for detailed discussions of the Zuma rape case.

[14] Murray's painting provoked sharply divided responses and a lengthy debate in the media about the politics of race and representation, particularly in light of the racialised sexual panics embedded in the country's history on the one hand, and on the other, the tensions between cultural sensitivity and freedom of expression.

[15] Kaizer Chiefs and Orlando Pirates are two of the prominent football clubs in South African soccer, with large fan bases.

masculinity whose sexuality is daring, uncontrollable, almost desirable. It is hard to laugh at the imagined fate the soccer fan in Gola's second joke would meet without evoking the growing statistics of taxi-rank assaults in which women deemed to be 'inappropriately dressed' get attacked. The three jokes here occupy a problematically ambivalent space where they simultaneously question and celebrate the brutal/ising black masculinities behind the sexual violence statistics in South Africa.

A related variation of this 'taming' of sexual violence as an object of laughter is evident in Conrad Koch's comedy, in the form of a particular appropriation of both the Zuma rape trial and homophobia as illustrated in the following joke, framed around a disagreement between Conrad Koch and his puppet Chester, who complains about not being consulted on whether he would like to be part of Koch's comedy performance:

> Chester: You can't ask after you have started. It is like the way Jacob Zuma has sex. DA: didn't ask. That *kak* ended in 1994 (Koch, *Just Because*).

The humour in Koch's joke lies in the play on the acronym DA which is also South Africa's official opposition party (Democratic Alliance). On its own, this linking of the DA to their sworn adversary, Jacob Zuma of the African National Congress, is a witty stroke of creativity. However, the cross-referencing of the Jacob Zuma rape trial – particularly his accuser's assertion that it was not consensual sex – with apartheid, in the phrase 'That *kak* ended in 1994' invites two possible critiques: first is a symbolic appropriation of rape broadly, and the Jacob Zuma rape trial specifically, as shorthand for commenting on apartheid-era human rights abuses. While arguably accurate, this connection diminishes the urgency of the problem of sexual violence by using it to make a vague comment on a broader and in some ways 'distanced' historical milieu. At the same time, when we consider the historical reality of various forms of sexual coercion of people of colour during apartheid, this joke becomes equally problematic in its apolitical allusion to history. But most literally, the juxtaposition of rape with the absence of consultation between Koch and his puppet trivialises the tragic reality of rape in South Africa. Koch's joke brings to mind the afore-mentioned controversial cartoon by celebrated South African cartoonist, Jonathan Zapiro, who used the Jacob Zuma alleged rape trial as a visual metaphor for what he considered to be the assault on the constitution, figured in the cartoon as Lady Justice.

Elsewhere, both Trevor Noah and Conrad Koch make jokes about athlete Caster Semenya and DA leader Helen Zille, relating to assumptions about hegemonic femininity:

> Chester (*addressing* Koch): Who did you vote for? He voted for a man in a dress: Helen Zille [...]. The truth is Helen Zille makes Caster Semenya look like Naomi Campbell (Conrad Koch, *Just Because*).

> (Trevor Noah *mimicking Julius Malema*) 'It's racist. Why doesn't IAAF test Venus and Serena Williams? Caster's a woman, 100% black woman'. 'So would you marry her?' (*Shakes his head*) 'Ah ah! She's not *that* type of woman. But I'm just saying.' (Trevor Noah, *Daywalker*)

Koch's joke, articulated through Chester, parodies the President of the Democratic Alliance, Helen Zille, and athlete Caster Semenya. The joke gels problematic gender stereotyping with an implicit dismissal of the strong-minded Zille. To a certain extent, the joke instantiates a form of appropriation: Koch implicitly crowns Zille as an honorary man, suggesting subscription to notions of strong, firm leadership as an essentially masculine trait; here reinforced by the referencing of Caster Semenya, believed by some to be an intersex person, whose performance at the Berlin World Athletics Championships was seen as aided by male hormones in her system. At the same time, the joke faults Zille for seemingly lacking both femininity and beauty, as suggested by the allusion to English supermodel, Naomi Campbell, who functions here as an icon of femininity. Similarly, Noah's joke, targeted at Julius Malema's outspoken defence of Caster Semenya has two gag points: firstly, Malema's assumed ignorance of the fact that by his logic of racism, the Williams sisters as black people would presumably be subject to the same racism to which he accuses the IAAF of subjecting Semenya. Secondly, for all his defence of Semenya, Noah suggests, Malema is not convinced she makes the cut of femininity, in this case measured through a vague notion of 'marriageability'.

Krijay Govender, one of the few women comedians in the South African comic industry, provides an example of the intersection between gender, sex and racial identity in her joke about the policing of female sexual purity in the South African Indian community, drawing on her observations as a member of that community:

> When I was moving to Johannesburg, my grandmother called me aside and told me: (*mimics her grandmother*) 'Your virginity is like a rosebud. Hold it tight; not to say you must not give away a few petals here and there. But let's say you are reaching the age of thirty and no bees are circling your flower? Give it away. Otherwise you'll be sitting with potpourri' (Krijay Govender, *Outrageous*).

Though based on the Indian community's gender values, Govender's joke references a broader policing of sexual purity that cuts across national and racial identities. As Meg Samuelson (2007: 2) reminds us elsewhere, nations are often imagined through gendered tropes in which 'women bear the symbolic weight of nationalism; their bodies are the contested sites on which national identities are erected and national unity is forged'.

On the whole, while South African comedians retain the prototypical use of sex/uality as a key trope in their comedy, a unique element in their work lies in the yoking of sex/uality together with race; and the ensuing insights into race politics in South Africa that their work offers, using sex/uality as the core lens.

'Black accents' and the ambiguities of the English rainbow

In *The Daywalker,* Trevor Noah explores the complexities of the interface between racial identity, language and culture, by indexing his personal experiences as a biracial man who often gets confused for a coloured[16] man from Cape Town:

> I always explain to people that I am coloured by colour but not by culture. Which is a difficult thing for people to understand. Being coloured is a cultural thing, not just a racial thing. I like to think of myself as a BEE baby: 51% black, 49% white. Although, I must admit, most of the time when I stand in the toilet with men from Venda, I wish I had a little more [black] empowerment (Trevor Noah, *The Daywalker*).

Drawing on the grammar of South African economic policy Black Economic Empowerment (BEE), which encourages the business sector to promote the creation of a racially inclusive economic landscape by ensuring black people's involvement and co-ownership in businesses, Noah jokes about his biracial identity as an example of 'BEE', signalling his cultural identification with blackness. At the same time, the joke taps into the discourse of stereotypical black male sexual virility through its allusion to the stereotypical Venda (a black South African community). Notable though is Noah's distinction between phenotypic racial identity and racial-cultural identity which renders him racially coloured but culturally black. In commenting on these distinctions, Noah explores the question of language as a politically charged coordinate in coloured identity, which encodes English, and especially particular English accents – coded as 'standard' English in South Africa – as an aspiration to whiteness. In the same joke series, Noah describes an encounter with a coloured man in Cape Town:

> '*Awe ma'se kind!*...[Afrikaans for 'hey child of my mother' *interjected with some mumbo jumbo*]'. I said 'sorry man, why are speaking so fast?' He responded '*Ek se bra* [Afrikaans for 'I say friend/brother], why are you thinking slow? And why are you talking funny?' I say, hey dude, I don't speak funny, you speak funny. He said, *nie* man [Afrikaans for 'no'], you talk funny. Where're you from? Are you from overseas? I

[16] Understandably, the grammar of racial identity is a constantly changing one across South African history, in ways that index various ideo-political milieus in the country, along with the attendant contestations around the terms 'African', 'black', 'coloured', 'Chinese' and 'Indian', each of which sometimes operate as stand-alone identities, while at other times are all framed as 'black' or 'African'. In recent years, the term 'brown' has gained currency in South African popular discourse, with similar contestations on its political implications. The term 'coloured' as Noah notes, is different from the term 'person of colour' in Euro-American contexts, as it is culturally specific, in addition to coinciding with a particular phenotypic racial identity.

> said, 'No, I'm actually from Johannesburg'. He's like 'Joburg? So why you talk like that?' I said, I guess I'm just different. 'Oh! You're those banana types, *ne*? You're *mos* yellow on the outside, but white on the inside, *ne?*' (Trevor Noah, *The Daywalker*).

Noah's joke here flags the articulation of racial identities through the lens of language, and particularly English. Beyond gesturing to the identity politics of the coloured community and its relationships to English and Afrikaans, Noah's joke further references the idea of whiteness, and specifically an English whiteness, as an aspirational identity. A similar set of ideas emerges around popular ideas of blackness in relation to English.

If, as Wylie Sypher observes, 'the ambivalence of comedy reappears in its social meaning, for comedy is both hatred and revel, rebellion and defense, attack and escape [...] revolutionary and conservative' (cited in Watkins 1994: iv), then perhaps more than the double-edged jokes about troubled histories or the ambiguities of racial stereotypes on sexuality, it is in South African comedians' use of the 'black accent' that we find the contradictions of laughing at the rainbow's cracks. In a sense, Seirlis' (2011: 516) suggestion that in contrast to 'the unattractiveness of Afrikaners and to their recurrent position as the butts of comedy [blackness] constitutes something with positive associations' and overlooks the class politics that continues to fracture blackness in South African social imaginaries, resulting in a complex variation of Bhabha's (1983: 19) 'productive ambivalence [towards] an object of desire and derision' with which I opened this discussion. If Jim came to Jo'burg in the 1940s South African bioscope[17], then Jim's descendants in the South African urbanscape remain largely split in two strains: the 'well-spoken' private school-educated 'coconut'[18], and the 'black accented' sibling, both of whom occupy the corridors of state power and the taxi ranks, corporate business and the informal sector, the leafy suburbs and the township. Contrary to Seirlis' perspective, the 'black' English accent is not only one of the core currencies of the contemporary South African comedian; it remains an excellent example of the ambivalent self-location of comedians.

This currency – the 'black' English accent – signals one of the fascinating contradictions of the South African laughter industry in so far as class politics is concerned. In large part – despite some self-reflexive examples examined below – most comedians across the race lines retain an uncritical stance on their parody of the 'black accent' and its implicit endorsement of a certain form of cultural whiteness, articulated (pun intended) through the notion of 'standard' English. This uncritical relationship to the intersection between race and class dynamics in comedy

[17] See Donald Swanson's 1949 film, *Jim Comes to Jo'burg*.

[18] This is a derogatory term in South African parlance, used to refer to black people perceived to aspire to cultural whiteness. See Kopano Matlwa's *Coconut* (2008) for a fictional portrait of the notion.

resonates with Grada Kilomba's (2008: 80) critique of the ways in which, through jokes, racist and patronising ideas 'are integrated in casual conversation and presented as casual comments in order to ventilate their real racist meanings [thus] power and hostility ...are exercised without being necessarily criticised or even identified – a joke is only a joke'.[19] In one of his performances, Trevor Noah critiques the attitudes attached to the 'black English accent':

> We've got people who judge our politicians based on how they sound; forgetting that there is such a thing as a black accent. So, the black accent is automatically associated with stupidity, which shouldn't be the case. Because, you know, there's French accents, there's Indian accents, there's Chinese accents and then there should be a black accent you know. When a French person says it, its sexy, it has that *Je ne sais quoi*; they can say anything. They can say (*mimics a heavy 'French' accent*): 'I have been really impressed with the ma-nage-ment of the company' and we'd go like, 'Wow! Oh wow! Take me now Jean-Pierre'. But then a black guy will say the same thing and we'll judge them (*mimics 'black' accent*): 'I have been very impressed. Eee, with the ma-nagement of the company'. And we'd be like (*in 'white' English accent*) 'No, no, no, Jabu, Jabu, it is not "management" its "management", no no, management, Jabu "Management"'. Now teach me, teach me (Trevor Noah, *Daywalker*).[20]

Noah's observations here, on the centrality of command of English and fluent articulation as a site of popular humour targeted at politicians, echoes similar patterns of humour in the Zimbabwean context where, as Wendy Willems' (2009) discussion suggests, politicians' fluency in English [or lack thereof] is keenly noted and mocked in popular media. The inconsistency of Noah's critique notwithstanding (a lot of his humour is anchored on the 'black accent'), his observations here nonetheless pinpoint the cultural ascendancy of hegemonic whiteness broadly, and Englishness in particular. In the South African comedic landscape, ironically, the hegemony of English both as a spoken language and a bedrock of the cultural topography remains largely unquestioned, as the Afrikaner and all accented people of colour come in for a peals of laughter for their deviance from 'standard' articulations of English. The cultural ascendancy of 'standard' English is so firmly established in both South African comedy, and South African imaginaries broadly, that a good number of popular jokes find their humour in ungrammatical English and 'non-standard' accents, as signalled by both the 'Don't touch me *on* my studio' episode, and Noah's two jokes about Malema cited above ('Can't you see? *He* is a woman' and 'They mustn't go, they must LEAVE'). Conrad Koch points this out in one of his

[19] I am grateful to Sharlene Khan for drawing my attention to Kilomba's work.

[20] Matlwa's novel *Coconut*, features a strikingly similar incident in which the protagonist, Fifi, a young black girl, is taught how to pronounce the word 'oven' 'properly': 'Say "uh-vin" Fifi. You bake a cake in an "uh-vin," not an "oh-vin," "uh-vin" [...] you have to learn to speak properly [...] Good. Now say "b-ird." Not "b-erd," but "b-ird" (p. 49). I am grateful to Lynda Spencer for drawing my attention to this example.

jokes based on one of the most commented-on racial-cultural idiosyncrasies in South African society:

> Chester: Your race and your accent are connected. The darker your skin, the slower the white guy talks to you (Conrad Koch, *Just Because*).

Koch's comedy offers yet another interesting instantiation of the slippery terrain of ambivalence mentioned above. Beyond the now-typical staple of the 'black' English accent deployed by comedians across race and gender lines, Conrad Koch's act is largely run through his puppet, Chester. Chester is a short, sharp-tongued coloured old man with a heavy Afrikaans accent. Interestingly, although Koch *is* the voice and brain behind Chester, their show is largely a conversation between this caustic coloured man and his more neutral white 'voice' who constantly differs with him, and often apologises to the audience for Chester's sharp, often 'tactless' views, articulated in an Afrikaans-accented English. This 'performed schizophrenia' is interesting for the ways in which it deploys staple racial stereotypes but simultaneously gels them in the two characters' joint identity.

A number of jokes across the repertoire of many of the comedians under study ostensibly critique the hegemony of both whiteness and English/ness which in a sense remain the predominant strand of aspirational whiteness in the South African public sphere. These two examples illustrate this:

> It is strike season in South Africa. The teachers have gone on strike again. I keep seeing teachers with placards with spelling errors. Spelling 'democracy' with an 's' (Loyiso Gola, *The Life and Times*).

I hate booking flights on phone. They give you these stupid reference numbers. Stop assuming I can spell. If I was the guy giving the reference number, I would just f**k with you. I would say, 'you got a pen? Ok, "K" for knowledge; "P" for physiotherapy' (Gola, *The Life and Times*).

The deployment of the 'black' accent as a vehicle of laughter – especially considering that the stock characters referenced include taxi drivers, *tsotsis*, Julius Malema, Jacob Zuma, and the poor – raises the question: where does the critical laughter end and complicity with class and racial condescension begin? This is a particularly urgent question in a country whose class politics intersect in problematic ways with hegemonic whiteness, in many ways retaining a white cultural hegemony as the aspirational identity for all 'non-whites'; an aspirational location that has more to do with the seeming coincidence of economic power and dignified life with hegemonic whiteness. Put differently, to what extent does the deployment of the 'black' accent as a staple in South African comedy become complicit with the continued endorsement of a white cultural hegemony as the desirable identity location, and by extension, an ongoing muting of critique of hegemonic white socio-economic and cultural ascendancy in South African public culture as black cultural scripts remain marginal and undesirable, except as deliberately oppositional praxis?

Conclusion

The prominence of contradiction and ambiguity in South African comedy offers a provocative interrogation of conventional notions of resistance as always necessarily oppositional. South African comedians' slippery self-location in relation to their material would seem to caution against rigid framings of resistance in favour of context-specific oppositional forms that strategically deploy ambivalence in their pursuit of platforms for convening conversations, thus side-stepping the minefields of taboo and self-censorship by a dominant script of a mythically cohesive rainbow nation.

The centrality of the stereotype as the vehicle of laughter in much South African comedy invites the question signalled by Simon Weaver (2010: 32–33): what does it mean to simultaneously rehash and challenge stereotypes? It is possible to read the use of racial stereotypes in the jokes discussed here as aligned with what Weaver describes as reverse discourse. According to Weaver (2010: 32), 'reverse discourses appear in comic acts that employ the sign-systems of embodied and cultural racism but develop, or seek to develop, a reverse semantic effect'. Yet Weaver warns against the dangers of the potential re-emergence of the very stereotypical discourse under question in the process of parodying it. As he writes, 'while we may see the reversed voice of the "Other" as the preferred meaning, there is a prior reliance on sign-systems of earlier racism. These earlier meanings have the potential to re-emerge, gain purchase and act rhetorically [...] Reversed meanings have a polysemic potential that can rearticulate the earlier racist meaning' (Weaver 2010: 33).

A second question that is invited by the very medium of comedy and particularly its deployment of laughter and ambivalence as its core transactional currencies is: to what extent does laughter enact a cathartic taming or domestication of critique? If, as Chinua Achebe (2011: 6) notes, the middle ground is 'the home of doubt and indecision, of suspension of disbelief, of make-believe, of playfulness, of the unpredictable, of irony', it is also the home of potential co-option, taming and appropriation. The latter question particularly invites careful reflection in the South African context, where, to a large extent, the rainbow project has been glued together by the adhesive of many silences around uncomfortable questions. It is in this context that comedy's ambiguities stand out starkly in its double act of de-closeting uncomfortable questions and simultaneously taming indignation with laughter. Ultimately though, stand-up comedy remains a robust podium for breaking taboos and silences that continue to shroud the race question in post-apartheid South Africa and, as audiences laugh at the cracks of the rainbow, taboo becomes speakable and thinkable. It is in this taboo-breaking that stand-up comedy enacts its resistance, albeit haunted by contradictions.

References

Achebe, C. ([2009]2011). *The education of a British-protected child.* New York: Penguin Classics.

Ashcroft, B., Griffiths, G. and Tiffin, H. (1998). *Key Concepts in Postcolonial Studies.* London and New York: Routledge.

Attwell, D. (2005). *Rewriting modernity: studies in black South African literary history.* Scottsville: University of KwaZulu-Natal Press.

Banjo, O. (2011). What are you laughing at? Examining white identity and enjoyment of black entertainment. *Journal of Broadcasting and Electronic Media,* 55(2), 137–59.

Brockman, J. M. (1986). Bitburg deconstruction. *Philosophical Forum,* 17(3), 159–74.

Bhabha, Homi (1983). The other question.... *Screen* 24(6): 18–36.

Bhabha, H. (1994). *The location of culture.* London: Routledge.

Gqola, P. D. (2006). *After the Zuma case: gender violence and our constitution.* Ruth First Lecture, Constitution Hill, Johannesburg, 15 November 2006.

Hamilton, C. *et al.* (2002). *Refiguring the archive.* Cape Town: David Phillip.

Kilomba, Grada (2008). *Plantation memories: episodes of everyday racism.* Munster: Unrast Verlag.

Matlwa, K. (2008). *Coconut.* Johannesburg: Jacana Media.

Mbembe, A. (1992). Provisional notes on the postcolony. *Africa: Journal of the International African Institute,* 62(1), 3–37.

McClintock, A. (1995). *Imperial leather: race, gender and sexuality in the colonial contest.* New York: Routledge.

Motsei, M. (2007). *The kanga and the kangaroo court: reflections on the rape trial of Jacob Zuma.* Johannesburg: Jacana Media.

Obadare, E. (2009). The uses of ridicule: humour, 'infrapolitics' and civil society in Nigeria. *African Affairs,* 108(431), 241–61.

Obadare, E. (2010). State of travesty: jokes and the logics of socio-cultural improvisation in Africa. *Critical African Studies,* 4, 1–21.

Parker, Z. (2002). Standing up for the nation: an investigation of stand-up comedy in South Africa post-1994 with specific reference to women's power and the body. *South African Theatre Journal,* 16(1), 8–29.

Samuelson, Meg (2007). Remembering the nation, dismembering women? Stories of the South African transition. Scottsville: University of Kwazulu-Natal Press.Seirlis, J. K. (2011). Laughing all the way to freedom? Contemporary stand-up comedy and democracy in South Africa. *Humor: International Journal of Humor Research,* 24(4), 513–30.

Staff reporter (2010). Terre'Blanche killed after row with workers, *Mail &*

Guardian Online, 4 April 2010, available from: www.mg.co.za/article/2010-04-04-terreblanche-hacked-to-death-after-row-with-workers (last accessed: 20 Aug 2012).

Watkins, M. (1994). *On the real side: a history of African American comedy from slavery to Chris Rock*. New York: Simon and Schuster.

Weaver, S. (2010). The 'other' laughs back: humour and resistance in anti-racist comedy. *Sociology*, 44(1), 31–48.

Willems, W. (2009). Joking via SMS: new publics and convergence culture in Zimbabwe, conference paper presented at 'Hidden Dimensions of the Zimbabwe Crisis Conference', University of the Witwatersrand, Johannesburg, 1–2 July 2009.

Yancy, G. and Ryser, T. A. (2008). Whiting up and blacking out: white privilege, race and *white chicks*. *African American Review*, 42(3–4), 731–46.

9 'Beasts of No Nation'
Resistance & Civic Activism in Fela Anikulapo-Kuti's Music

Jendele Hungbo

Introduction

This chapter examines resistance and civic activism in the music of Fela Anikulapo-Kuti. Using Fela's album 'Beasts of No Nation' (1989) as entry point, I seek to create an understanding of African music and popular culture in general as 'sites of ideological struggle and resistance' (Darts 2004: 316). The chapter locates Fela's music within the sphere of nationalist resistance to hegemony and shows how he uses the popular art form to undermine the production and reproduction of dominant power structures at both the local and the global levels. Making use of interpretive textual analysis as analytical device, the chapter calls attention to the possibility of popular cultural forms relating to civil society discourses, making them more relevant beyond the common ascription of entertainment. It urges a move away from the normative search for civil society within the praxis of formal non-state institutions to a more nuanced appreciation of the potential of popular cultural forms as embodiment of the kinds of activism and resistance practice which define contemporary civil society. An incorporation of popular cultural forms within the scope of civil society will benefit the literature in many regards and 'not only extend the boundaries of the idea, but also enrich our understanding of the (often inert) culture of protest in many African societies' (Obadare 2009: 244).

Fela Anikulapo-Kuti (1938–1997) remains one of the greatest musicians to have come out of Nigeria in recent times. His music, which he called 'Afro-beat', is an eclectic one, combining mainly highlife, funk and jazz. His 'greatness' on the music scene can be attributed to three major factors. While his iconoclastic creation of a unique musical form (Afro-beat) made him stand out as a musician of note, his political activism and deviant personal life seemed to spice up the Fela brand, making him a ubiquitous subject in the media. The significance of Fela is further evidenced by the interest that his songs continue to generate in social and academic circles years after his death in 1997 (see for instance Idowu 2003; Olaniyan 2004). His activism constantly reflects in his music through the composition of confrontational lyrics, creating a kind of symbiosis between his political life and his art. This complex mix is perhaps what informs Kelefa Sanneh's (2000: 114) description of Fela as 'legendary hedonist, and implacable foe of Nigeria's numerous dictatorships'. His music constantly responds to the socio-political developments in his country, the African continent and indeed the world at large. In short, it mirrors both personal and collective experience, especially in matters relating to the lives of Africans across borders.

Fela was imprisoned many times as a result of his constant opposition to successive regimes in Nigeria. In 1984, he was jailed five years on charges of foreign currency violations. He served only two out of the five years before he was released at the inception of a new military administration which overthrew the one that sent him to jail. The two-year prison experience appeared to have given him the impetus to write a song which he released as 'Beasts of No Nation' in 1989 under the label of his own recording company, Kalakuta Records. This chapter focuses primarily on the title track of the album. The track, a little over sixteen minutes in length, features confrontational lyrics which seem to give an insight into the kind of political ideology that underlined much of Fela's creative enterprise.

This chapter uses interpretive textual analysis as an entry point into the music of Fela Anikulapo-Kuti (Schutz 1973; Lee 1991; Gephart 1997). Interpretive textual analysis gives consideration to the intersubjectivity of meaning-making in the interpretation of social or empirical reality. In a way, it is largely premised upon the idea of 'doing an interpretation of the behaviour of human subjects in their local settings' (Lee 1991: 349). Though interpretive textual analysis incorporates different sub-fields like phenomenology, hermeneutics and ethnography, this chapter leans more towards the ethnographical approach. This way, I attempt to explore Fela's response to local and global hegemonic power relations through a close reading of his lyrics in relation to historical experience and social conditions existing at the time of production of the work in question. This is in recognition of the contention that 'people create and attach their own meanings to the world around them and to the behaviour that they manifest in that world' (Lee 1991: 347). The artistic work, in this case Fela's 'Beasts of No Nation', therefore, becomes what Michael Baxandall (1988: 1) describes as 'the deposit of a social relationship'. In dealing with popular artistic forms in Africa, methodological approaches like interpretive textual analysis become crucial in that they offer tools with which to analyse important popular cultural forms emerging from less normative civil society institutions. The lyrics of Fela's music then become texts through which his intellectual essence becomes accessible to the audience. As texts, such lyrics can be said to 'constitute a rich archive of local thought and experience, experiment and commentary [shedding] a fascinating light on life on the ground in Africa, past and present' (Barber 2011: 174).

Theorising Africa's postcolonial moment

The postcolonial moment in Africa has continued to generate discourses on the adoption of cultural values best suited for the progress of the continent as well as the fashioning of an identity that will – at least in the sight of the rest of the world – hold up certain minimum moral codes seen as indices of a 'welcome' civilisation. Such discourses often implicate the colonial experience of Africa and the potential of an unrepentant direct and indirect prescription of modes of behaviour which symbolise a cultural reorientation befitting of redeemed civility. This chapter relies largely on aspects of postcolonial theory which deal in some way with the emergence of cultures and the relations of power in formerly colonised societies. Culture is a central analytical category in postcolonial theorising, and key figures in the field like Edward Said (1994), Homi Bhabha (1995) and Gayatri Spivak (1988) have demonstrated the importance of power in the understanding of relationships between different categories of people locally and globally. In Bhabha's estimation, for instance, the colony will always remain a site of contestation since ambivalence and conflict are necessary conditions of the hybrid space (Bhabha 1995).

It is in this regard that elements like hybridity, multiculturalism, marginality and alterity/otherness will be useful in this study. Similarly, Ilan Kapoor's (2008: xiii) deployment of postcolonial criticism as a 'lens to question development's dominant cultural representations and institutional practices' reinforces the importance of postcolonial discourse in situations of cultural diversity typified by contemporary African society. In dealing with the conflicts of nation-building arising from both local and global power relations defined by inequality and mistrust, Kapoor (2008: xiii) 'explore[s] the possibilities for a transformatory postcolonial politics'. The emergence of independent African states governed by Africans themselves after the experience of colonialism naturally lays the premise for new expectations and hopeful projections into the future of African nations. Such expectations, apart from being a forlorn wait, have often extended into despondency resulting from maladministration in most of the states in post-independence Africa. In Nigeria specifically, the slow pace of development had ostensibly occasioned a series of military interventions and constant questioning of the moral credentials of leaders who, like their European counterparts, were in Fela's estimation, no better than 'animal in human skin'.

Resistance, generally speaking, can be described as a form of 'ideological insubordination of subordinate groups' (Scott 1990: 157) aimed towards an alteration of the status quo in an attempt to create a new order which is often perceived as either more beneficial or more equitable. Resistance itself has become a common feature of everyday life in postcolonial Africa. As a result, there have been various approaches to the idea of resistance. In almost all these approaches, one thing that comes out clearly is that resistance is often generated by a desire to reject a particular social order that is seen as antithetical to the achievement of certain objectives in structuring society. In this chapter, I follow the trajectory of resistance theory as it has developed as a branch of critical pedagogy from the 1970s. This is not to assume that a historical periodisation of resistance or resistance theory would be such an easy task. What this limiting to a particular category and temporality does is just to provide a safety valve for understanding the idea of resistance as it relates to cultural forms, especially in postcolonial societies where critical pedagogy itself has been a major factor in determining the socio-political directions of the people. In this regard, resistance, it should be noted, has been embedded in popular or indigenous cultural forms long before it came unto the academic stage as a branch of critical pedagogy in the 1970s. Harry West and Jo Fair (1993: 99) have argued for instance that 'many forms of song, dance, theatre, sculpture, and so forth, originated within the context of resistance to a dominant social order'. This argument is a reinforcement of the ubiquity of resistance practices, even in performances which predate modernity (see for instance Duncombe 2002; Moore 1995; Scott 1990).

Popular music and civil society

It will be difficult to ignore popular culture, especially music, in the emerging civil society discourse in Africa. In addition to this, the processes of making Africa 'modern' through different kinds of artistic representation, making use of everyday life, seem to have enjoyed minimal attention in civil society scholarship. This is in spite of the important role which popular media forms continue to play in influencing people's understanding of themselves and the world around them (Wasserman 2011). In their study of the link between popular music and political action in the United Kingdom, for instance, John Street *et al.* (2008: 270) emphasise 'the ways in which music has traditionally been connected to forms of political participation' as it constitutes 'a prime example of public expression of feelings' about events going on in society at particular historic moments. The ubiquity of popular forms generally places them at an advantage when it comes to mobilising or reaching the people, especially in societies where literacy rates remain generally low. Popular musical forms like Afro-beat tend to provide a kind of consciousness built around the prevailing problems that society needs to deal with for its own good.

In trying to conceptualise popular music, I turn to the definition offered by Nabeel Zuberi who appropriates John Corbett's (1994) exploration of popularity in music as entry point. According to Zuberi (2004: 431):

> [T]he term *popular music* remains a floating signifier that can mean any or all of the following: music liked by many people, music seen to represent particular populations, specific music genres usually derived from American and British rock and roll music, music that sells in large numbers or figures in polls and charts, or simply any music that is recorded and manufactured as a mass re-produced commodity for the market-place.

What is interesting about this approach to understanding popular music is the recognition it gives to mass production and consumption. In addition, it factors in the reception of such music as one of the things to be considered in judging popularity. The eclectic nature of Fela's 'Beasts of No Nation' is perhaps a pointer to its ability to fit into the kind of description given by Zuberi. In any case, Zuberi's definition is not the only way to go in finding popular musical forms which deal with the everyday concerns of people in any society. Fela's music is a politically active art which has continued to maintain relevance through both its diversity and local significance (Barber 1994). It is executed via a peculiar aesthetic that speaks to its own particular audience. It creates discourses that key into the major concerns of contemporary society, thereby creating a unique civil society platform through which patrons are able to grapple with the relations of power evolving around them. In other words, the music has the potential not just for cultural agency but also for playing a pedagogical role in the lives of the consumers as it 'provides tools to unsettle commonsense assumptions, theorise matters of self and social agency, and engage the ever-changing demands and promises of a democratic polity' (Giroux 2011: 1).

'Beasts of No Nation' displays a characteristic feature of African popular performances which gain their strength from the active participation of an audience which can be present or imagined. At the beginning of the song, Fela invites his audience to join him in a philosophical assessment of the postcolonial African world:

> *Ah! Let's get down into another underground spiritual game*
> *Just go dey help me dey answer, you go dey say, 'ayakata' – O ya*
> (You will join me in chorus, just say 'ayakata' – let's go)

Such invitation is often an opportunity for citizen involvement in the public sphere which has the capacity of translating into political agency. The recognition given to the audience, or an imaginary audience, in this song seems to validate the assumption that the discursive space made possible by popular cultural and media forms like music are often made vibrant by people when given the opportunity to participate. As Maria Bakardjieva (2011: 67) argues in her discussion of new media and civic agency, 'the mediapolis is more than a space of representation. It is a living space inhabited not only by images and discourses, but also by people with daily thought and action'. The role of the audience is played in this instance by the chorus whom Fela drills for a moment, perhaps to ensure that they are attentive enough and ready to follow his narrative before embarking on his musical journey:

O f'ese luu
Chorus: *ayakata*
O f'ese gbon on
Chorus: *ayakata*
...

Though this call and response teaser, which is rendered in the singer's Yoruba language, is difficult to translate directly into English, it implies a situation of confusion where things scatter and become fragmented. After this teaser, Fela recalls the role of the agentic popular performer who never keeps quiet whenever he sees things go amiss around him. Such performers are usually, in a sense, bearing the responsibility of alerting society to dystopian developments which have implications for its growth and direction. Their roles, as Henry Giroux (2011: 1) argues, involve being 'discerning and attentive to those places and practices in which social agency has been denied and produced'. The metaphor of the 'basket mouth' with which Fela introduces the idea of the sentinel performer in this song is a popular one in Nigeria. It is often used either positively, to refer to a social reformer, or negatively to describe gossip:

Basket mouth wan start to leak again oh, oh, oh, oh
(Basket mouth is about to leak again)
Chorus: *basket mouth wan open mouth again oh*
(Basket mouth is about to speak again)
Abi you don forget say I sing, e e oh
(Have you forgotten I'm a musician)
Chorus: *basket mouth wan open mouth again oh*

'Beasts of No Nation' mirrors the curiosity of the audience in the way they keep asking Fela about what he intended to sing about after his prison experience. As he puts it:

Fela, wetin you go sing about? Chorus: *dem go worry me (x3)*
(Fela, what's your next song about?)
Dem go worry me, worry me, worry, worry, worry, worry
(People keep asking)
Chorus: *dem go worry me*
(They keep asking me)
Dem want make I sing about prison
(They want me to sing about prison)
Chorus: *dem go worry me*

Against his fans' expectation that Fela would present a narrative of his prison experience ('inside world') in this post-prison album, he chooses to sing about the free world ('outside world') which he constructs as a space crazier than prison and devoid of the basic civil liberties that ordinary citizens in any free society are entitled to:

The time weh I dey for prison
(When I was in prison)
I call am inside world
(I called it inside world)
The time weh I dey outside prison
(When I came out of prison)
I call am outside world
(I called it outside world)
Na craze world, no be outside world
(It's a crazy world, not outside world)
Chorus: *craze world*
(Crazy world)

Fela then calls attention to the dysfunction in contemporary Nigerian society epitomised by the bankruptcy of institutions of state, especially those related to the realisation of a just and egalitarian social order. In making clear his objection to the modus operandi of such institutions, he lists some of them in the track:

No be outside police dey?
(Isn't it outside you find the police?)
Chorus: *craze world*
(Crazy world)
No be outside soldier dey?
(Isn't it outside you find soldiers?)
Chorus: *craze world*
No be outside court dem dey?
(Isn't it outside you find the courts?)
Chorus: *craze world*
No be outside magistrate dey?
(Isn't it outside you find the magistrates?)
Chorus: *craze world*
No be outside judge dem dey?
(Isn't it outside you find the judges)
Chorus: *craze world*

In 'Beasts of No Nation', Fela specifically draws attention to the justice system narrating his own victimhood as an exemplar of the miscarriage of justice characteristic of a militarised judicial system. This offers him a seemingly authentic background into the moral crises he hopes to present before the audience through a refraction of realities confronting the Nigerian nation. Fela therefore voices his concern for the less privileged, among whom he categorises himself, in the face of an already compromised system where decisions of upholders of the law can be swayed by those in authority. A practical example in Fela's personal experience is in the confession of the judge who had incarcerated him. The judge during a secret visit to Fela in prison admitted to having been pressured by the state to convict him. While the judge was fired by the military government following a media leak of the visit, there had been a general belief that Fela's release might have been hastened by the public knowledge of his innocence.

In spite of his emphasis on the world outside, however, the 'inside world' cannot be discounted in the totality of Fela's experience as reflected in the song. The prison experience, it can be seen, provides him an opportunity for a comparative consideration of the two 'worlds' he sings about in the album.

In his list of failed state establishments, Fela includes the military leadership of the country as a major statement on the broader challenge of the post-independence political predicament in most African states at the time. In representing the monstrosity of a local (Nigerian) military regime, 'Beasts of No Nation' hints at the bigger problem of incessant military interventions across postcolonial Africa. The specific example of the Nigerian military rulers at the time is also quite instructive. Apart from being the regime under which Fela himself was sentenced to a five year jail term, the Buhari/Idiagbon dictatorship was famous for its flagrant disregard for citizens' rights and brute high-handedness. Such brutality, in Fela's estimation, makes the world outside the walls of the prison worse:

No be outside Buhari dey?
(Isn't it outside you find Buhari?)
Chorus: *craze world*
Na craze man be dat
(That's a lunatic)
Chorus: *craze world*
Animal in craze-man skin
(Animal in crazy man skin)
Chorus: *craze world*
Na craze world be dat
Chorus: *craze world*
No be outside Idiagbon dey?
(Isn't it outside you find Idiagbon?)

In this section of the song, Fela undertakes an assessment of one of the major policies of the regime aimed at 'civilising' Nigerians through the inculcation of a culture of discipline which was said to be lacking in the people at that time. He concludes that such policies, and the way they were communicated by the regime, fell far short of expectation in human society. In other words, any attempt to coerce the people into a disciplined behaviour which necessitates an infringement on the basic human rights would fall short of decent human behaviour. In addition, such would be even more reprehensible where it is being implemented by a military regime, which not only in the first instance lacked the moral justification to be in power but also had demonstrated marks of indiscipline both in personal conduct and at the level of policy. As Fela implies in the song, the attempt to instil discipline through the War Against Indiscipline (WAI) instituted by the regime can be considered at its best an act of sheer hypocrisy.

Fela's lyrics show a serious objection to the way and manner in which the government fails to respect its own citizens, a discounting of them if you will. He reinforces his dismay by expressing the strangeness with which he regards the reference the government had made to its own citizens as a 'useless' people. The implication here is that Fela expects the government to show respect for its citizens, even if it had identified a culture of indiscipline among them which it hopes to curb. This is a reference to the idea of sovereignty, which is expected to be bestowed on any government by the people it claims to represent. This section of the song seems to point out the aberration which military regimes in themselves constitute in any society. For Fela, any government that fails to recognise the source of its sovereignty in the people and then treat them with the respect they deserve cannot be considered civil or even human. It is no wonder then that he concludes that only animals could refer to their subjects as 'useless' or 'undisciplined'. In Fela's reckoning, it takes a beastly character for leaders under any guise to make public their disgust for the people over whom they rule especially when issues border on a culture of indiscipline, a failing for which the then military establishment was known to be more guilty than any other individual or group.

History, solidarity and resistance

Although 'Beasts of No Nation' is inspired by a personal experience, Fela presents the audience with a dramatic re-enactment of collective agony applicable to colonised and oppressed people across Africa. The song reconstructs the agonies of liberation struggles in different parts of Africa in a show of solidarity with subalterns throughout the continent. In this way, it can be interpreted as a response to the oppression of the defenceless masses which characterised colonial rule as well as post-independence dictatorships in Africa. The song in itself acquires meaning beyond entertainment to become a musical idiom deployed creatively towards the articulation of the traumatic experience visited on the people from time to time. Thus, Fela functions in the mould of radical artists who, as Douglas Kellner (1995: 174) observes, 'have traditionally used music and musical idiom as a privileged form of resistance to oppression'. This is evidenced in the way Fela talks about the brutality of state forces against students in different parts of the continent.

While his reference in the song to Zaria and Ife respectively recalls police brutality against protesting Nigerian students in 1978, the mention of Soweto in this part of the song is an apparent reference to the 1976 students uprising in South Africa which marked a watershed in the struggle against apartheid in that country. There is in this reference a noticeable hybridity and multiculturalism which provides a broader conceptual base for Fela to deal with some of the major concerns he has raised in his song. In addition to this is the recourse to history and memory as major tools with which he re-enacts the narrative of oppression and the brutal deployment of violence by the state against the people which has characterised much of postcolonial Africa. This approach largely underscores the significance of history in the attempt to understand the present. So, the past does not break away from the present. It leads into it. In memorialising the history of government's clampdown on youth, represented by students across different parts of the continent, Fela seems to 'look back at the liberation struggle and the euphoria of the present with a view to composing an elegy for the past' (Olaoluwa 2012: 2).

The past, in this instance, becomes a sobering monument or a cost that needs to be weighed seriously against whatever are considered the gains of the present, which are often brandished by those in authority as a trophy in the rhetoric of transformation. Such rhetoric often ignores history, urging an unquestioning forward march in an attempt to create a form of amnesia or insulate the public from the goriness of the realities that led them to their current position. As Olaoluwa (2012: 2) further argues, 'it is not enough to make encomiastic comments about the merits of the present transformation without a sober reflection on the past'. Such sober reflection, which features as part of a resistance strategy, is evident in Fela's deployment of memory and historical facts in his interrogation of the way the state exercises power in dealing with its own citizens. The reference itself, which is an expression of solidarity with the victims, serves two basic purposes. First, it is a condemnation of the state's act of killing students during protest in the different instances cited. Second, it serves as a kind of commendation for the sacrifices made by the victims of the struggles that produced the calamity. Though such tribute may imply a mourning of the passage of the various victims, it at the same time suggests a kind of heroism occasioned by the bravery of a few who dare to challenge the status quo. In some other instances, these historical accounts may also serve the purpose of challenging official history or grand narratives, thereby trying to set issues in proper perspective as a form of challenge to the position of hegemonic institutions. This, in other words, is a form of resistance which seeks to reclaim the domain of history which ordinarily should belong to the people who are part and parcel of the making of such histories.

In a practical sense, Fela's 'Beasts of No Nation' touches on three major historical moments that have dealt major blows on the African continent, especially on the psyche of the people. Slavery, colonialism, and apartheid (in South Africa) have remained dark spots whose ghosts continue to haunt, not just Africa, but the rest of the world in different ways. Fela enters the historical discourse by calling into question the relevance of the United Nations as a global mediator among states, chiefly by drawing an analogy between 'beastly' nature and 'human' behaviour. Man's beastly nature is cited as the bastion of bad behaviour.

The song exposes a contradiction in the idea of 'giving' human rights to subjects of the different countries of the world which was a major rhetoric of the United Nations and almost every new regime that assumed power in postcolonial Africa. As Fela argues, human rights in essence are basically constitutive of man. They are an inalienable property, and as such never a privilege to be granted by any individual or institution. Any promise to give human rights is therefore not just political duplicity but rather self-serving rhetoric meant to hood-wink the masses. In claiming '*human rights na my property*' Fela speaks to the contentions raised by the insinuations of the need to grant human rights to citizens of different countries across the world. The argument that you do not 'give' to a person what naturally belongs to him signals a resistance to the appropriation by the state of fundamental or inalienable rights of citizens which the United nations, perhaps inadvertently, endorses through its crusades asking dictatorial regimes to concede some human rights to citizens. In implicating the apartheid regime in South Africa, Fela hinges his bitterness in the song on a statement credited in the media to former South African Prime Minister, Pieter Willem Botha. Botha was Prime Minister from 1978 to 1984. He also served as the country's first executive president from 1984 to 1989.

One of the strategies of resistance deployed by Fela in this song is the naming of the fault lines of imperialist ideas which claim to possess an agenda for global peace and development. This is clearly evident in his comments about the United Nations in which he points out the hypocrisy inherent in the very idea of nations which are ordinarily not at peace with one another claiming to come together to form a 'united' front in an organisation.

Another dimension of such hypocrisy as pointed out in the song is the veto power for members of the Security Council of the United Nations which translates into skewed power relations among member states. In exposing these hypocrisies through his music, especially as they concern the experience of struggling postcolonial countries in Africa, Fela extends his radical evaluation of power relations to those within the United Nations. In doing this, he articulates the warped logic of the use of veto votes within the fold of the United Nations as a body.

Apart from laying bare the illogicality of the modus operandi of an international organisation that seeks to universalise the idea of a just and egalitarian society, comments made by Fela in the song also shatter the heritage of Western philosophy and recipes for modernisation which have become dominant templates in different parts of the world. They expose, as Achille Mbembe (2008) argues, 'both the violence inherent in a particular concept of reason, and the gulf separating European moral philosophy from its practical, political and symbolic outcomes'. They take on the reality of the African, and indeed the global, condition as a narrative that points to social fractures belying the optimism that hegemonic Western ideologies tend to propagate. In other words, this section of the song critically interrogates 'the hope in the advent of a universal brotherly community' (Mbembe 2008) being sold to the world in the guise of a global body like the United Nations, providing an opportunity of representation for different states and their culturally and historically diverse populations across the world.

Resistance, music and postcolonial African experience

Generally speaking, resistance is often a reaction to a particular experience. Even intellectuals and scholars of resistance cannot possibly be excluded from this reaction paradigm that illustrates critical approaches to realities of the human condition. As David Jefferess (2008: 3) argues: 'For others, drawing upon the theories of anticolonial intellectuals, resistance constitutes organised political and military struggle against colonial rule and structures of the colonial economy.' So, a particular form of domination usually triggers off a response which may come in different shades of resistance. 'Beasts of No Nation' is therefore an attempt to challenge a grand narrative while opening the eyes of the public to the sources of the quotidian failures bedevilling postcolonial Africa or the less developed countries in general. It brings to the fore an alternative narrative which creates the possibility of making the voice of the 'subaltern' heard. Fela produces in the song a radical entertainment form embedded with clear political messages drawn from contemporary issues across the world. Therefore, he subverts 'the essentialist identities produced by colonial knowledge' (Jefferess, 2008: 3) and espouses a consciousness which is difficult to ignore in discourses of the fate of the African continent and its people.

Resistance, in other words, is a product of experience just as much as it is intended to produce a new identity both individually and collectively. As Troy Catterson (2008: 404) contends, individuals and, by extension, different groups of people, exist 'as continuing subjects of experience over time'. In a sense therefore, though the experience over time might not produce a completely different person or subject, it alters the composition of the self and invariably results in a different version of the subject. The opposition inherent in resistance is in most cases the product of a particular experience which the subject might have gone through at a particular point in time. It is in this regard that Fela's 'Beasts of No Nation' can be understood as a reflection of personal, national as well as continental experience which elicits a form of resistance expressed through the medium of music. As Karin Barber (2009: 6) has argued, the media in Africa – as agents of civil society and civic activism – have 'brought texts and performances to new audiences, within Africa as well as beyond the continent'.

Conclusion

This chapter has explored both resistance and civic activism in Fela's 'Beasts of No Nation'. In so doing, it has spoken to the decolonisation of Africa discourse which is mainly premised upon the liberation of the different countries of the continent and its people, including leaders who have emerged after the colonial experience. I have explored Fela Anikulapo-Kuti's response to a hegemonic tradition which proclaims freedom for the hitherto oppressed and at the same time seeks to advocate a dominant modernisation paradigm skewed in favour of global power blocs. The chapter has also shown the way popular music becomes useful as an instrument of resistance and civic activism or, in the words of Tejumola Olaniyan (2004: 2), 'the peculiar character of the relations between art, specifically oppositional music, and a postcolonial African state'. Fela, in different ways, takes a critical look at the practice of democracy by world powers in the present global age. In his estimation, the structures of power which dominate the social and political landscape at the moment not only fall short of expectation, but also place Africa at a great disadvantage in the global scheme of things.

His resistance to what is generally considered 'modern' in this sense should therefore be understood against the background of general rejection of the hegemonic deployment of the modernisation discourse in such a way that the weak countries of the world continue to remain at the receiving end of the politicking that goes on through different power blocs represented in global institutions. In other words, the lyrical composition of 'Beasts of No Nation' signals a rejection of the reproduction of dominance which seems to characterise postcolonial Africa. In addition, there seems to be an attempt to invoke postcolonial guilt which ascribes responsibility for the failures of African democracies to powerful external forces and local leaders produced by systems and civilisations put in place and sustained by such exogenous entities. Above all, Fela's 'Beasts of No Nation' represents, to a large extent, an opportunity to rethink Africa's 'modernity' viewed through the tropes of 'democracy' and 'development'. Fela's cultural nationalism should be understood against the understanding of the concept as an avenue for contesting neo-liberal versions of globalisation and modernity that threaten institutions of social interrelations meant to advance the cause of a more equitable society (see for instance Calhoun 2007). The song is a negation of hegemony and its practice couched in the aesthetics of dissidence.

References

Bakardjieva, M. (2011). Reconfiguring the mediapolis: new media and civic agency. *New Media and Society*, 14(1), 63–79.

Barber, K. (1994). African popular music: Review of *Sweet mother: modern African music* by Wolfgang Bender. *Journal of African History*, 35(1), 161–2.

Barber, K. (2009). Orality, the media and new popular cultures in Africa (pp. 3–18). In K. Njogu and J. Middleton (eds), *Media and identity in Africa*. Edinburgh: Edinburgh University Press.

Barber, K. (2011). Editorial note: local intellectuals in Africa. *Africa*, 81(2), 173–4.

Baxandall, M. (1988). *Painting and experience in fifteenth-century Italy*. Oxford: Oxford University Press.

Bhabha, H. (1995). Signs taken for wonders. In: B. Ashcroft, G. Griffiths and H. Tiffin (eds), *The postcolonial studies reader*. New York: Routledge.

Calhoun, C. (2007). *Nations matter: culture, history and the cosmopolitan dream*. New York: Routledge.

Catterson, T. (2008). Changing the subject: on the subject of subjectivity. *Synthese*, 162(3), 385–404.

Corbett, J. (1994). *Extended play: sounding off from John Cage to Dr. Funkenstein*. Durham, NC: Duke University Press.

Darts, D. (2004) Visual Culture Jam: Art, Pedagogy, and Creative Resistance. *Studies in Art Education*, 45(4), 313–27.

Duncombe, S. (2002). *Cultural resistance reader*. London: Verso.

Gephart, R. (1997). Hazardous measures: an interpretive textual analysis of quantitative sensemaking during crises. *Journal of Organizational Behaviour*, 18(S1), 583–622.

Giroux, H. (2011). *On critical pedagogy*. New York: Continuum.

Idowu, M. (2003). African who sang and saw tomorrow (pp. 16–24). In T. Schoonmaker (ed.), *Fela: from West Africa to West Broadway*. New York: Palgrave Macmillan.

Jefferess, D. (2008). *Postcolonial resistance: culture, liberation and transformation*. Toronto: University of Toronto Press.

Kapoor, I. (2008). *The postcolonial politics of development*. London: Routledge.

Kellner, D. (1995). *Media culture: cultural studies, identity and politics between the modern and the postmodern*. London: Routledge.

Lazarus, N. (1999). *Nationalism and cultural practice in the postcolonial world*. Cambridge: Cambridge University Press.

Lee, A. (1991). Integrating positivist and interpretive approaches to organizational research. *Organization Science*, 2(4), 342–65.

Marshall-Andrews, B. (2011). Manipulation is a two-way street. *British Journalism Review*, 22(3), 65–72.

Mbembe, A. (2008). What is postcolonial thinking? An interview with Achille Mbembe. *Eurozine*, available from: www.eurozine.com/articles/2008-01-

09-mbembe-en.html(last accessed: 2 April 2012).
Moore, B. (1995). *Cultural power, resistance and pluralism: colonial Guyana, 1838–1900*. Montreal: McGill-Queen's University Press.
Moore, C. (2009). *Fela: this bitch of a life*. Chicago, IL: Lawrence Hill Books.
Obadare, E. (2009). The uses of ridicule: humour, 'infrapolitics' and civil society in Nigeria. *African Affairs*, 108(431), 241–61.
Olaniyan, T. (2004). *Arrest the music! Fela and his rebel art and politics*. Bloomington, IN: Indiana University Press.
Olaoluwa, S. (2012). Liberation struggle, memory and freedom in Mongane Serote's *Freedom Lament and Song*. *African Identities*, 10(1), 1–15.
Said, E. (1994). *Culture and imperialism*. London: Vintage Books.
Sanneh, K. (2000). Here comes the son: a conversation with Femi Kuti. *Transition*, 10(1), 114–39.
Schutz, A. (1973). Concept and theory formation in the social sciences (pp. 48–66). In M. Natanson (ed.), *Collected papers I: the problem of social reality*. Dordrecht: Kluwer Academic Publishers.
Scott, J. (1990). *Domination and the arts of resistance: hidden transcripts*. New Haven, CT: Yale University Press.
Spivak, G. (1988). Can the subaltern speak? (pp. 271–313). In C. Nelson and L. Grossberg (eds), *Marxism and the interpretation of culture*. Basingstoke: Macmillan.
Street, J., Savigny, H. and Hague, S. (2008). Playing to the crowd: the role of music and musicians in political participation. *British Journal of Politics and International Relations* 10(2), 269–85.
Wasserman, H. (2011). Taking it to the streets (pp. 1–16). In H. Wasserman (ed.), *Popular media, democracy and development in Africa*. New York: Routledge.
West, H. and Fair, J. (1993). Development communication and popular resistance in Africa: an examination of the struggle over tradition and modernity through media. *African Studies Review*, 36(1), 91–114.
Zuberi, N. (2004). Sound exchange: media and music cultures (pp. 429–46). In J. Downing, D. McQuail, P. Schlesinger, and E. Wartella (eds), *The Sage handbook of media studies*. London: Sage.

[illegible]

Part IV

PUBLICS AS EVERYDAY SITES OF RESISTANCE

10 The Power of Resonance
Music, Local Radio Stations & the Sounds of Cultural Belonging in Mali

Dorothea Schulz

Introduction

Political liberalisation in Africa has spawned a growing literature on 'media and democracy' in Africa. Characteristic of much of this literature on private/local radio stations, and more generally on (new) media in Africa, is a focus on the supposed democratising potential of these media institutions (e.g. Senghor 1996; Opoku-Mensah 2000; Hungbo 2008; Hyden *et al.* 2002; see Randall 1998).[1] Whether working on countries with a liberalised mediascape (e.g. Bosch 2006; Graetz 2000; Myers 2000; Mwesige 2009) or on those countries whose political conditions remain adverse to a diversified media landscape, such as in Zimbabwe and Cameroon (Nyamnjoh 2005; Hungbo 2008: 9), scholars often centre attention on the 'alternative' spaces these media institutions create for civic activism and for the capacity of groups of civil society to resist autocratic state power. Along with the preoccupation of scholarship with critical opinion-making and resistance, there is a notable focus on programmes that provide a platform for political information and debate. Music and other cultural programmes are considered mostly with regard to their potential to extend beyond 'mere entertainment' by clearing a space for democratic debate (e.g. Hungbo 2008). Even analyses of interactive radio formats, such as talk radio, often concentrate on their potential to generate political awareness (Bosch 2006; Mwesige 2009). The idea that vernacular broadcasts may have significance beyond their instrumental role in facilitating understanding and accessibility goes largely unnoticed (but see Kawoya and Makokha 2009).

It is certainly important to understand how local radio stations operate in political settings defined by state censure, and to assess the role of vernacular radio stations in generating new spheres of local

[1] Authors who reflect on the potential of 'the media' to transform the nature of state power tend to generalise about the democratising potential of 'the media' without paying sufficient attention to the specifics of individual media technologies and institutions and the political context within which they operate (e.g. Nyamnjoh 2005). Authors who focus on specific media institutions, such as private radio stations, argue that they serve as a primary means for popular communication. Yet other authors highlight the potential of local radio stations for political manipulation (e.g. Chrétien 1995; Mitchell 2007).

communication, and potentially politically subversive, communication. Yet, the question remains as to whether purely instrumentalist readings of cultural radio programmes can account for the popularity of these programmes. This question is of central import to studies of state-making and nation-building as a 'cultural process' (Corrigan and Sayer 1985; see Steinmetz 1999). Whereas anthropologists and historians have stressed the importance of culture to the formation of post-independent nations in Africa (Turino 2000; Askew 2002; Apter 2005; Moorman 2008; White 2008), much of the literature on local radio stations does not recognise the complex social repercussions that the mass-mediatisation of 'culture' might generate and that might allow scholars to interpret these cultural forms beyond narrowly conceived understandings of local radio stations as sites for political resistance or subversion.

Karin Barber's work on popular theatre in Nigeria (2000) and Gunner's (2000) study of Zulu radio drama hint at the insights that an investigation of cultural programmes on local radio might offer. Barber and Gunner do not address processes of mass mediation per se but they maintain that genres of popular drama resonate with spectators' 'real-time' life experiences, concerns and dilemmas. Both authors highlight the importance of language as a 'thick medium' that turns it into 'a carrier of multiple signs and discourses and as a medium for the transformation of consciousness' (Gunner 2000: 228). Arguing that language itself is essential to the popularity of radio-mediated oral genres, Gunner demonstrates that the relevance of these popular genres extends beyond the immediate political 'message' they might, or might not, formulate (also see Ligaga 2005; Englund 2011). What these studies suggest then is that talk radio and music programmes, while seemingly geared toward 'mere entertainment', may resonate deeply with the aesthetic preferences and moral concerns of radio listeners. Consumption of these radio broadcasts generates, if only temporarily and fleetingly, experiences of a collective 'we'.

I want to take up these authors' arguments about the sense of community that emerges out of shared practices of radio consumption and moral appreciation. But I also move beyond analysis of the texts of radio broadcasts. Surely, if we want to understand the role of radio broadcasting in generating a sense of shared experience and community, we need to pay closer attention to the social and material practices that accompany listeners' engagements with these broadcasts (Spitulnik 2002). In a second step, this chapter situates the significance of local radio broadcasting in a setting in which political liberalisation since the early 1990s – notably the introduction of multi-party democracy – posed new challenges to the central state to perform (in the double sense of the word) its capacity to ensure the common good by containing the centrifugal trends inherent in present-day politics of difference (Comaroff and Comaroff 2004). Here, a guiding concern of the chapter is to understand the socially productive effects of local radio stations in the context of a politics of local particularity and identity that has gained momentum with administrative decentralisation since the mid-1990s. Among the repercussions of this administrative reform are various idioms of belonging, such as the one of 'autochthony' (see Geschiere and Nyamnjoh 2000; Nijenhuis 2003, 2005), that are closely associated with a search for 'authentic' origins and are often related to competition over shrinking resources. Examining the role interactive formats and cultural programmes on local radio assume in these claims and dynamics will allow us to come up with a more differentiated portrayal of the 'affective effects' of local radio broadcasting, and of culture as a site for a more complex politics of identity.

The diversification of the Malian media landscape: local radio stations

The multiplication of private media institutions in and around Mali's urban arenas since the early 1990s has been among the most significant consequences of the new civil liberties granted by the 1991 Transition Regime and endorsed by the subsequent democratically elected governments of Presidents Alpha Oumar Konaré (1992–2002) and Amadou Toumani Touré (2002–2012). Accordingly, it would be tempting to interpret the mushrooming culture of local radio broadcasting in Mali along the lines proposed by comparative studies that stress the new possibilities for popular participation, democratic access and transparency afforded by local radio stations. However, although local radio stations certainly contributed to the disruption of a former state monopoly over media discourse and promotion of national culture, the prevailing scholarly emphasis on the liberating effects of local radio stations and hence their potential for political resistance deserves further probing.

As Warner (1990, 2002) argues in his work on public discourse in eighteenth-century North America, the effects of a particular media technology depend on the ideologies of mediation and the specific construction of the collectivity into which the technology becomes embedded. In the present situation of globally extending media institutions and apparatuses, technologies arrive in new settings with certain, though not fixed, meanings and ideologies, and these meanings affect and shape in turn the ideological context within which they are integrated and employed. Jonathan Sterne (2003) similarly highlights the often-arbitrary relationship between particular technologies, their domains of employment, and the cultural and moral values associated with their use. Only with the institutionalisation of certain protocols and conventions of media use do individual technologies become recognised as 'media'. My intention is therefore to understand how local radio in Mali, as a particular institution, a set of technical devices with attendant protocols of use, acquired the meanings and workings it currently performs in particular localities. Into what conventional understandings of the 'function' of communication were local radio stations integrated, and how did they transform them? What – possibly conflicting – expectations about these stations exist and how do they circumscribe the operation and effects of these media institutions?

We can decipher these ideologies of communication by tracing debates surrounding the adoption of new media technology and institutions; by looking at radio producers' performative constructions of audiences (cf. Spitulnik ms: ch. 10); and, finally, by examining how listeners engage with radio broadcasts (Schulz 2012: ch.7). Because these processes are to be understood in their interplay with the political and technical parameters of radio broadcasting in contemporary Mali, these parameters shall be briefly sketched out below.

Since 1992, local radio stations – many of them serving towns and their immediate surroundings – have grown in number, with varying programme quality and sustainability. Apart from new local relay stations of national radio and other officially registered radio stations[2], numerous undocumented '*bricolage*' radio stations were launched by young men who, with minimalist equipment, disseminate music, debates, and local news to local audiences. Although many of these radio initiatives did not survive, they testify to the great excitement surrounding local radio broadcasting in Mali's urban and semi-urban areas. Although formally, commercial radio stations need to be distinguished from community radio and other non-commercial stations[3], they all bear striking resemblances with respect to programme structure, financial and technical constraints and limited professional expertise[4]

Political constraints further impede the 'democratic' potential that many Malian intellectuals and outside observers attributed to local radio stations in the first years of their existence. The Ministry of Communication exerts a considerable amount of control over the non-govern-

[2] From twenty local radio stations officially registered in early 1994, the number of local stations rose to more than eighty in 1997, and to more than two hundred in 2011 (Friedrich Ebert Stiftung 1997; Media Sustainability Index 2006–07; personal communication, director of URTEL (*Union de Radio et Télévision Libres*), Bamako, January 2011). Since 1996, the number of local radio stations in the Northern areas has increased considerably, with radio stations in Kidal, Gao, Menarka, and Timbuktu. Still, many more local stations serve populations in the Southern triangle of Mali than those in the Northern regions.

[3] The different statutes accorded to radio stations categorise them as either corporations with limited liability ('*Société anonyme à responsabilité limitée*'), radio stations financed by individuals who are not organised in the form of a company, or as radio stations organised as cooperatives.

[4] Most private radio stations, whether nominally commercial or non-commercial, generate only limited income through advertisements and other private-sector services. State extension services and international development projects sometimes rely on local radio stations, as do some merchants. But the economically most-powerful actors are international enterprises such as Maggi, Nestle, and Jumbo that cooperate exclusively with the national broadcast station because of its wider coverage of the national territory (Friedrich Ebert Stiftung 1997: 21).

mental media market through the *Conseil Supérieur de la Communication*, a governmental commission in charge of allocating frequencies (Friedrich Ebert Stiftung 1997: 16–17). Organisational reforms within the national broadcast station, and the revision of many programme formats of the state radio in response to a more competitive market situation, have worked to the disadvantage of local radio stations that suffer from budgetary constraints and a lack of professional expertise. No legal framework has been implemented that could ensure a diverse and truly competitive media landscape. Also, so far, private media entrepreneurs have been largely unsuccessful in their attempts to formalise structures capable of representing their interests vis-à-vis the state.[5]

Despite these setbacks, local radio stations have been enormously successful with broad segments of Mali's urban and rural populations. So unparalleled was their popularity that it induced the Ministry of Communication to revise programmes of national radio in line with the more interactive and vernacular language-based media formats of local commercial and community radio stations.

How can we explain the remarkable popularity of local radio stations? What connections exist between their success and a thriving politics of local belonging that have shaped Malian national and regional arenas since the mid-1990s, following the implementation of a large-scale administration decentralisation policy?

Radio-mediated sociality

Leclerc-Olive (1997) notes that in Mali, the relegation of certain administrative powers to newly created rural communities in the context of the *Politique de la Decentralisation* implemented since 1995 coincided with a reinvigoration of traditional authority institutions. Whilst we might not agree with Leclerc-Olive's approach to 'traditional' authority, he does point to a possible nexus between a new appeal of the traditional and the values and forms of social interaction that have been invigorated by local radio broadcasting.

In Mali, local radio stations, and the contentions that emerged around their functions and effects, need to be understood against the backdrop of the heated atmosphere reigning in public life in the early 1990s, when President Alpha Konaré and his party Alliance Démocratique au Mali (ADEMA) had just been voted into office and the former Democracy Movement split into those who gained power, and those relegated to the political opposition. Many early private local radio initiatives were closely associated with either the new ruling party or its major political oppo-

[5] Supported by the USAID and other donor organisations, private, independent radio stations have organised themselves in the association URTEL (*Union de Radio et Télévision Libres*) to represent their interests vis-à-vis the state and establish contacts with international donor organisations. So far, however, internal frictions of the association have limited its success.

nents who at that time coalesced around the party Congrès National d'Initiative Démocratique (CNID).[6] Political opponents stressed the political-critical vocation of local radio stations and thus took up the then-prevailing pan-African rhetoric of a 'civil society against the state'. Those in support of the new ruling party ADEMA, on the other hand, stressed the 'enlightenment' local radio stations offered to the people. Debates about the function of local radio stations involved not just the political elite but diverse segments of local audiences. The controversial reception among these audiences of 'political information' broadcast on local radio shows that to them, the ultimate goal ('use', *nafa*) of local radio broadcasting was by no means evident. A major divide between listeners of different age and educational backgrounds, and between men and women, was evident. Whereas many younger male listeners felt that local radio stations should strive towards greater transparency and a critical public, most older listeners welcomed the opportunities provided by local radio stations to foster 'social bonding' and a spirit of 'solidarity'. Clearly, there did not exist any uniform attitude among listeners toward local radio stations with regard to their vocation as a site of political criticism, even less so of resistance.

The town of Segu, a centre of opposition coordinated by the party CNID, was a good place to assess listeners' conflicting views of the 'vocation' of local radio in 1994. Radio Foko, the radio station of the 'cooperative Jamana' founded by leading members of the ruling party ADEMA, competed for audience attention with Radio Sido, financed by CNID party members. In the early days of my research in Segu in 1994, debates about the significance of local radio always centred on questions of the social function (and effects) of radio programmes – as captured in the recurrent notion of 'use' (*nafa*, 'advantage'). These questions were addressed in everyday conversations and, though less frequently and in more indirect fashion, on the airwaves. Many younger male listeners – a significant segment of these radio stations' audiences – felt that it was the 'civic duty' of local radio stations to offer critical political information. Supporting this idea were the producers (and listeners) of Radio Sido who – driven by their opposition to the ruling party – defended their preference for political criticism as a way to offer 'the politically ignorant' information that would allow them to assert their rights. Regardless of their 'civil-society-against-the-state-rhetoric', the parallels between these radio makers' stress on the educational function of radio broadcasting and the long-standing, top-down approach of state radio were striking. Producers of Radio Foko, on the other hand, strongly disagreed. They, as well as many older listeners (among them many intellectuals) charged Radio Sido with 'mixing up politics with personal defamation', hence contrasting disinterested information to partisan politics.

6 Although radio directors generally played down their affiliation with, or financial dependence on, individual political parties, in some cases their political leanings were nevertheless evident.

These divergent approaches to local radio broadcasting suggested that no clear contrast can be posited between an 'intellectual', 'liberal-minded' vision of radio as the site of emancipatory politics on one hand, and a 'traditional' view of radio communication on the other. This point was also driven home by many adult (male) listeners from Segu's rural environs who, irrespective of their educational background, often criticised what they deemed the 'political' uses of local radio that, they felt, would not foster 'political participation'. To them, the principal goal of local radio was to broadcast 'conversation' and 'our music' for the purpose of 'furthering social bonds'. These rural listeners thus conceived 'useful' radio communication as an extension of what they considered 'good', that is, socially productive, conversation (*baro*): a communication defined by its capacity to refer to and foster 'togetherness' (Schulz 2002). 'Political information' and 'critical speech' were considered the antitheses of this kind of sociable conversation. As a farmer of approximately 55 years from a village 30 kilometres from Segu asked me (rhetorically):

> Why should I listen to their [Radio Sido] talk? It is without use (*nafa*) to me. They talk a great deal but what they say is disrespectful and creates social uproar [...]. That's why I enjoy listening to '*aradjo efem*', when they play music. Music is good, it lifts our burden and brings us together. But this *politiki* talk [...] is a waste of batteries, so (when it starts) I switch off my radio post.

This farmer associated the political information offered by Radio Sido with the in-fighting characteristic of multi-party democracy. He also offered an incisive commentary on the socially and morally productive functions of local radio: its capacity to sustain sociability and (what listeners envision as) social harmony. His remark also reflects the perception that 'out there', in the shared realm of broadcast consumption, there is a larger community of people who share one's own societal headaches. Local radio thus mediates a simultaneity of shared experience (Schulz 1999).

Rather than viewing local radio communication as a realm of politically critical activity, listeners accord to local radio stations a key function in playing their 'own music' and in making – or restoring – an idealised rural *gemeinschaft*. Local radio stations do acquire a politically relevant meaning but one that cannot be identified as a matter of 'resistance' to the state or political power. The importance listeners attribute to hearing their 'own traditions' being broadcast on local radio reflects on their newly invigorated concern with one's own location within the nation. Local radio broadcasts are actively engaged in *making* local 'traditions' that enhance listeners' sense of their own position within the national territory. Yet, as I realised while conducting a survey on local radio reception in different towns of Southern Mali in 1994 and 1995, the potential of these 'traditions' to influence people's particular identity depends on the location of individual radio stations in the nation's geographical, linguistic, and ethnic topographies. Whether listeners frame their expectations toward local radio broadcasting as a matter of cultural and political marginality depends on their reception of national radio that has historically privileged Bamanakan as the main national language.[7] There thus exist important regional differences with respect to the degree in which local radio stations support a sense of one's own situatedness vis-à-vis a national 'community' of listeners (see Schulz ms: ch.7).

Since the late 1990s, the political situation in Segu and in other southern towns that boast the presence of local radio stations has become more stable. The function of local radio stations is no longer a matter of public controversy, partly because local radio stations devote major chunks of time to the broadcasting of talk-radio programmes and of what listeners consider their 'truly own' (*yèrèyèrè*) musical traditions. Rather than interpret this development as proof of their failure to generate a critical public through the broadcasting of information about politics, the substantial amount of airtime reserved for music and oral traditions deserves to be understood in its own right.

As I will argue, the current appeal of local music and 'tradition' is rooted in the mutually constitutive relationship between the new appeal of an idiom of local particularity and the thriving of local radio stations. Local radio-mediated communication itself acquires a new meaning that points beyond a politically critical function in the narrow sense; it affects listeners' perceptions of themselves and of their place in a community.

Invoking the 'morally concerned' citizen-listener

One way in which to assess the communicative spaces generated through radio reception, is to retrace the circulation of media discourse outside the immediate listening event and examine how pieces and bits of this discourse are inserted into and animate various everyday conversations and settings (see Spitulnik ms: 161). I therefore trace the *recycling* of elements of talk radio in everyday life because it is undoubtedly the most successful programme type on local radio.[8] Talk-radio programmes in Mali are often set up as a dialogue between two speakers; they comprise a mix of music, greetings, staged debates between announcers and invited guests or listeners who call in, and announce-

[7] My account of programme choices by listeners living within a radius of 40 kilometres of Segu and Bandiagara is based on quantitative and qualitative data collected in 1988, 1994, 1995, 1996, 1998 and 2011 (Schulz 1999, 2000).

[8] I borrow the term 'talk radio' from call-in programmes first introduced in U.S. commercial radio broadcasting in the 1920s (cf. Laufer 1995). Based on the programme schedules I collected in 1994, 1996, 1998 and 2011 and on my own observations, I estimate that talk radio takes up between 30 and 45 per cent of daily broadcasting time.

ments of local events. The main group of consumers of talk radio are urban youth and women, but depending on the music and topics it features, it may also attract adult men from town and its surroundings.

Although the popularity of talk-radio programmes is ubiquitous and therefore not a peculiar characteristic of radio reception in Mali, it is important to note the emotions this format invokes and generates among listeners in Southern Mali. By taking a closer look at how radio announcers in Mali invoke and thereby actually mould a particular listener-consumer, I want to demonstrate that talk radio resonates deeply with the social function that listeners tend to attribute to radio broadcasting: to generate a sense of 'being together'.

Lila Abu-Lughod (2005), in her discussion of Egyptian state television series, argues that displaying a particular emotional expressivity is key to the production of citizens as subjects with a specific, 'melodramatic' sensibility. Egyptian soap opera productions interpellate, create, and synchronise a citizen-consumer with a specifically modern sensibility. Along similar lines, we might inquire into the specific emotionality that local talk-radio programmes generate and that clearly reverberate deeply with the expectations of female and young radio listeners. Talk-radio programmes in Mali address and generate a particular subject: the 'socially and morally concerned' listener-subject. Pivotal to this process of mediating a particular kind of subjectivity, is the generation of a particular 'mood' (Spitulnik ms: 276) or, in Raymond Williams' words, a 'structure of feeling' (1977). This structure of feeling depends (and reflects) on a particular kind of subjectivity, that is, one of emotional receptivity. It also generates a particular type of interaction and constitutes a particular form of imagining, belonging and of shared intimacy. In other words, what emerges from the engagements of 'morally concerned' listeners with talk radio is a shared 'public intimacy', a sense of belonging to an 'intimate public'.

A key factor in the success of many talk-radio programmes in Southern Mali is the rhetorical skills of individual radio announcers[9], illustrated in their ability to infuse their dialogues and addresses with a mix of gravity and flirtation condoned in interactions between men and women of the same generation.[10] The popularity of Radio Sido's morning talk-radio programme 'Debates' (*Causeries*) among urban women and youth in 1994 is a good illustration.[11] Set up as a conversation between the two announcers, a man (Adama) and a woman (Kadiatou), the programme addressed all kinds of topics pertaining to

9 About 70 per cent of the announcers are men. Female speakers often run programmes that are more specifically oriented towards women. When women host talk-radio shows, they usually do it together with a male announcer.

10 Joking relationships or *senankuya*, as it is called in Bamana/Maninka, constitute an institutionalised form of mocking interaction between matrimonially related family members who are otherwise subject to strict rules of mutual respect and distant behaviour.

11 The name of the programme, a direct translation of "(good) conversation" (*baro*) suggests the producer's intent to distinguish it from any kind of '*politiki* programme'.

family life in town. The speakers' quick-wittedness, voice modulation, and their half-joking, half-flirtatious interactions were considered 'funny' and entertaining by most listeners. Also relevant was the announcers' display of the 'social knowledge' that proved them to be insiders to the gossipy talk that fuels everyday conversations in town (Schulz 2002, 2012b). By articulating listeners' aesthetic and topical expectations, Kadiatou and Adama 'synchronised' listeners in a shared framework of expectations and appreciative responses. The discussions their talk show generates among listeners illustrate that the two speakers very deftly prompt the social circulation and 'recycling' (Spitulnik ms: 164) of titbits of the broadcast conversation, and thereby extend the relevance of their call-in programme into different domains of daily life (see Schulz ms: ch.7).

While listeners' responses to this and other call-in formats vary with topic and time of the day, common to the radio-mediated 'debates', such as those featured by Radio Sido, is their potential to draw people into joint conversation and an experience of simultaneity. This experiential space, generated through a shared mood rather than through 'common opinion', forms the ground upon which listeners perceive themselves as belonging to a community that extends beyond immediate face-to-face interaction. The sense of public intimacy that this 'community of sentiment' (Appadurai 1990: 107) radiates is not all-inclusive; nor does it represent some pristine form of community. Still, as listeners commonly stress, it is based on shared moral concerns and social headaches.

Popular radio announcers play an important role in these experiences of commonality when they act as focal points of emotional identification with a wider group of people (see Spitulnik ms: 130). This identification, though experienced as 'spontaneous' and immediate, is predicated on existing norms and expectations. Listeners' engagements with talk radio may take the form of an imaginary dialogue with an announcer who, in this fashion, becomes their confidant, a confidant whose opinions one discusses without necessarily sharing them. Radio announcers may thus be pivotal in mediating listeners' sense of belonging to a broader public that emerges around simultaneous listening and a sharing of social headaches.

Letters written by listeners to be read aloud on radio show a similar process of affective identification with radio personalities and, through them, with a broader community of listeners. The envisioned commonality is based on shared origins, language, or local dialect; it is articulated through 'congratulations' extended to radio personnel for their familiarity with local custom ('the ways our ancestors used to do it'). Here again, announcers personify listeners' attachments to their 'true' origins and an audience 'community' (see Schulz 1999).

The letters frequently capture the spirit of moral consensus that listeners declare and generate in their role as letter writers. Although references to the state are missing, it frequently provides an implicit backdrop against which listeners articulate their sense of shared experience. What demarcates this community of sentiment is not territorial boundaries but, as the term implies, a consensus based on shared taste and daily experience and framed in moral terms. What we witness, here, is an emergent 'moral public' (Schulz 2000) that people claim to be distinctively local. Local radio stations thus participate in sustaining a particular construction of the public (see Spitulnik ms: 142).

'Making one's name great'

To understand the community-generating effects of 'entertainment' radio programmes, we need to include into our analysis the social and material practices in which their reception is embedded. As I have argued elsewhere (Schulz 1999, Schulz ms: ch.7), key to the success of talk radio in Mali is that it allows and prompts announcers and their fans to extend their interactions beyond the broadcasting event. Announcers regularly 'greet' individual radio listeners whom they already met in 'real life'. They detail with great relish listeners' family background, profession, marital status, and why they deserve the attention of a wider public, and thus claim a familiarity that further adds to the renown of the person in question. Listeners engage in a similar kind of reputation enhancement. They call in to 'give their greetings' to announcers, and approach them off-stage to 'compliment them on their work'. Initial 'greeting' encounters are thus extended to 'off-stage' settings, into subsequent conversations among listeners, and between announcer and listeners.

When I first observed these interactions in the mid- and late 1990s, I found particularly noteworthy the great relish with which listeners scrutinised the 'greetings' offered by individual broadcasters. Listeners would discuss the exact phrasing of individual announcements, and what jokes and allusions the broadcaster had woven into his greetings. Greetings thus feed into existing networks of social relations and obligations among members of the radio audience and, in this way, constitute the audience by invoking it.

That people feel gratified when hearing their name broadcast on radio is certainly not unique to Malian audiences but accounts for the success of call-in radio programmes in the USA and Europe, too (e.g. Laufer 1995: 41–43). Peculiar to the listeners' responses in Southern Mali is that their satisfaction about hearing 'their names being aggrandised' links up with older conventions of reputation-making and with aesthetic expectations about 'skilful speech'. These conventional forms of reputation management are closely associated with *jeli* singers (praise singers, *griots*) and speakers whose public mentioning of an individual's 'name' (*tògò*) or 'reputation' is essential for a person's publicity and prestige (e.g. Zobel 1997; Schulz 1999, 2012).

Also distinctive about radio-mediated forms of reputation-making in Mali is that the forms of network-building in which announcers and listeners engage moves a sense of connectedness beyond the immediate broadcast event. Broadcast interactions *and* 'off-stage' interactions both contribute to the making of a local public. Personal prestige becomes an ingredient of imaginations of a local radio audience and hence, a 'technology' of mediating 'community' in arenas of communication established by local radio stations.[12]

Local radio programmes designed for rural listeners often invite them to send letters and suggestions to be read out 'live' on radio. These letters, while leaving out any mention of politics, are most often addressed to the radio personnel and to fellow listeners who are envisioned as 'equal minded people' with similar moral concerns. The letters often convey the author's[13] sense of pride about the prospect of hearing his or her name being mentioned on the airwaves and thus of being recognised by friends and acquaintances. In this, the letters hint at the social practices that accompany listeners' media engagements and that foster a sense of intimacy typical of these emergent local publics.[14]

By highlighting their sense of local belonging and sharing, letter writers implicitly claim that that marginality vis-à-vis the central state is not the principal factor of 'binding' local listeners together. Instead, they identify as common sources of attachment shared descent, tradition, and language. Objectified notions of 'genuine' local origins and tradition thus figure as points of reference for listeners' 'communal' attachment. Mass-mediated speech and music broadcast play a pivotal role in mediating these emotional attachments, in ways that resemble the nocturnal 'soul talks' of Israeli pioneers that, in the 1920s, became a platform, 'a communicative practice, a symbol and a medium for an experience of *gemeinschaft* and egalitarianism' (Katriel 1998: 114).

A fractured sound community

Listeners, regardless of educational background and rural or urban location, often spontaneously assert that what marks out a genre as 'their own' is its territorial roots. 'Being rooted' implies *rural* origins. The 'earth' is the marker of 'true', uncontestable and undeniable belonging; it generates and justifies deep emotional attachment. These assertions, made during spontaneous assessments of individual musical pieces

[12] National radio rural extension programmes include a similar "response format", but they cannot compete with the greater immediacy of exchange granted by local radio stations.

[13] These letters are usually 'co-authored' because they have been dictated to a literate person who does not present himself as the author of the letter, but sometimes adds his name, greetings, or opinion.

[14] Most of them (ca. 80 per cent) were written in different dialects of Dogon, others were written in Fulfulde, the second local language, and in French. About 60 per cent of the letters were sent by listeners from Bandiagara, and the rest were from villages around Bandiagara.

broadcast on local radio, reveal specific norms and criteria for a successful performance, and hence what, according to listeners, distinguishes a genuine performance of their 'true origins' from 'useless' performances.

Evaluations of musical and oral poetry performances are commonly based on several criteria, among them the familiarity of the language or dialect employed, the singer's or speaker's rhetorical prowess, and whether listeners 'feel moved' by the rhythm and melody. Still, as I show elsewhere (Schulz ms: ch. 4, 5), formal characteristics *per se* are insufficient to explain why listeners recognise a performance as 'genuinely theirs'. Closer attention is warranted to the affective dimensions of the processes by which listeners come to acknowledge, and validate, a performance as genuine. Inquiring into the role of the affective in this process allows us to study listeners' expression of attachment not as 'mere claims' and 'constructions', but as sensuously mediated, visceral experiences.

Birgit Meyer (2009: 9ff) has coined the terms 'aesthetic formations' and 'sensational forms' to analyse how 'religious mediations address and mobilise people and form them aesthetically'. She proposes a more encompassing, embodied understanding of aesthetics that, drawing on the Aristotelian notion of *aisthesis*, makes room for the 'affective power of images, sounds, and texts' that intervene in, and enable, mediation processes (Meyer 2009: 9–11; see Verrips 2006; Meyer and Verrips 2008; see also Hirschkind 2006: 100–102). By taking into account the embodied nature of aesthetic perception, we are in a better position to scrutinise the relationship between mediated cultural forms and the forms of community to which they give rise, and on whose existence the operation of the cultural forms depends. Maffesoli's (1996: 31ff) notion of 'aesthetic style', Meyer (2009: 9) argues, allows scholars to recognise its simultaneously structuring and structured effects, and hence its capacity to induce a 'shared sensory mode of perceiving and experiencing the world that produces community'. Meyer's approach promises insight into the highly transient experiences of emotional attachment that listeners spontaneously articulate when hearing 'their' musical and oral traditions being broadcast on local radio stations in Southern Mali. But this perspective also confronts us with several challenges.

One is how Maffesoli's (1996: 5) focus on the structuring form of images can be made relevant to aural aesthetic 'impressions'. Here we might ask how the melodic-rhythmic patterns of music and oral art shape and resonate with listeners' expectations and perceptions of what is, as listeners put it, 'agreeable'. But Maffesoli's privileging of the ideational dimensions of experiencing community also needs to be balanced by paying closer attention to the social and material practices that give these community formations more permanent form. I already pointed to certain social and material practices that mediate experiences of community and a sense of 'public intimacy' among listeners. I shall now apply a similar perspective to music broadcasts, by exploring their 'affective effects' on the social relations they affirm and potentially transform.

Following Greg Urban's (1996: 22) argument that '[p]erceptions and feelings [...] precede their formulation in publicly accessible words [...] [and] cannot be studied directly but only indirectly through the words in which they are encoded', I examine the terms by which radio listeners in Mali narrate their hearing experience. My argument is that listeners' experience of 'genuine' (*yèrèyèrè*) attachment is best rendered by the term 'resonance'. In physics and acoustics, the term 'sympathetic resonance' refers to a harmonic process in which a container or string moves in response to vibrations to which it is harmonically alike. By referring to the perception processes induced by broadcast music as a matter of 'resonance', I want to capture the sensual and emotional experiences and the socially creative effects that listeners ascribe to, and expect from, the music to which they listen. 'Resonance' highlights the working of the 'forming forms' of music broadcasts, that is, how they inform listeners' recognition, and contestations of certain broadcasts as their 'truly own' tradition.

Listeners describe the embodied effects produced by music but also the 'genuine' nature of a song with the verb *bèn*, 'to come together', 'to meet', and 'to agree'. This term bears very strong connotations of social connectedness. *Bèn* is used to describe meetings, a consensus achieved or desired; it describes the process of 'coming together' of something (or someone) else with one's own perception of what is right, proper, and acceptable. It also expresses the satisfaction generated by a resonance between what is said, performed, and articulated, and one's own aesthetic and moral expectations.

Listeners' assessments of the 'genuine' nature of a music broadcast, whether they are articulated through words or in embodied enactments (see Urban 1996: 240–2), centre on the 'coming together' of expected form and their own moral and aesthetic norms. *A bè bèn an'w ma* (this is agreeable to us, this is something on which we can agree) highlights that a performance 'is agreeable' to one's senses and aesthetic preferences but also to one's moral values. By claiming that an 'agreeable' performance shows in its 'binding and bonding' effects (cf. Meyer 2009: 13), listeners also stress the socially productive implications of a performance. A song should not simply invoke belonging but actually produce feelings of attachment. Music becomes embodied in a both physical and social sense: a song's resonance in the physical, individual body mirrors its productive resonances in the social body.

What validates a song performance as 'genuine' and 'truly our own', is that it achieves these effects: that it establishes 'agreement' between a performance's aesthetically pleasing, embodied effects and its socially and morally productive results. The stress on the intertwining among the moral, the social, and the aesthetic is noteworthy. Listeners identify a performance as 'truly their own' tradition not because it is a faithful rendition of an original version. Rather, in their eyes, a song is validated by its multiple productive effects; that is, by its capacity to generate community, to evoke and make moral consensus, and to speak to shared aesthetic expectations. These appreciations are contingent on the circumstances under which a song is received and evaluated. For instance, political considerations may prompt some listeners to discount a rendition as less-than-genuine, even if it meets the formal and aesthetic standards (see Schulz ms: ch.7). Therefore, broadcast songs – even if they draw on the musical elements of a particular locality – do not mediate community in any simple or unproblematic way. Their reception reveals and reproduces fractures within the local community. Some listeners may even 'opt out' and disengage from the 'community of sentiment' that is evoked by a broadcast performance. They may do so by simply refusing to use their batteries for a programme that 'does not agree with them'. However, even in cases where listeners question that a broadcast song is an uncorrupted rendering of their 'truly own' traditions or contest the genuine nature of a performance, their way of questioning it reconfirms the validity of the criteria themselves; it also confirms the expectation that a song should enable a resonance among its social, moral, and aesthetic reverberations.

In the semi-urban environments covered by local radio stations in Southern Mali, occasions on which listeners question the validity of a musical performance range from moments in which listeners allege that their own family history has not been properly represented to situations in which listeners may place their evaluations in the context of local political dynamics. Here, musical broadcasts prompt responses that reflect long-standing divisions within a local 'community' or within a family. Listeners' frequent insistence on the 'genuine' nature of songs and oral traditions seem to take on a new significance in the present situation characterised by the 'revalidation' of the local and of local belonging. Local radio stations thus assume a vital role. They allow listeners to express and reflect on their positions within a national 'community', and on the multiple forms of connectedness within and across local spheres of communication.

All of this suggests that listeners' acts of validating *jeli* music that is broadcast on local radio stations follow complex trajectories with often unexpected outcomes. The social circumstances may feed into the validation process as much as the sensuously mediated, discursively prefigured experiences of 'genuine' attachment. Herein lies an insight that moves us beyond the framework proposed by Maffesoli. To understand the – possibly paradoxical – effects of shared aesthetic formats on the making of community, more attention should be paid, first, to the internal refractions of these experiences of community, and second, to the social and political dynamics within which these internal frictions gain new momentum.

Conclusion

The purpose of this chapter has been to assess the astounding popularity of cultural programmes broadcast on local radio by examining what social and political meanings and functions listeners attribute to them. The rationale for this discussion was to probe a prevalent trend in the literature on media in Africa to interpret local radio stations as sites of politically critical action. I have argued that a narrow focus on resistance or political subversion does not capture the complex resonances that interactive radio formats and music broadcasts generate as a medium for feelings of attachment and belonging. Listeners' engagements with these specific local radio programmes constitute moments in which a particular political subjectivity of citizens emerges, at the interface between official constructions of national community, and listeners' responses to these constructions. These media engagements do not constitute moments of resistance. Rather, they are moments in which particular forms of community construction, such as the invocation of a national community and sentiment, are achieved and contested in daily practice.

In the contemporary context of a revalidation of tradition and the 'local', local radio stations, by virtue of the particular programme formats and contents they favour, mediate constructions of local community as a 'moral public' but also reflect, and sometimes deepen, divisions within this community. Historically, in the context of live oral performances, claims to social rootedness and belonging were often validated through linguistic registers, music, and oral tradition that were recognised as specifically local. In the contemporary context of a 'resurgence of the local', invigorated by decentralisation politics, these assertions of local particularity and belonging take on a new significance. Local radio stations play an instrumental role in mediating these assertions and the underlying imaginations of 'local' community.

The enthusiastic responses by listeners to the possibilities of sociability and reputation management offered by local radio stations, and their concomitant refusal to use these stations for purposes of political participation, point to the ongoing disjuncture between official constructions of national community and people's own sense of belonging. At the same time, listeners, by contrasting the 'sociable' character of local radio broadcasting to the 'alien' and impersonal forms of exchange characteristic of a national public, do situate themselves within a wider political community. Official constructions of national community in their most recent variant, that is, through the staging of local particularity and belonging, might not yield the intended effects; yet they nevertheless mould listeners' self-understandings as both citizens and *subjects* of the state.

References

Abu-Lughod, L. (2005). *Dramas of nationhood: the politics of television in Egypt*. Chicago, IL: University of Chicago Press.

Appadurai, A. (1990). Topographies of the self: Praise and emotion in Hindu India (pp. 92–112). In L. Abu-Lughod and C. Lutz (eds), *Language and the politics of emotion*. Cambridge: Cambridge University Press.

Apter, A. (2005). *The pan-African nation: oil and the spectacle of culture in Nigeria*. Chicago, IL: University of Chicago Press.

Askew, K. (2002). *Performing the nation: Swahili music and cultural politics in Tanzania*. Chicago, IL: University of Chicago Press.

Barber, K. (2000). *The generation of plays: Yoruba popular life in theater*. Bloomington, IN: Indiana University Press.

Bosch, T. E. (2006). Radio as an instrument of protest: the history of Bush Radio. *Journal of Radio & Audio Media*, 13(2), 249–65.

Chrétien, Jean- Pierre (ed.) (1995). *Rwanda: les médias du génocide*. Paris: Editions Karthala.

Comaroff, J. and Comaroff, J. (2004). Criminal justice, cultural justice: the limits of liberalism and the pragmatics of difference in the new South Africa. *American Ethnologist*, 31(2), 188–204.

Corrigan, P. and Sayer, D. (1985). *The great arch: English state formation as cultural revolution*. Oxford: Basil Blackwell.

Englund, H. (2011). *Human rights and African airwaves: mediating equality on the Chichewa radio*. Bloomington, IN: Indiana University Press.

Friedrich Ebert Stiftung (1997). *Rapport sur la situation des radio libres au Mali*. Bamako: Friedrich Ebert Stiftung.

Geschiere, P. and Nyamnjoh, F. B. (2000). Capitalism and autochthony: the seesaw of mobility and belonging. *Public Culture*, 12(2), 423–52.

Graetz, T. (2000). New local radio stations in African languages and the process of political transformation in the Republic of Benin: the case of Radio Rurale Locale Tanguiéta (Northern Benin) (pp. 110–27). In R. Fardon and G. Furniss (eds), *African broadcast cultures*. Oxford: James Currey.

Gunner, L. (2000). Wrestling with the present, beckoning the past: contemporary Zulu radio drama. *Journal of Southern African Studies*, 26(2), 223–37.

Hirschkind, C. (2006). *The ethical soundscape: cassette sermons and Islamic counterpublics*. New York: Columbia University Press.

Hungbo, J. (2008). *The wilderness of the public sphere: clandestine radio in Africa*, paper presented at the CODESRIA 12th General Assembly 'Governing the African Public Sphere', Yaoundé, Cameroon, 7–11 November 2008.

Hyden, G., Leslie, M., Ogundimu, F. (2002). *Media and democracy in Africa*. New Brunswick, NJ: Transaction Publishers.

IREX (2010). *Media sustainability index Mali*, available from: www.irex.org/resource/mali-media-sustainability-index-msi (last accessed: 16 September 2012).

Katriel, T. (1998). The dialogic community: 'soul talks' among early Israeli communal groups (pp. 114–35). In T. Liebes and J. Curran (eds), *Media, ritual, and identity*. London: Routledge.

Kawoya, V. and Makokha, J. S. (2009). The case for Kiswahili as a regional broadcasting language in East Africa. *The Journal of Pan African Studies*, 2(8), 11–35.

Laufer, P. (1995). *Inside talk radio. America's voice or just hot air?* New York: Birch Lane Press.

Leclerc-Olive, M. (1997). Espaces 'métisses' et légitimité de l'état: l'expérience Malienne (pp. 177–92). In GEMDEV (ed.), *Les avatars de l'état en Afrique*. Paris: Karthala.

Ligaga, D. (2005). Enacting the quotidian in Kenyan radio drama: 'Not Now' and the narrative of forced marriage. *The Radio Journal – International Studies in Broadcast and Audio Media*, 3(2), 107–19.

Maffesoli, M. (1996). *The contemplation of the world: figures of community style*. Minneapolis, MN: University of Minnesota Press.

Meyer, B. (2009). Introduction. From imagined communities to aesthetic formations: religious mediations, sensational forms, and styles of binding (pp. 1–28). In B. Meyer (ed.), *Aesthetic formations. Media, religion, and the senses*. New York: Palgrave Macmillan.

Meyer, B. and Verrips, J. (2008). Aesthetics (pp. 20–30). In D. Morgan (ed.), *Keywords in religion and media*. New York: Routledge.

Mitchell, Jolyon (2007). *Media Violence and Christian Ethics*. Cambridge: Cambridge University Press.

Moorman, M. (2008). *Intonations: a social history of music and nation in Luanda, Angola, from 1945 to recent times*. Athens, OH: Ohio University Press.

Mwesige, P. G. (2009). The democratic functions and dysfunctions of political talk radio: the case of Uganda. *Journal of African Media Studies*, 1(2), 221–45.

Myers, M. (2000). Community radio and development (pp. 90–101). In R. Fardon and G. Furniss (eds.), *African broadcast cultures: radio in transition*. Oxford: James Curry.

Nijenhuis, K. (2003). Does decentralisation serve everyone? The struggle for power in a Malian village. *The European Journal of Development Research*, 15(2), 67–92.

Nijenhuis, K. (2005). Migratory drift of Dogon farmers to Southern Mali (Koutiala) (pp. 190–215). In M. E. de Bruijn, M. M. A. Kaag, K. van Til and J. W. M. van Dijk (eds), *Sahelian pathways. Climate and society in Central and South Mali*. Research Report 78. Leiden: African Studies Centre.

Nyamnjoh, F. (2005). *Africa's media: democracy and the politics of belonging*. London: Zed Books.

Opoku-Mensah, A. (2000). The future of community radio in Africa (pp. 165–73). In R. Fardon and G. Furniss (eds.), *African broadcast cultures*. Oxford: James Currey.

Randall, V. (ed.) (1998). *Democratization and the media*. London: Routledge.

Schulz, D. (1999). In pursuit of publicity: talk radio and the imagination of a moral public in Mali. *Africa Spectrum*, 34(2), 161–85.

Schulz, D. (2000). Communities of sentiment: local radio stations and the emergence of new spheres of public communication in Mali (Vol. 2, pp. 36–62). In S. Brühne (ed.): *Neue Medien und öffentlichkeiten: politik und telekommunikation in Asien, Afrika, und Lateinamerika*, Vols 1 and 2. Hamburg: Übersee-Institut.

Schulz, D. (2002). The world is made by talk: female youth culture, pop music consumption, and mass-mediated forms of sociality in urban Mali. *Cahiers d'Études Africaines*, 42(168), 797–829.
Schulz, D. (2012a). *Muslims and new media in West Africa: pathways to God*. Bloomington, IN: Indiana University Press.
Schulz, D. (2012b). Mapping cosmopolitan identities: rap music and male youth culture in Mali (pp. 192–217). In E. Charry (ed.), *Hip Hop Africa. New African music in a globalizing world*. Bloomington, IN: Indiana University Press.
Schulz, D. (ms). *Music, media and political mediation in Mali* (book-length manuscript, under review).
Senghor, D, (1996). Radio stations in Africa: issues of democracy and culture (pp. 79–108). In P. G. Altbach and S. M. Hassan (eds), *The muse of modernity: essays on culture as development in Africa*. Trenton, NJ: Africa World Press.
Spitulnik, D. (2002). Alternative small media and communicative spaces (pp. 177–205). In G. Hyden, M. Leslie and F. Ogundimu (eds), *Media and democracy in Africa*. New Brunswick: Transaction Publishers.
Spitulnik, D. (ms). *Media connections and disconnections. Radio culture and the public sphere in Zambia* (book-length manuscript).
Steinmetz, G. (1999). *State/culture: state-formation after the cultural turn*. Ithaca, NY: Cornell University Press.
Sterne, J. (2003). *The audible past: cultural origins of sound reproduction*. Durham, NC: Duke University Press.
Turino, T. (2000). *Nationalists, cosmopolitans, and popular music in Zimbabwe*. Chicago, IL: University of Chicago Press.
Urban, G. (1996). *Metaphysical community: the interplay of the sense and the intellect*. Austin, TX: University of Texas Press.
Verrips, Jojada (2006). Aisthesis and An-aesthesia. *Ethnologia Europea*, 35 (1–2): 27–33.
Warner, M. (1990). *The letters of the republic*. Cambridge, MA: Harvard University Press.
Warner, M. (2002). Publics and counterpublics. *Public Culture*, 14(1), 49–90.
White, B. (2008). *Rumba rules: the politics of dance music in Mobutu's Zaire*. Durham, NC: Duke University Press.
Williams, R. (1977). *Marxism and literature*. London: Oxford University Press.
Zobel, C. (1997). *Das Gewicht der Rede. Kulturelle Reinterpretation, Geschichte und Vermittlung bei den Mande Westafrikas*. Frankfurt: Peter Lang.

11 Narrating the Contested Public Sphere

Zapiro, Zuma & Freedom of Expression in South Africa

Daniel Hammett

Political cartoons and other forms of political satire are widely regarded as key indicators of the health of a democracy. Cartoonists and satirists are important social and political actors whose work can hold elites to account and challenge excesses of state power. Critical and popular scholars of geopolitics view expressions of state power and of resistance to state power in political cartoons and popular culture as a vital and active component of discursive networks through which meaning and understanding are constructed. Individual cartoons and films can be used to 'read' or 'decode' a particular moment or event, acting as a window on a nation's *zeitgeist*. Analysis of the narratives contained within a series of cartoons, comics or films can provide a more nuanced, diachronic account of the shifting geopolitical landscape. These foci, however, remain preoccupied with elites – not the political elites of concern in formal and practical geopolitics, but media elites – and overlook the importance of audience reception and responses to these geopolitical messengers.

This chapter therefore considers audience responses to several controversial cartoons by Zapiro, South Africa's leading post-apartheid cartoonist, in order to develop further insights into the contested process of democracy in South Africa. Such an engagement provides a basis from which to identify and analyse the complex mosaic of resistance, recognising that subjective decoding of cartoons and satire elicits a range of reactions and interpretations that do not generate a single mode of resistance. Rather, a multiplicity of engagements and competing readings of the product are identified as contributing to a heterogeneous array of resistances – including resistance to the expression of resistance. In unpacking the dynamics and ideologies inherent within these engagements, both the producer *and* audience are conceptualised as active agents in the development, expression, enactment and response to moments of resistance. In order to consider audience (re)interpretations of resistance, the chapter proceeds through an outline of critical geopolitical engagements with political cartoons and humour, followed by an overview of the political and media context framing the cartoons' production and reception, and a note on Zapiro and the specific cartoons addressed. Analysis of audience responses to these cartoons is then presented, focusing on debates around race and racism, freedom of speech and expression, and of the role of independent media in a post-authoritarian context. This analysis points to the need to recognise resistance as contested, multifaceted and heterogeneous. Further engagement with these complexities is vital to understand the many forms, experiences and expressions of resistance in African public spheres under varying conditions of curtailment and surveillance.

Political cartoons in popular geopolitics

The fields of popular and critical geopolitics have expanded in the past twenty years, diversifying geopolitical interest beyond the formal and practical elements of the discipline to explore the everyday nature of geopolitics and spatialising of international relations through popular culture and media (Dodds 2010). These efforts have sought to shift attention away from the state and academic geopolitical practices to their expressions and encounters in daily life by providing insights into the role of the media in reinforcing elite discourses (Dittmer and Gray 2010). These engagements have focused upon understanding the power of popular culture as a component of discursive networks of power and knowledge that inform everyday political engagements (Dodds 2010: 2). Scholars have considered the ways in which political ideals and representations are communicated and contested in films (notably in relation to Hollywood and the media-military-entertainment complex) (Carter and Dodds 2011; Carter and McCormack 2006; Dalby 2008; Dodds 2008), radio broadcasting (Pinkerton and Dodds 2009), comic strips (Dittmer 2005, 2007), political cartoons (Dodds 2007; Eko 2007; Hammett 2010a, 2011), comedy acts (Purcell *et al.* 2010) and magazines (Sharp 1996). Popular culture is recognised as a sphere that is utilised both to support and perpetuate specific geopolitical visions *and* to challenge excesses of state power and deploy a 'critical geopolitical eye' (Dodds 1996). Despite these engagements, popular geopolitics has remained 'focussed on the elite visions of media moguls, movie directors, and lower-level yet still relatively empowered media functionaries' (Dittmer and Gray 2010: 1664), overlooking audience engagements with and responses to these discourses.

Recognition of this shortcoming has contributed to Dittmer and Gray's (2010) argument for a 'popular geopolitics 2.0', incorporating ideas, methods and theories from feminist geopolitics, non-representational theory and audience studies to uncover other elements of geopolitical encounters in everyday life. Drawing in ideas of embodiment and affect, they argue, would reinvigorate debates around notions of the a/political public/private distinction, enhance understandings of the multiple actors, spatialities and relationalities of geopolitics and recognise consumers of geopolitical messages as active, political agents (Dittmer and Gray 2010). Recognising the importance of viewing 'audiences as active and central to the construction of geopolitical imaginations' (Dittmer 2011: 115), or as Barber (1997: 356) outlines, that audiences 'have a hand in the constitution of the "meaning" of a performance, text or utterance [...] [we] need to look not only at the utterance but also at the interpretation of that utterance'. A number of recent interventions have sought to explore audience reception and dispositions to geopolitical content in popular culture and political satire (see Dittmer and Dodds 2008; Dodds 2006; Johnson *et al.* 2010). In many ways these efforts reflect the 'ethnographic turn' within media studies in the 1980s, where scholars began to recognise audiences as active participants in meaning-making, and perceptions of passive audiences and linearity of media communication were acknowledged as flawed and replaced with analysis of the circularity inherent in communication (cf. Barber 1997; Morley 2006; Pillai 1992).

While concerns have been raised of an essentialising of audiences as always active (Morley 2006), critical engagements have sought to explore how the diversification of audiences due to the development of media technologies have resulted in a range of responses to preferred meanings within media content (Pillai 1992). Such concerns have emphasised the subjective and contextual nature of audience's decoding and reading of texts and (geopolitical) meanings produced (Barber 1997; Newell 1997; Pillai 1992), while continuing to recognise how the construction of media content continues to influence and shape audience reactions (Jacobs 2007). In this regard, there are moves to recognise the agency and power not only of the producers of media but also the audiences and consumers of media products, both in determining what to watch/read/listen to but also through the co-production of meaning between the producer and consumer in interpreting this content. Despite these efforts, there remains a distinct lack of engagement with audience studies within popular geopolitics (cf. Dittmer and Gray 2010; Refaie 2009). Such studies are vital to understanding how subjective interpretations and understandings of images and text are formed, and how these inform the meanings readers take from them and give to the world around them, as these processes of decoding and interpreting can result in (mis)interpretations that produce meanings different from those intended by the producer (Dittmer and Gray 2010; Johnson *et al.* 2010; Mason 2010). In these situations, it is vital to recognise the mosaic of power relations and expressions that inform and frame (re)interpretations of resistance – a mosaic that includes state and non-state elite power, including media elites, civil society and community or faith-based organisations, as well as individual agency.

The context and circumstances in which a geopolitical message is received and understood, along with the readers' political disposition, general knowledge, personal experience and political literacy is vital to the meanings rendered from popular culture. Cartoons are complex and contentious: the interpretation of a cartoon or satirical moment involves a complex process of (de)coding that draws upon the viewer's literacies and contextual framing (cf. Refaie 2009). Producing meaning from a cartoon involves the conceptualisation and construction of the image by the cartoonist *and* the viewer's decoding and processing of the image and the multiple meanings, languages and semiotics contained therein. The producer and consumer are intimately involved in this process; audiences cannot be viewed as passive or reactive recipients or consumers, they are active agents and constituents (Bratich 2005; Dittmer 2010; Pillai 1992; Refaie 2009; Ruddock 2008). These processes involve multiple negotiations of subjective and contextual verbal, visual and symbolic language to construct meanings. It is unsurprising, therefore, that controversies and discrepancies of understandings or interpretations erupt around cartoons, both between different audiences and between the cartoonist and the audience as the intended and received meanings of a cartoon may differ greatly.

The challenges posed by an unintended divergence in understanding can be exacerbated in situations where a particular reading of a cultural product is deliberately used for political ends. In South Africa, Mason (2010: 207) has commented that while cartoons are subject to multiple interpretations, there have been occasions where those of Zapiro have been deliberately manipulated and used for political ends in efforts to, or which inadvertently served to, delegitimise his position as a critical political observer: 'there were sections of the public who wilfully misrepresented Zapiro's attacks on government incompetence and corruption to bolster their right-wing opinions, undermining the integrity of his position' (Mason 2010: 207). These encounters underline the need for further exploration of the range of audience responses to Zapiro's cartoons, not least as the post-conflict, post-authoritarian situation in South Africa invokes critical concerns with elite and popular negotiations of the meanings and practices of the public sphere in a young democracy (cf. Hammett 2010b).

The shifting political and media context in South Africa

The freedom afforded to political cartoonists, and the media more broadly, is recognised as a barometer of the health of a democratic nation and as an indicator of the excesses of state power in totalitarian and authoritarian states (Sparks 2011). An independent media performs a vital democratic role, providing a public sphere in which critical political debates can be held and political and economic elites held to account. In authoritarian or totalitarian contexts, media freedoms are often severely curtailed and journalists harassed and attacked (cf.

Hammett 2011). In apartheid-era South Africa, state control over print and broadcast media limited the public sphere and curtailed expressions of opposition to the state, reflecting a democratic deficit.

Within this constrained mediascape there was limited scope for the publication of overtly anti-apartheid materials. Historically, South Africa had enjoyed a strong culture of caricature and satire with a range of British and Afrikaner cartoonists emerging as strident critics of imperial power and the political and economic power of small elites (Mason 2010). By the 1940s, a darker strand of Afrikaner cartooning developed as a precursor to the apartheid period, expressing racist ideologies and fostering popular belief amongst white South Africans over the threat posed by the *swart gevaar* (black peril) (Mason 2010). During the apartheid era the majority of Afrikaner cartoonists in the mainstream press maintained these narratives and supported the segregationist policies of the National Party government, while liberal English cartoonists struggled to negotiate a paradoxical position of opposition to apartheid and fear of black nationalism (Mason 2010). Government control and censorship of the press did not stop critical political satire: a vibrant underground and alternative press developed, giving expression to anti-apartheid ideals in underground comics, educational comics and other publications (cf. Krüger 2011; Mason 2010).

The role of the media in South Africa underwent radical change with the democratic transition, from a state-controlled tool of division and oppression to a medium for nation-building and reconciliation, with a broader array of stakeholders and reduced government oversight. New legislation resulted in the partial privatisation of the South African Broadcasting Corporation (SABC), the introduction of new broadcasting licenses and emergence of new print media outlets. This expansion of voices in the public sphere, evidence of press diversification and freedom, demonstrated an early movement towards Western norms and expectations of media independence (Jacobs 2004; Krüger 2011; Sparks 2011). This process has witnessed both elite continuity in control over the media and a renewal of a media elite with the emergence of a new cohort of media owners and operators (often aligned to the new political elite), with private capital continuing to dominate the print media (Sparks 2011). Meanwhile, the state has retained a central position in broadcast media through the SABC, which, critics argue, has evolved into an uncritical pro-government agency (Tomaselli and Teer-Tomaselli 2008).

This allegation is only one factor in the complex transition of the political and media landscapes in South Africa. In common with many other post-transitional states, tensions surrounding the entrenchment of the public sphere and role of the media have emerged, often coalesced around the media's role in nation-building projects. In such contexts, the media is often viewed by the state as having a responsibility to promote the state's nation-building agenda rather than as an independent arena for critical political engagement (Dorman 2006; Eko 2007; Hammett 2011; Tomaselli 2009). In South Africa, these tensions have been exacerbated by the need to reconcile the promotion of multi-culturalism with the depoliticisation of ethnicity, and the state has increasingly sought to intervene and regain greater press control – notably over an increasingly critical print media (Barnett 1999; Botma 2011; Tomaselli and Teer-Tomaselli 2008). The role of the political satirist in these situations, to expose and critique power relations and excesses of power, has been subject to pressure from elites seeking to maintain powerful positions and marginalise dissenting voices (cf. Hammett 2010b). These endeavours have posed challenges to the media's independence and role as a critical public sphere as South Africa's mediascape has shifted towards a polarised plurality marred by increasing state intervention and declining media professionalism rather than a (Western) utopian media liberalism (Botma 2011; Duncan 2009; Jacobs 2004; Krüger 2011).

The proposed introduction of a Media Appeals Tribunal, to oversee media content, and passing of the Protection of Information Act by the lower house of the South African Parliament on 22 November 2011, are both widely viewed as threats to media freedom. The Act, according to the ANC, is designed to protect against espionage and is in the 'national interest' but critics argue it will limit the autonomy and freedom of the press and could be used to protect elites from critical investigative reporting, with Sparks (2011: 14) observing 'it is very hard not to see these measures as designed to ensure that the media can no longer play a campaigning role against corruption and the abuse of power'. McDonald (2011), while cautioning that polemical hysteria that the Act is akin to apartheid-era censorship is over-simplistic and cynical, signals that these developments are of concern and pose a threat to the public sphere and recently realised rights to freedom of expression. In many ways, the Act has emerged as a touchstone issue relating to the continued (re)negotiation of power between state and civil society actors. Thus, while the media retains some protection under Section 16 of the South African Constitution (freedom of expression), fears remain that the scope of the Act, which 'promote[s] secrecy not just as a security matter [...] but in the name of justice, democracy and the economy' under catch-all labels of the 'national interest' and 'public good' (McDonald 2011: 124), will serve to curtail press freedom and hinder critics such as Zapiro.

Zapiro and Zuma: a battle over a democratic public sphere?

Jonathan Shapiro (Zapiro)'s active engagement with progressive politics began in earnest with his two-year conscription into the South African army at the age of 24 in 1982. In 1983 he joined the United Democratic

Front (UDF), played a prominent role in the End Conscription Campaign and was later arrested under the Illegal Gatherings Act. The values of the UDF provided Zapiro with a political frame that informed, and continues to frame, his cartooning for a range of progressive political organisations (Zapiro 2009: 6). In 1987, Zapiro gained his first taste of editorial cartooning, providing images for the anti-apartheid paper *South* in which he developed a style combining opposition to apartheid with the promotion of democracy (Zapiro 2009: 8). In 1989 Zapiro accepted a two-year Fulbright Scholarship to study at the School of Visual Arts in New York before returning to South Africa in 1991 when he focused on producing educational cartoons for a range of civil society organisations. It was not until 1994, when he took up the position of editorial cartoonist for *The Sowetan* (until 2005) and *Mail & Guardian* newspapers, that Zapiro returned to regularly producing political cartoons. He also drew cartoons for *The Cape Argus* from 1996 to 1997, and produces cartoons for the *Sunday Times* (since 1998), *The Cape Times*, *The Star*, *The Mercury* and *Pretoria News* (all since 2005).

During the course of his career, Zapiro's approach has evolved – reflecting the shifting socio-political context – from a concerted anti-apartheid focus, through an accessible pro-nation-building approach (reflected in his continued beneficent caricature of Nelson Mandela) to a more critical 'patriotic sceptic' position (Hammett 2010a). This repositioning, due to Zapiro's growing scepticism of the new elite's values and actions, has resulted in conflicts between Zapiro and many he regarded as comrades during the struggle (Hammett 2010a; Mason 2009). Zapiro's depictions of Jacob Zuma, the current ANC and South African President, in particular have resulted in the cartoonist facing the ire of the political elite and court cases for defamation of character.[1] Zapiro's trademark caricature of Zuma with a showerhead attached to his skull emerged in 2006 in response to Zuma's testimony during his trial for raping an HIV-positive family friend – a charge he was acquitted of. Under cross-examination, Zuma – then head of the South African National AIDS Council – admitted to having unprotected consensual sex with his accuser and stated that he showered afterwards in order to minimise his risk of infection (see Hammett 2010a).

A more controversial depiction of Zuma followed in September 2008 when Zapiro, reflecting on the furore surrounding the National Prosecuting Authority's attempted prosecution and subsequent decision to drop charges of fraud and corruption against Zuma in relation to a 1998 multi-billion Rand arms deal, depicted Zuma and his allies as preparing to rape the metaphorical figure of Lady Justice (symbolising the independence and fairness of the judiciary). In this cartoon, Zuma

1 Zuma initiated two civil cases against Zapiro in 2008, amounting to claims for over R5 million for defamation of character. However, he withdrew both cases in 2012, terminating proceedings against Zapiro and the *Sunday Times* over the cartoons and agreeing to pay half of the *Sunday Times*' legal costs.

is shown, trousers unbuckled, standing in front of Lady Justice who is restrained by Zuma's allies in the ANC, the ANC Youth League, the South African Communist Party and the Congress of South African Trade Unions. This image quickly gained notoriety as controversy erupted around allegations of racism, insensitivity to rape victims and attacks on Zapiro for failing to show respect for the country's President (for detailed analysis see Hammett 2010a, b). Zapiro has reprised the 'rape of' motif to comment critically on Zuma's claims of respect for the independence of the judiciary as a democratic institution (11 September 2008), as well as on Thabo Mbeki's interference in the National Prosecuting Authority's (NPA) procedure against Zuma (14 September 2008), on Zuma's proposals to issue presidential pardons for both Eugene de Kock and Shabir Shaik (14 January 2010)[2], and in opposition to the Protection of Information Act (9 June 2011). The questions provoked by this motif are complex, setting the cartoonist's right to freedom of expression (as enshrined in the constitution) against debates over the limits of taste and decency and of the extent to which a cartoonist has the right to mock and ridicule political leaders (cf. Hammett 2010a; Mason 2010: 211). Despite the amount of reaction these cartoons have provoked, academic interest has failed to explore the sentiments and responses expressed. Academic work, instead, has addressed the ways these cartoons have affected Zuma's political brand (Bal *et al.* 2009), how social media can extend the life of a political cartoon (Terblanche 2011) and the broader political debates emanating from a specific image (Hammett 2010a). More detailed engagements with audience responses to political cartoons and satire – circulating both in the formal and hidden or informal press, and public spheres – are vital. Such engagements provide for deeper understandings of the ways in which resistance and opposition may be mobilised, as well as the ways in which ideas and ideologies are received and contested by different audiences. Such consideration moves beyond the assumption that satire mobilises and/or reflects resistance and dissent, to question how the processes implicit in critical engagements and citizenship are engaged and played out.

The final section of this chapter provides a preliminary, and partial, analysis of audience responses to Zapiro's September 2008 'Rape of Justice' cartoons (Zapiro 2008a, b, c), his January 2010 'Zuma: Unfinished business – begging your pardon' cartoon (Zapiro 2010) relating to the proposed presidential pardoning of Shabir Shaik and Eugene de Kock, and the June 2011 'Pressure on Lady Freedom to fight back as ANC push forward with "Secrecy" Bill' cartoon (Zapiro 2011). The September 2008 cartoons began with the 7 September depiction of

[2] Eugene de Kock, also known as 'Prime Evil', was an apartheid-era police colonel who commanded the notorious Vlakplaas counter-insurgency unit of the South African Police Service. His testimony during the Truth and Reconciliation Commission hearings revealed details of the kidnapping, torture and murder of hundreds of ANC activists. He was later convicted of crimes against humanity and sentenced to 212 years in prison. Shabir Shaik was Zuma's financial advisor during the 1998 arms deal and was convicted of corruption charges relating to this deal in 2005.

Zuma preparing to rape Lady Justice (Zapiro 2008a), who was restrained by ANC Youth League President Julius Malema, ANC Secretary General Gwede Mantashe, the South African Communist Party General Secretary Blade Nzimande, and Congress of South African Trade Unions General Secretary Zwelinzima Vavi. Two further cartoons in the same vein quickly followed. The first, on 11 September (Zapiro 2008b), replicated the 7 September image but with Zuma saying 'Before we start, I just want to say how much we *respect* you!' to question the validity of political leaders' attempts to reaffirm their respect for the independence of democratic institutions. A cartoon on 14 September (Zapiro 2008c) reprised the 'Rape of Justice', this time acknowledging that the NPA's procedure in the corruption case had been invalid while replicating the 7 September image with Zuma and his allies, as well as a second version of Mbeki and his allies in the same context.

Zapiro's reprise of the 'Rape of Justice' on 14 January 2010 depicted Zuma unbuckling his trousers in front of Lady Justice, this time restrained by Shabir Shaik and Eugene de Kock, with Zuma saying 'Begging your pardon', a comment in relation to the proposed pardoning of the other protagonists. The 9 June 2011 cartoon depicts a defeated Lady Justice, her robes torn, calling out 'Fight, sister, fight!!' to an allegorical figure of Lady Freedom/Free Speech. This second figure, holding aloft a flaming torch – the flame of freedom, to cast light (truth) into darkness – is held back by Gwede Mantashe while Jacob Zuma (representing the government) unbuckles his trousers in front of her. Drawn in response to the Protection of Information Bill, the cartoon graphically demonstrates the threat this Bill is seen as posing to the constitutional right to freedom of expression and the independence of the media.

Audience responses considered here, posted both directly to the cartoons and in response to media commentaries, are drawn from the online comment threads hosted on the *Mail & Guardian* and *Sunday Times* websites and the South African media website the *Daily Maverick*.[3] In addition, responses to Zuma's confirmation in December 2010 of his defamation action against Zapiro are considered as these, *inter alia*, relate the cartoons under consideration. Comment threads varied from individual posts to hundreds of postings, including exchanges between individual posters. This approach has several limitations. Those who posted in response to the cartoons required access to the internet (a major barrier for many in South Africa, where only 10 per cent of the population were internet users in 2009, see Marishane and Shackleton

[3] The *Mail & Guardian* was established in 1985 as the *Weekly Mail* as an alternative, critical press and was the first South African newspaper without a racially defined target market. The United Kingdom's *Guardian* newspaper acquired a majority shareholding in the paper, leading to the rebranding as *Mail & Guardian*. The paper and its online version are targeted at a well-educated, professional readership, interested in politics and current affairs, with a readership of 500,000. The *Sunday Times* was founded in 1906 and is South Africa's most widely read weekly paper, with a circulation of 504,000 and a readership of 3.2 million. The *Daily Maverick* is an online news, comment, opinion and satire website focusing on South African politics and current affairs.

2009), had engaged with the *Mail & Guardian* website (generally seen as a middle-class weekly newspaper), and were politically engaged and mobilised. This material is therefore not drawn from a representative sample but serves to highlight a number of key, evocative concerns raised in the public sphere surrounding the cartoons and the political and constitutional questions addressed therein. The use of posts relating to opinion pieces written about the cartoons poses a further dilemma in understanding how audience responses towards a specific cartoon can be informed or influenced by commentators' own interpretations of and reactions to the image. In this instance, however, the content of the posts – as a partial sample of audience responses – provides useful insights into the varying reception of these cartoons.

Audience reception and freedom of expression in post-apartheid South Africa

The popular responses to Zapiro's cartoons coalesce around a number of key themes: race, gender, violence, democracy and freedom of expression. These reactions resonate with broader, ongoing political discussions and reflect how historical experience and contemporary conditions inform audience engagements with and responses to these moments of political satire. The vibrancy of the responses posted reflects the existence of a dynamic public sphere, emphasising the socially subjective nature of the decoding of cartoons (as acts of resistance), although the demagogy and intolerance of certain posters towards differing viewpoints, as well as calls for a less critical media, indicate potential challenges to this space.

These exchanges drew on claims to struggle-heritage and history as well as Western ideals of media liberalism. On one side of the debate, a series of posters argued that the realisation of the right to freedom of expression was due to the ANC and the anti-apartheid struggle, meaning South Africans were indebted to the party for this right. Therefore, the argument went, the media should not abuse this right in attacking the ANC (and its members) but should focus on contributing to the government's nation-building agenda. Senzo Selebe's post captured many of the ideas contained in this strand of argument while criticising the media for, as Senzo perceives it, serving an anti-government agenda based upon fabricated stories of corruption:

> [P]eople should never abuse their right that the ANC has fought for in so many years. The right of freedom of speech, the right to express views of your own. The cartoon above doesn't build the nation, the media always complain that the organisation [ANC] is corrupt and is not capable to lead the nation. So as the media is misleading the country for the price of sales, at the expense of the citizen of South Africa. I appreciate the work that Zapiro has done all these years, wish him all the best and the

> strength to see more than what the eye can see. For the nation depends on the power that the media possess (Senzo Selebe 7 September 2008).[4]

Complaints of a biased (print) media agenda against the government are well-noted and feed into broader debates around elite and popular understandings of the role of the media in democracy, and the continued challenges faced by the ANC in the party's transition from a revolutionary to a governing party (Dorman 2006; Hammett 2010a; Maré 2001; Tomaselli and Teer-Tomaselli 2008). These challenges are evidenced by the vitriolic press statement issued by the ANC and allies in response to the first 'Rape of Justice' cartoon, which attacked both Zapiro and Mondli Makhanya (editor of the *Sunday Times* in which the cartoon was published), 'We can only hope that the newspaper will find a suitable leadership other than the ranting dictator who finds joy in manipulating the truth. [...] The ANC is keen that the public should get Makhanya to answer for abuse of press freedom by the *Sunday Times*' (cited in van Hoorn 2008). Such passionate responses were not the sole preserve of political elites, as several posters launched their own polemical attacks on the cartoonist. Admittedly drawn from the more extreme end of the spectrum of responses, Mvikeni kaNxamala Zuma's post gave a sense of the depth of feelings and emotions triggered by the cartoon, the role of historical experience in framing this response, as well as an underlying understanding that the print media (and Zapiro) were not only failing in their duty to support the government but were biased against Zuma and the ANC government:

> Know one thing my friend, some people would kill and die for ZUMA so please don't stir SA up for World War 3. My friends we are tired of wars, we really need peace in this country, it things like these that could lead to bombing of shopping malls and casinos (Mvikeni kaNxamala Zuma 8 September 2008).

The resonance between the militarised rhetoric of this posting and the threats made by members of the ANC Youth League and Umkhonto we Sizwe (MK)[5] veterans against the judiciary, and to make the country ungovernable if Zuma were found guilty of the charges made against him, is notable (cf. Hammett 2010a). These pronouncements not only call into question understandings of the nature and role of various institutions of democracy, but also highlight the continued divisions within South African society and the power of historical experience in fomenting these. They also demonstrate the need for nuanced, contextual understandings of power and resistance as framed by history and ideology, and highlight that both the powerful and the marginalised are imbricate in negotiations of what constitutes 'valid/appropriate' dissent and resistance.

4 Names of commenters occur in the References alphabetically by first name/nickname.

5 Umkhonto we Sizwe ('Spear of the Nation') was the military wing of the ANC during the struggle against apartheid.

Ranged against audience responses calling, either directly or indirectly, for a less critical media and closing down of the public sphere, were other posters who argued for the importance of such critical and provocative commentaries. This viewpoint was captured in Lee Cahill's post, who argued for the need for critical and creative political interventions within the public sphere as essential to the health of South Africa's democracy:

> John Lennon said it is the role of creative people in a society to express what we all feel; to act as a reflection of the environment. No-one does this better than Zapiro. I, for one, am deeply grateful that his eye is turned on the disturbing events unfolding here. It is voices like his – hopefully – that will prevent us from sliding into latter-day Stalinism (Lee Cahill 8 September 2008).

The essence of Cahill's argument was reflected in other postings, both from the general public and in 'Thought Leader' blogs on the *Mail & Guardian* website on which Jonathan Berger opined:

> Zapiro's cartoon does push the boundaries of what we may consider acceptable [...]. It's the nature of the medium – it's supposed to do what it does. It's not meant to make us feel warm and fuzzy and patriotic and ready to take up arms to defend the leader. It's designed to get us talking. At least we're now talking (Berger 2008).

The importance of the cartoons was, for many, not simply their commentary on a political event or narrative, but in generating discussion and debate, as Berger noted above. This aspect is important to note as this implicitly recognises not only the power of political cartoons within a post-transitional democracy and the existing freedom of expression but the importance of these, and the need to defend them in South Africa:

> The cartoon made me a little uncomfortable, but it was so accurate [...]. [Zapiro] did it well, judging by all the reactions (Kandi 8 September 2008).
>
> If Zapiro intended that people talk more openly about what they REALLY believe is REALLY going on with JZ's trial – then, judging from the comments above, I would say that the end has already justified the means (Baba Umfundisi, 8 September 2008).

These sentiments were echoed by the then editor of the *Mail & Guardian*, Ferial Haffajee, who made an impassioned plea for the need for greater popular understanding of the role of the political cartoonist in a democratic public sphere:

> Of greater concern is the ignorance of the role we give to cartooning in modern liberal societies, such as we like to claim we are. They are our *imbongi*, the patriots who speak truth to power when necessary [...]. Cartooning needs to be neither accurate nor

> truthful, the measures of other forms of journalism. It is an art that is meant to push the envelope, to cause discomfort, to exaggerate threat and mock most everything. It ensures that we do not forget [...]. In the pantheon of free expression, cartooning has a special place (Haffajee 2008).

Underpinning these commentaries are two key concerns: the role of the media as a component of the democratic public sphere was problematically understood, and while the debate provoked by the cartoon(s) demonstrated the health of the public sphere at that moment there were concerns that this was threatened by popular belief and political will. The content of the comment threads themselves provided evidence of existing underlying factionalism and division that limited the potentially constructive nature of discussion and debate. Divergent opinions and attitudes were evident in the postings, with numerous instances of posters' replying not only to the original cartoon or press story but to the comments of previous contributors. These exchanges often served to highlight entrenched social and political divisions, stifling open and critical discussion, much to the dismay of several contributors:

> It's amazing how polarised responses [to the cartoon] have become [...] as long as we are polarised between those factions, we will have great fun stirring the shit-pot! So, prepare for years of pot-stirring to come, because we will never cross over to the other side (Gerry 9 September 2008).

> Nothing depresses me quite as much as the quality and tone of comments on this site. Regardless of the article, regardless of the topic, as soon as the thread starts, this country's dark heart is exposed. The petty, bitter, vindictive and downright stupid comments, by supposed 'thought leaders', just takes my breath away (Bruce 11 September 2008).

Powerful divisions also appeared around the ways in which race and allegations of racism were mobilised in readings of Zapiro's cartoons. On the one side, posters such as MFB (9 September 2008) argued that the images were simply reflections of Zapiro's racist mindset and apartheid upbringing: '[O]f course the cartoon is racist. Shapiro writes for a white right-wing audience. No surprise there that he depicts blacks as genetically disposed rapists'. Also Dave Harris (22 January 2010), who stated: 'I can understand Zapiro's fear of Zuma stemming from racism and the loss of white-AA privileges'. These responses are rooted in both South Africa's historical experiences of colonialism and apartheid and the deployment of narratives of racial superiority and inferiority during these periods, and in a contemporary context wherein the government has failed to provide leadership in reconciliation and to offer an alternative to race in discussions of development, politics or society. These shortcomings are reflected in a sense amongst sections of

South African society that race is problematically deployed in political ways to silence critics and dissenters (cf. Hammett 2008; Maré 2001). In these exchanges, Zapiro's supporters frequently utilised his earlier anti-apartheid works to repudiate allegations of racism made against Zapiro and as a justification for his critical depictions of Zuma and the ANC. Contributors sought to question the validity of reading race/racism into Zapiro's cartoons, arguing that the cartoon had nothing to do with race but was solely concerned with the actions of the protagonists:

> The cartoon isn't about race, it's about the actions of the people involved. Get the race chip off your shoulder and stand up and be counted on the basis of belief and action, just as the politicians you defend should be doing. Um, and by the way, turning that mirror back on you, what do you mean by 'you people'? Isn't that the generalised discriminatory comment that is profoundly and fundamentally racist? (Lee Cahill 8 September 2008).

Such responses failed to acknowledge the complexities and powerful nature of historical experiences of racism and oppression, which contributed to readings of the cartoon that invoked these histories and rebuttals of associated stereotypes. While many of these exchanges were divided along racial lines, this division was not absolute, with several posters using these exchanges as opportunities to call for greater engagement with the politics and processes of integration and reconciliation:

> It saddnes [*sic*] me that still up to now, there is a black opinion and a white opinion, it does not matter how well we now blacks speak English, how we now suddenlt [*sic*] live in the suburbs and have acquired tastes and opinions [...] we are still divided as ever and that wond [won't, *sic*] change until the day we stop our SA window dressing (Itumeleng 8 September 2008).

> How is the cartoon an insult to black people as a whole. Am I missing something here, I am labeled 'black' and I took no offense. This is not a black or white issue, why can't people get that through their heads? (khathutshelo 8 September 2008).

These exchanges, and many others, demonstrate how powerful political cartoons remain and the range of readings they are subjected to and interpretations that are produced from these. The reading of race/racism into the cartoons also drew from historical experiences wherein the majority of South Africans endured a deficit of respect in their dealings with the minority elite, such that perceptions of an injury to one (through being accorded a lack of respect) was an injury to all:

> i [*sic*, and hereafter] hear a cry from zapiro and his elite of how anc/alliance are going to abuse judiciary, what about zapiro respecting members of this organisation for

> him to insult this leaders means he is attacking masses that are led by these leaders. zapiro represent the view of rich towards the masses, ignorant, violent and abusive, he might as well be groot krokodile [apartheid leader P. W. Botha] (sabelo njoko 9 September 2008).

Sabelo's comment reminds us of the power of historical experience and division in shaping the current nation-building project and the challenges faced by the new nation, as well as underlying tensions surrounding media freedom, ownership and government control. Alongside the divergent readings of race onto the cartoons, another major trend in audience response focused upon the appropriateness of depicting an impending act of sexual violence. For several posters, the metaphor was too vivid to be acceptable:

> When you live in a township where a gang is on every street corner preying on young and old subjecting any person to unimaginable abuse one wonders how a violent image of a young black woman about to be gang-raped can ever be acceptable in communities who live through the trauma of rape on a daily basis. I am a young black woman who live in a township. I frequent public transport and live in a shack. Gang rape is a daily fear. RAPE is a daily fear (Kitty Kat 25 January 2010).

For others, an assumption that the cartoon was intended to provoke laughter or humour meant that this image was unsuitable:

> Politics aside: I consider the cartoon – (ANY cartoon) visually depicting a bound woman awaiting rape with the expectation that I will LAUGH about it, what EVER the context – extremely distasteful, insensitive and crude. Rape is no laughing matter' (Geri 8 September 2008).

What this last quote reminds us is that while the cartoonist may understand the important of 'unlaughter' (Billig 2005) in satire, their audience may not but may rather be seeking laughter. The importance of unlaughter as a cartoonist's tool was noted by a number of readers, who felt that the opposition to the cartoon mobilised by ANC politicians was due to a failure to understand that political cartoons do not need to be humorous to be powerful, but that the invoking of discomfort through unlaughter was an important contributor to robust democratic debate:

> Duarte and co, like members of the previous Government, don't understand irony. It's not supposed to be funny. There's nothing funny about Jacob and his cronies trying to hijack our country and run roughshod over our constitution and legal system. There is nothing funny about rape either [...]. This discourse is important. The cartoon stimulates debate. It is brilliant. We need this (Warrick Sony 8 September 2008).

This layer of understanding of the nature and power of political cartoons requires a particular form of literacy, of knowledge and understanding of the ways in which political satire and cartoons are conceived and conceptualised. This literacy is not universal but, as with the symbolic and other language deployed within cartoons, is subjective and acquired through experience and exposure. Therefore, the allegations of racism surrounding Zapiro's depiction of Zuma in these cartoons are informed not only by the racism of colonial and apartheid experience, but also by differing knowledge and literacy regarding traditionally Western metaphorical figures. So, Citizen Mntu's comment that 'rape of' cartoons were 'nothing new' may be accurate for observers with exposure to Western art, literature, history and metaphors:

> People, the use and the purpose of metaphor is nothing new, nothing to be surprised and shocked about. Every word, every term, every concept in any language, is available for use as metaphor or symbol, or archetype. Nice & pretty or alarming & ugly. Thus is reality also reflected. Would you condemn Alexander Pope ('The Rape of the Lock')? Or the painting 'The Rape of the Sabine Maidens'? And many, many more examples, going back to Antiquity? Sheer literalism is wholly out of place when it's quite clear that we have an artist at work. And when his socio-political intent is clear (Citizen Mntu 11 June 2011).

To those without this literacy, however, these meanings would be lost, and alternative understandings developed – which, in this context, invoked histories of racism and oppression.

Such unintended responses to and readings of the cartoons are implicated in their affective power. Scholars of affect such as Mbembe (2001) and Thrift (2004) would argue that even the moment of ridicule and the effort to undermine a political elite presented by a cartoon can serve to reinscribe and reinforce elite power. This concern over affect was noted by one contributor who pondered how Zuma would respond to the cartoon and whether the outcry around it would increase his popular support:

> I wonder how Zuma himself will respond. If I were him, I would maintain a dignified silence and look like a noble martyr. The irony is that by attacking Zuma in this way, Zapiro may well prompt sympathy for the man from people who are not in his core support base (Sarah Britten 9 September 2008).

There was evidence in the postings that Zapiro's attempts to delegitimise and criticise Zuma had served to reinscribe loyalty to and entrench the power of the political leader amongst his supporters, who viewed the attacks upon him as illegitimate and the work of a cabal of disenchanted white, right-wing anti-revolutionaries.

While this may have entrenched Zuma's strength for one constituency, the increasingly demagogic reaction from Zuma and his supporters inverted this affect by reinforcing another constituency's sense that Zuma's credibility was declining and these strident efforts to prop up his powerbase simply reflected its growing insecurity. These exchanges underscored the complex and contested networks of power relations that exist within South Africa's nascent democracy: collective and individual power and agency are exercised in support of and opposition to both the state and its critics, resulting in ongoing (re-)interpretations of acts and expressions of resistance. While the state is often implicated, of critical concern are the ways in which both elite and, importantly, non-elite groups co-construct – often divergent – meanings in their interpretations of (un)civil expressions of resistance within a public sphere where the limits of power, agency and resistance continue to be negotiated. These developments were reflected in a number of postings from contributors whose interest in the cartoons and controversy was sparked and maintained by Zuma's allies' responses to it: 'Zapiro zapped 'em... The more they squeal about the zappery, the better the cartoon becomes' (Jon 9 September 2008) and 'The more argument the better the cartoon becomes! I agree. I had actually thrown the paper away – then went through the trash to find the cartoon and have pasted it on my fridge!' (Lyndall Beddy 9 September 2008). These reactions serve to reinforce the power of the political cartoon(ist) in the post-apartheid period while revealing/reinforcing awareness of key socio-political issues through awareness of audience responses to moments of satire.

Conclusion

Political cartoons lie at the heart of contestations over the meanings and processes of democracy in postcolonial states. The threats posed to media freedom in these contexts underscore the importance of, and necessity to protect, the media as a public sphere in which critical citizens can engage the practices of democratic citizenship. Political cartoons provide vital moments and narratives of resistance to excesses of state power from the perspective of members of the media elite. The responses to these cartoons, the reception of the images, offer further insights into the hitherto under-explored arena of popular understandings of, and sentiments towards, the meanings and practices of democracy and citizenship.

The range of responses provoked by Zapiro's cartoons highlights a number of concerns in popular understandings of the socio-political situation in post-apartheid South Africa. The emotive and, at times, vitriolic reactions remind us of the power of political cartoons in mobilising popular political engagement and, therefore, the necessity of protecting the public sphere as a space for freedom of political expression and dissent in a democratic society. Political cartoons, in other words, can create and mobilise popular politics: while they may speak the truth to power, more often their power lies in the contestation of 'truths' and the ensuing deliberation of these concerns. The continued persecution of political cartoonists and efforts to censor and censure their works – see the persecution of cartoonists in Syria in 2012 – further underscores the power of such images in mobilising political discussion and resistance to excesses of state power. The rhetoric of the responses, however, sounds a note of caution as to the depth of understanding of the media's role in this guise in South Africa. The invoking of calls for the media, and Zapiro, to – in essence – focus on contributing to a particular nation-building discourse and to refrain from attacking Zuma out of respect for his status are at odds with Western expectations of media liberalism. The negotiation of these dilemmas is a core part of the process of democracy. The continued entrenchment of democracy, and efforts to co-opt organised civil society as a partner within these processes, renders a popular uprising akin to those witnessed in North Africa in 2010/11 unlikely in South Africa, but does challenge the spaces and forms of resistance. However, the state's (albeit at times partial) acceptance that (un)organised civil society provide expressions of agency and opposition to the state, not necessarily with 'civility', provides a continual release of public and private dissent in ways that prompt state attention and response.

The invoking of race and racism, and arguments over the claiming of anti-apartheid struggle history and values to bolster conflicting views on Zapiro's cartoons, underlines both continued struggles over the meanings and practices of democratic citizenship *and* the power and importance of historical experience and memory in shaping contemporary political views, engagements and actions. The emotions and vitriol contained within the responses remind us of the continued challenges facing South Africa as a consolidating democracy and demonstrate the necessity not only for the public sphere to remain a space for critical expression and exchange, but the imperative for government to assist in facilitating non-demagogic dialogue in order to foster greater tolerance and understanding as part of the continued process of nation-building. The fractures and fault lines in post-apartheid society and social relations in the responses evidence continued underlying divisions within the nation-building project, not least around the depoliticisation of race and deployment of race in profoundly political ways (cf. Hammett 2008), and the pressing need for constructive dialogue to overcome these. The political cartoons and responses considered here demonstrate not only how the cartoon itself can provide a (partial) momentary insight into a nation's *zeitgeist* but also how analysis of audience responses provides deeper insights into the popular psyche and the pressing concerns, fears and desires of citizens.

More broadly, it is apparent that detailed readings of audience responses to such moments and expressions of dissent are necessary to unpack the complex networks and dynamics of power and resistance in Africa. Whether satire is expressed and circulated in public or private, it is political and is subject to multiple interpretations and understandings. Recognising and unpacking this range of reactions emphasises the need to recognise the importance of agency, even in conditions of a curtailed public sphere, which results in a largely overlooked mosaic of heterogeneous forms of resistance. It is in these complexities that nuanced understandings of the contested practices, power and performance of resistance need to be understood not only in relation to state-society relations but also between and within communities and society.

References

Baba Umfundisi, comment in Vilakazi (2008), Why, Zapiro?

Bal, A., Pitt, L., Berthon, P. and DesAutels, P. (2009). Caricatures, cartoons, spoofs and satires: political brands as butts. *Journal of Public Affairs*, 9(4), 229–37.

Barber, K. (1997). Preliminary notes on audiences in Africa. *Africa*, 67(3), 347–62.

Barnett, C. (1999). Broadcasting the rainbow nation: media, democracy and nation building in South Africa, *Antipode*, 31(3), 274–303.

Berger, Jonathan (2008). In defence of Zapiro. *Mail & Guardian*, 9 September. Available at www.thoughtleader.co.za/jonathanberger/2008/09/09/in-defence-of-zapiro, (last accessed: 20 January 2012).

Billig, M. (2005). *Laughter and ridicule: towards a social critique of humour*. London: Sage.

Botma, G. (2011). Going back to the crossroads: visions of a democratic media future at the dawn of the New South Africa. *Ecquid Novi: African Journalism Studies*, 32(2), 75–89.

Bratich, J. (2005). Amassing the Multitude: Revisiting Early Audience Studies. *Communication Theory*, 15(3), 242–65.

Bruce, comment in Haffajee (2008), Cartoons speak the truth in our society.

Carter, S. and Dodds, K. (2011). Hollywood and the 'war on terror': genre-geopolitics and 'Jacksonianism' in *The Kingdom*. *Environment and Planning D: Society and Space*, 29(1), 98–113.

Carter, S. and McCormack, D. (2006). Film, geopolitics and the affective logics of intervention. *Political Geography*, 25(2), 228–45.

Citizen Mntu, comment in Thorpe (2011), Zapiro used rape to show severity.

Dalby, S. (2008). Warrior geopolitics: *Gladiator*, *Black Hawk Down* and *The Kingdom of Heaven*. *Political Geography*, 27(4), 439–55.

Dave Harris, comment in Tabane (2010), Zapiro shouldn't apologise.

Dittmer, J. (2005). Captain America's Empire: reflections on identity, popular culture and post-9/11 geopolitics. *Annals of the Association of American Geographers*, 95(3), 626–43.

Dittmer, J. (2007). The tyranny of the serial: popular geopolitics, the nation and comic book discourse. *Antipode*, 39(2), 247–68.

Dittmer, J. (2010). Comic book visualities: a methodological manifesto on geography, montage and narration. *Transactions of the Institute of British Geographers*, 35(2), 222–36.

Dittmer, J. (2011). American exceptionalism, visual effects, and the post-9/11

cinematic superhero boom. *Environment and Planning D: Society and Space*, 29(1), 114–30.
Dittmer, J. and Dodds, K. (2008). Popular geopolitics past and future: fandom, identities and audiences. *Geopolitics*, 13(3), 437–57.
Dittmer, J. and Gray, N. (2010). Popular geopolitics 2.0: towards new methodologies of the everyday. *Geography Compass*, 4(11), 1664–77.
Dodds, K. (1996). The 1982 Falklands War and a critical geopolitical eye: Steve Bell and the If ... Cartoons. *Political Geography*, 15(6–7), 571–92.
Dodds, K. (2006). Popular geopolitics and audience dispositions: James Bond and the Internet Movie Database (IMDb). *Transactions of the Institute of British Geographers*, 31(2), 116–30.
Dodds, K. (2007). Steve Bell's eye: cartoons, geopolitics and the visualization of the 'war on terror'. *Security Dialogue*, 38(2), 157–77.
Dodds, K. (2008). Hollywood and the popular geopolitics of the war on terror. *Third World Quarterly*, 29(8), 1621–37.
Dodds, K. (2010). Popular geopolitics and cartoons: representing power relations, repetition and resistance. *Critical African Studies*, 4, 1–19.
Dorman, S. (2006). Post-liberation politics in Africa: examining the political legacy of struggle. *Third World Quarterly*, 27(6), 1085–1101.
Duncan, J. (2009). The uses and abuses of political economy: the ANC's media policy. *Transformations: Critical Perspectives on Southern Africa*, 70, 1–30.
Eko, L. (2007). It's a political jungle out there: how four African newspaper cartoons dehumanized and 'deterritorialized' African political leaders in the post-Cold War era. *International Communications Gazette*, 69(3), 219–38.
Geri, comment in Vilakazi (2008), Why, Zapiro?
Gerry, comment in Berger (2008), In defence of Zapiro.
Haffajee, Ferial (2008). Cartoons speak the truth in our society. *Mail & Guardian*, 11 September. Available at www.thoughtleader.co.za/ferialhaffajee/2008/09/11/cartoons-speak-the-truth-in-our-society, (last accessed: 20 January 2012).
Hammett, D. (2008). Disrespecting teacher: the decline in social standing of teachers in Cape Town, South Africa. *International Journal of Educational Development*, 28(3), 340–47.
Hammett, D. (2010a). Zapiro and Zuma: a symptom of an emerging constitutional crisis in South Africa? *Political Geography*, 29, 88–96.
Hammett, D. (2010b). Political cartoons, post-colonialism and critical African Studies. *Critical African Studies*, 4, 1–26.
Hammett, D. (2011). Resistance, power and geopolitics in Zimbabwe. *Area*, 43(2), 202–10.
Hammett, D. and Staeheli, L. (2011). Respect and responsibility: teaching citizenship in South African high schools. *International Journal of Educational Development*, 31(3), 269–76.
Hughes, R. (2007). Through the looking blast: geopolitics and visual culture. *Geography Compass*, 1(5), 976–94.
Itumeleng, comment in Vilakazi (2008), Why, Zapiro?
Jacobs, S. (2004). Media during South Africa's first decade of liberal democracy: some short impressions. *Ecquid Novi: African Journalism Studies*, 25(2), 346–50.
Jacobs, S. (2007). Big Brother, Africa is watching. *Media, Culture and Society*, 29(6), 851–68.

Johnson, A., del Rio, E. and Kemmitt, A. (2010). Missing the joke: a reception analysis of satirical texts. *Communication, Culture and Critique*, 3(3), 396–415.

Jon, comment in Berger (2008), In defence of Zapiro.

Kandi, comment in Vilakazi (2008), Why, Zapiro?

Khathutshelo, comment in Vilakazi (2008), Why, Zapiro?

Kitty Kat, comment in Tabane (2010), Zapiro shouldn't apologise.

Lee Cahill, comment in Vilakazi (2008), Why, Zapiro?

Lyndall Beddy, comment in Berger (2008), In defence of Zapiro.

Krüger, F. (2011). News broadcasting on South African community radio: in search of new public spheres. *Ecquid Novi: African Journalism Studies*, 32(3), 61–79.

Maré, G. (2001). Race, democracy and opposition in South African politics: as other a way as possible. *Democratization*, 8(1), 85–102.

Marishane, L. and Shackleton, S.-J. (2009). *South Africa: access to on-line information and knowledge*, GISWatch Report, available from: www.giswatch.org/country-report/20/south-africa (last accessed: 23 July 2012).

Mason, A. (2009). Ten years after: South African cartooning and the politics of liberation (pp. 247–302). In J. Lent (ed.), *Cartooning in Africa*. Cresskill, NJ: Hampton Press.

Mason, A. (2010). *What's so funny? Under the skin of South African cartooning*. Claremont: Double Storey.

Mbembe, A. (2001). *On the postcolony*. Berkeley, CA: University of California Press.

McDonald, P. (2011). The present is another country: a comment on the 2010 media freedom debate. *Ecquid Novi: African Journalism Studies*, 32(2), 122–34.

MFB, comment in Berger (2008), In defence of Zapiro.

Morley, D. (1993). Active audience theory: pendulums and pitfalls. *Journal of Communication*, 43(4), 13–19.

Mvikeni kaNxamala Zuma, comment in Vilakazi (2008), Why, Zapiro?

Newell, S. (1997). Making up their own minds: readers, interpretations and the difference of view in Ghanaian popular narratives. *Africa*, 67(3), 389–405.

Pillai, P. (1992). Rereading Stuart Hall's encoding/decoding model. *Communication Theory*, 2(3), 221–33.

Pinkerton, A. and Dodds, K. (2009). Radio geopolitics: broadcasting, listening and the struggle for acoustic space, *Progress in Human Geography*, 33(1), 10–27.

Purcell, D., Brown, M. and Gokmen, M. (2010). Achmed the dead terrorist and humor in popular geopolitics. *GeoJournal*, 75(4), 373–85.

Refaie, E. El (2009). Multiliteracies: how readers interpret political cartoons. *Visual Communication*, 8(2), 181–205.

Ruddock, A. (2008). Media Studies 2.0? Binge drinking and why audiences still matter. *Sociology Compass*, 2(1), 1–15.

sabelo njoko, comment in Berger (2008), In defence of Zapiro.

Sarah Britten, comment in Trapido (2008), Will Mondli fire Zapiro?

Senzo Selebe, comment in Zapiro (2008a), Rape of Justice cartoon 1.

Sharp, J. (1996). Hegemony, popular culture and geopolitics: the *Reader's Digest* and the construction of danger. *Political Geography*, 15(6–7), 557–70.

Sparks, C. (2011). South African media in comparative perspective. *Ecquid Novi: African Journalism Studies*, 32(2), 5–19.

Tabane, Onkgopotse J. J. (2010). Zapiro shouldn't apologise. *Mail & Guardian*, 21 January. Available at www.thoughtleader.co.za/onkgopotsejjtabane/2010/01/21/zapiros-rape-cartoon-free-expression, (last accessed: 20 January 2012).

Terblanche, N. (2011). You cannot run or hide from social media – ask a politician. *Journal of Public Affairs*, 11(3), 156–67.

Thorpe, Jen (2011). Zapiro used rape to show severity. *Mail & Guardian*, June 15. Available at www.thoughtleader.co.za/jenniferthorpe/2011/06/15/zapiro-used-rape-to-show-severity, (last accessed: 20 January 2012).

Thrift, N. (2004). Intensities of feeling: towards a spatial politics of affect. *Geografiska Annaler: Series B*, 86(1), 57–78.

Tomaselli, K. (2009). Repositioning African Media Studies: thoughts and provocations. *Journal of African Media Studies*, 1(1), 9–21.

Tomaselli, K. and Teer-Tomaselli, R. (2008). Exogenous and endogenous democracy: South African politics and media. *The International Journal of Press/Politics*, 13(2), 171–80.

Trapido, Michael (2008). Will Mondli fire Zapiro? *Mail & Guardian*, 8 September. Available at www.thoughtleader.co.za/traps/2008/09/08/will-mondli-fire-zapiro, (last accessed: 20 January 2012).

Van Hoorn, I. (2008). Zapiro in Zuma cartoon uproar, *Mail & Guardian*, 8 September.

Vernon, K. (2000). *Penpricks: the drawing of South Africa's political battle lines*. Claremont: Spearhead Press.

Vilakazi, Sandisiwe (2008). Why, Zapiro? *Mail & Guardian* blog, 8 September. Available at www.thoughtleader.co.za/readerblog/2008/09/08/why-zapiro, (last accessed: 20 January 2012).

Warrick Sony, comment in Trapido (2008), Will Mondli fire Zapiro?

Zapiro (2008a). Rape of Justice cartoon 1, published in South African *Sunday Times* on 7 September. Available at www.zapiro.com/cartoon/122794-080907st and http://mg.co.za/cartoon/zapiro_2099, both last accessed 20 January 2012.

Zapiro (2008b). Rape of Justice cartoon 2, published in *Mail & Guardian* on 11 September. Available at www.zapiro.com/cartoon/122793-080911mg, last accessed 16 August 2013.

Zapiro (2008c). Rape of Justice cartoon 3, published in *Sunday Times* on 14 September. Available at www.zapiro.com/cartoon/122792-080914st, last accessed 16 August 2013.

Zapiro (2009). *The Mandela files*. Cape Town: Double Storey.

Zapiro (2010). Zuma: Unfinished business – Begging your pardon cartoon, published in *Mail & Guardian* on 14 January. Available at www.zapiro.com/cartoon/118053-100114mg, last accessed 16 August 2013.

Zapiro (2011). Pressure on Lady Freedom to fight back as ANC push forward with 'Secrecy' Bill, published in *Mail & Guardian* on 9 June. Available at www.zapiro.com/cartoon/361477-110609mg, last accessed 16 August 2013.

Index

Abahlali baseMjondolo 140, 141
abasazi 109
Abbink, J. 5, 30
Abrahamsen, R. 3
Abu-Lughod, L. 7, 111, 193
accommodation 6, 31, 66
accountability xiii, xv, 41, 59, 61, 104, 105, 128, 207
Achebe, Chinua 164
action, citizen 4–11 *passim*, 17, 19, 20, 49–62, 106–10, 116–18, 127–9 *passim*, 132, 136, 167–81, 185
Adebanwi, W. 1
adjustment, structural 5, 10–12 *passim*, 19, 27, 29, 85, 87, 99, 128
Afewerki, Isaias 43
Africa Centre for Strategic Studies 44
African Peer Review Mechanism 43
African Union 43
Afrikaner Weerstandsbeweging 147
Agamben, G. 79
Agbese, Pita Ogaba 34
age factors 35, 190, 193 *see also* youth
Agglioti, Glen 136
agriculture 11, 13, 57, 104, 105, 118
Ahmad, A. 31
aid 4, 41, 49, 58
Ake, Claude 34–7 *passim*
Algeria 30
Angola 10, 11, 30, 50, 51, 56–61; economy 57; Federation of Representative Associations (NRA) 11, 51, 58, 59; MPLA 57
Ansoms, A. 105
anthropology 5, 31
apartheid 14, 16, 27, 32, 128, 129, 142, 148, 151–3 *passim*, 156, 158, 177, 208, 210, 216, 219; anti- 53, 133,140, 176, 208, 210, 213, 217, 221
Appadurai, A. 52, 194
Apter, A. 86, 91, 95–6, 99, 186
Arab Spring xvii, 16, 28, 29, 42–4, 106, 118, 122
Archer, M. 113
Arnold, D. 130, 132
Asikhulume 130
Askew, K. 186
associations 1, 5, 10–12 *passim*, 40, 49, 51, 55, 57–60, 69–75 *passim*, 77, 79, 80, 81
Attwell, David 156
audiences 17, 18, 131, 147, 171–2, 188, 190–201, 205–7, 211–21 *passim*
authoritarianism xviii, 3, 13, 14, 37, 41, 52, 104–25, 207–8
autochthony 187
autonomy xv, 6, 7, 19, 35, 36, 42, 67, 133, 149, 209
Azarya, Victor 34, 40

Bafo, K. 54–6 *passim*
Bahl, V. 132
Bakardjieva, Maria 171–2
Bakhtin, Mikhail 134
Bal, A. 211
Bamileke 88, 89
Banda, Kamusu 41
banks/banking 13, 93, 96
Barber, K. 168, 171, 179, 186, 206
Barrett, G. 53, 59

Bauman, Z. 85
Baxandall, Michael 168
Bayart, J.-F. 5, 78, 85, 86, 88, 90, 92, 94, 97, 99
Bayat, Asef 66
Bayly, C.A. 132
'Beasts of No Nation' xvi, 15–16, 168, 171–9 *passim*
Beauchamp, T. 98
Beddy, Lyndall 220
behaviour 9, 11, 67, 169, 175, 177
Belgium 96
belonging 17, 81, 88, 89, 187, 189, 193, 194, 196–200 *passim*
Benin xvii, 41, 44
Berger, Jonathan 215
Bhabha, Homi 31, 100, 149–50, 152, 161, 169
Bible 31
Biko, Steve 140, 141
Billig, M. 218
Binza, Professor 130
Biya, Paul xvii, 87, 88
Black Consciousness 139–40
blackness 148, 151, 152, 154, 160, 161
Blackwash 140
Bosch, T.E. 185
Botma, G. 209
Botha, P.W. 152–3, 177
Bowie, N. 98
Brady, B. 96
Brandes, S.H. 135
Bratich, J. 207
Bratton, M.P. 59
Braudel, Fernand 97
British South Africa Co. 30
Brittan, S. 95
Britten, Sarah 219
Brockman, J.M. 147
Bromley, R. 68
Brown, A. 66, 76
Bruce 216
Bruijn, M. de 5
Bucciferro, C. 133, 135, 136
Burkina Faso 44
Byerley, A. 66

Cahill, Lee 215, 217
Calhoun, C. 180
Campbell, Naomi 158–9
Cameroon xvi, xvii, 12–13, 44, 85–9, 91–6 *passim*, 99–100, 153–4, 185; Bamileke 88, 89; Beti 88–9; CPDM 89, 92; economy 87
Canada 96
capitalism 13, 20, 28, 40, 43, 86, 94–100 *passim*, 141, 148
Carter, S. 205
cartoons xvi, 18, 158, 204–5, 207–20 *passim*
Catan, T. 93
Catterson, Troy 178
Cele, Bheki 136–8 *passim*
censorship 14–16 *passim*, 134, 150, 208, 221; self–164
Chabal, Patrick xii–xviii, xx, 5
Chan, S. 4
Chatterjee, P. 132
Chaturvedi, V. 139
Chazan, N. 3, 34, 40
Chile 133
Chinweizu 35
Christianity 29, 31
churches xvi, 41, 55, 57
citizenisation 91–4 *passim*
citizenship 1,10–11, 13, 34, 43, 49–62, 66, 79, 80, 88, 91, 220, 221; Development Research Centre on 50
civil society xii–xiv passim, xvii, xix, 2–4, 8, 9, 18, 35, 41, 50–1, 53, 55–7 *passim*, 60–1, 128, 149,167–75 *passim*, 185, 190, 206, 209, 221; organisations xiii, xiv, 1, 3–5 *passim*, 41, 51–3 *passim*, 58, 61, 210
Clark, K. 134
class factors 39, 113–14, 121, 130–3 passim, 144, 148,161, 163
clientelism xviii, 5, 42, 49, 52, 57, 78, 85, 86, 93
Clifford, James 97
Cobus de Wet 142
Coelho, V.S. 52, 60
Colombo 66
colonialism xiv, 2–5 *passim*, 10, 14, 16, 19, 27–35, 110, 142, 149, 150, 156, 169, 175, 177, 216, 219; anti- 2–5 *passim*, 10, 31, 178;

neo- xiv, 27, 29; post- xiii, 2–10 *passim*, 14, 19, 29, 31–42 *passim*, 149, 150, 169–70, 176–9 *passim*
coloniality 27–9 *passim*, 32, 38
Comaroff, J.L. and J. 4–6 *passim*, 31, 41, 95, 186
comedy/comedians 14–15, 20, 37, 127, 130–9, 143–4, 147–66 *passim*, 205 *see also individual entries*
Congo 96; Congo-Brazzaville xvii–xviii
Cooper, Frederick 31
Corbett, John 170
Cornwall, A. 52
Corrigan, P. 186
corruption 5, 42, 104, 129, 130, 136–8 *passim*, 210, 213
Côte d'Ivoire 96
creativity 5, 7, 66
credit 58, 113; associations 69, 74
crime/criminalisation 13, 20, 85–103, 136
Crisufulli, P. 118
Crossa, V. 67, 78
culture 14–17 *passim*, 29, 32, 37, 52, 60, 99, 127–81, 185–7, 200, 201, 204, 204–7 *passim*

Dalby, S. 205
Darts, D. 167
Davis, M. 63
Dawson, M.C. 127
decentralisation 42, 53, 57, 187, 189, 200
decitizenisation 85
decolonisation 10, 27, 30–6 *passim*, 39, 179
democracy/democratisation xiii, xviii, 2, 3, 5, 28, 30, 34, 37, 41–4 *passim*, 52, 59, 60, 89, 179, 185, 186, 191, 207, 210, 213, 220, 221
depoliticisation 14, 121, 127, 135, 140, 143, 209, 221
Desrosiers, E.-M. 105
development xiii, 34, 41–3 *passim*, 54, 105, 114, 122, 128, 169, 179
dialogue 7, 9, 59, 221
Diamond, Larry 34
dictatorships xix, 1, 14, 16, 43, 44, 168, 174, 175
dignity xix, 19, 31, 116–21 *passim*
disenfranchisement 85–7 *passim*, 128, 140
disobedience, civil xiv, 44, 55, 89
displacement 56, 68, 76, 118
Dittmer, S. 205–7 *passim*
Djibouti 44
Dodds, K. 205, 206
domination 2, 6, 7, 10, 19, 27–48, 149, 178, 179
donors xiii, xix, 3–4, 58
Dorman, S. 208, 214
Douala/New Bell 87–9 *passim*
dress 9, 11
Duncan, J. 209
Duncombe, S. 170

East Africa 30 *see also individual country entries*
economic factors 3, 6, 11–13 *passim*, 54, 57, 87, 94–100 *passim*, 105, 123, 160; growth 3, 13, 54, 57, 104, 105, 118
Economist Intelligence Unit 104
education 4, 31, 54, 55, 57, 190
Egypt 34, 42, 44, 193
Eko, L. 205
elections xv–xviii *passim*, 3, 54, 56, 57, 104, 129
elites xiii–xvi *passim*, 10, 13, 14, 33, 36–42 *passim*, 80, 85, 89, 92, 94, 97, 99, 105–7, 112–14 *passim*, 128, 131, 133, 134, 143, 204–9 *passim*, 214, 219, 220
Ellis, S. 5
emigration 37
employment 12, 87, 114, 118
empowerment, citizen 1, 52–3, 55–6, 59, 109; self- 117
engagement, citizen 52, 53, 57–61 *passim*
Engel, U. 5
Englebert, Pierre 34
Englishness 151, 160–3
Englund, H. 18
Eritrea 43
Esedebe, P.O. 31
Ethiopia 41, 43

ethnicity xiv, xv, 4, 12, 27, 37, 87, 90, 209
Europe 4, 29, 36, 43, 86, 96, 178, 195; Eastern xiii, 3; Euro-American factors 29, 44; Euro-Christian-Modernist factors 29
expectations 169, 173, 174, 188, 194, 197–9 *passim*

'419' scams 85, 86, 90–100 *passim*
Fabian, J. 14
Fair, Jo 170
Fanon, Frantz 33
FAO 112
Ferguson, J. 85
Ferreira, I. 57–9 *passim*
feymen xvii, 12–13, 85–100 *passim*
Fikeni, Somadoda 130
films 204, 205
Foeken, D. 5
Foltz, W.J. 33, 40
Foucault, M. 6, 7, 19, 77, 110
France 33, 86, 89, 96; Francophone Africa 35, 41
fractured sovereignty 6
fraud 12–13, 85–103 *passim*; advance fee 91–3, 95–9 *passim*
freedom xiv, 33–4, 36–7, 39–44 *passim*; of expression 213–20
Friedrich Ebert Stiftung 188
Fung, A. 52

Gabon 44
Gaddafi, Muammar 28, 44
Garveyism 31
Gatimu, D. 70, 71
Gaventa, J. 52, 53, 59
gender issues 42, 69, 156, 159, 190, 193, 213
genocide 104, 106, 108, 109, 112, 115–22 *passim*
geopolitics 204–7
Gephart, R. 168
Geri 218
Germany 86, 93
Gerry 216
Geschiere, P. 94, 98, 187
Ghana xviii, 40
Giroux, H. 171, 172
Gitlin, T. 1
Glassman, J. 30
Glickman, H. 93, 96, 99
globalisation xiv, 28, 38, 96, 179
Gnacos 88
Gola, Loyiso 134, 150–4 *passim*, 156–7, 163
Gordon, D. 141
Govender, Krijay 150, 159
governance 3, 36, 41, 42, 50–1
Graeber, D. 1
Graetz, T. 185
Gramsci, Antonio 8, 130
Gravel, P. 105
Gray, N. 205, 206
Grosfoguel, R. 28, 32
Gugulethu 153
Guha, Ranajit 8, 67
Guinea 35, 40
Guinea-Bissau 30, 44
Gunner, L. 186
Gwala, Xolani 130

Haan, L. de 5
Habermas, J. 17
Habimana, A. 121
Haffajee, Ferial 215–16
Hall, S. 130, 136, 140–1
Hamlin, A. 95
Hammett, Daniel 18, 204–25
Handelman, S. 95
Harbeson, J.W. 3
Harcourt, B.E. 1
Harris, Dave 216
Harvey, D. 98
Haynes, D. 8, 132, 134, 139
health care 4, 49, 54, 55, 57, 112
hegemony 9, 37, 81, 128, 130, 136, 149, 163–4, 167, 168, 176, 178–80 *passim*
Hibou, B. 5, 85, 86, 88–9, 92, 96, 97, 99
hierarchy, social 105, 107, 111–14 *passim*, 121–2 *see also* class
Hirschkind, C. 197
historiography 2–4, 8, 30, 133
history 30, 133, 151–6, 161, 176–8, 213, 214, 216–18 *passim*, 221
HIV/AIDS 10–11, 54–6 *passim*
Holquist, M. 134
Holston, James 12, 65–6

Houtzager, H. 52
Howe, G. 105, 108
Huggins, C. 105
Human Rights Watch 104
humanitarianism 28, 30
humour xiv, xix, xx, 2, 9, 14–15, 18, 37, 127, 130, 133–9, 147–66, 204–20 *passim*
Hungbo, Jendele 15–16, 167–81, 185
Huntington, S. P. 3, 41
'hustling' 20, 85–100
Hyden, G. 185
hypocrisy 16, 175, 177

ibyihebe 109
ICT 43–4
Idowa, M. 167
identity 17, 31, 37, 51, 67, 80, 97, 160–4 *passim*, 169, 178
ideology 15, 18, 19, 29–32, 36–8, 130–3, 139–42, 167–9 *passim*, 178, 187, 188, 204, 208, 211, 214
Ihalailen, Markus 11–12, 15, 65–84
illicit cohabitation 149, 150
IMF 3, 19, 27
imperialism 10, 27–33 *passim*, 44, 149, 177
income 111
independence 30–9 *passim*; 'second' 37
India 8
inequality 54, 111–14 *passim*, 128, 140, 169
informality xii–iv, xvi, xvii, 65–71 *passim*, 76, 80
Ingelaere, B. 105, 109
institutions 36, 42, 43, 51, 54, 57, 60, 173, 174, 176; international financial 6, 19, 27, 28, 87, 99; *see also individual entries*
internet 11, 16, 85, 93, 212
Israel 196
Itumeleng 217

Jackson, Michael 157
Jackson, R.H. 6, 40
Jacobs, S. 206, 208, 209
Jean-Bosco 107, 108, 112, 118–21
Jeanne 107–8, 112, 115–18
Jefferess, David 178
Jensen, D. 1
John Everyman 142
Johnson, A. 206
jokes 14, 134, 138, 139, 150–64 *passim*, 195
Jon 220
Joya, A. 43
justice 173–4; social 54, 152, 153

Kabila, Laurent-Désiré 36
Kagame, Paul 43, 104
Kamete, A. 76
Kamunyori, S. 69
Kandi 215
Kapoor, Ilan 169
Karlstrom, Mikael 38
Katriel, T. 196
Kau, David 135
Kaunda, Kenneth 41
Kawoya, V. 185
Kaya FM radio station 136
Keita, Modibo 36
Kellner, Douglas 175–6
Kenya 11–12, 19, 30, 44, 68–82 *passim*; KENASVIT 81; Republic of 69
Kérékou, Mathieu xvii, 41
Khathutshelo 217
Khoza, Eugene 14, 127, 132, 134, 136–9, 143
Khoza, Irvin 157
Kibuuka, David 135
Kieh, George Klay 34
Kilomba, Grada 162
kinship 4, 51, 90
Kinyanjui, M.N. 69, 81
Kitty Kat 218
Kiura, C.M. 69
Koch, Conrad 150, 157–9, 162–3
Kock, Eugene de 211, 212
Konaré, Alpha Oumar 187, 189
Konings, P. 5, 87, 89, 91, 94, 98
Krüger, E. 208, 209
Kuti, Fela xvi, 14–16 *passim*, 167–81
Kwa-Zulu Natal 138

Laakso, L. 34
labourers 8, 108, 113, 118, 147, 149

land 11, 35, 105, 107, 113–14, 118, 141
Landless People's Movement 140, 141
language 129–31 *passim*, 133, 136, 143, 160–3, 186, 192, 196, 197
Laufer, P. 195
laughter 14, 127, 132, 134–6 *passim*, 139, 143, 147–66 *passim*, 218
Lavalle, A. 52
Leclerc-Olive, M. 189
Lediga, Kagiso 135
Lee, A. 168
Lefebvre, H. 66
legitimacy xiii, xv, xvi, 10, 38–9, 104
Lewis, D. 3
liberalisation 11, 16, 17, 185, 186
Libya 28, 34, 42, 44
Lieres, Bettina von 10–11, 49–62
Ligaga, D. 186
Lindell, Ilda 11–12, 15, 65–84
literacy 170, 218, 219
livelihoods 5, 11, 59, 105
local authorities 11–12, 58–60 *passim*, 69, 71–6 *passim*, 106, 110, 111, 116–18 *passim*, 122
Longman, T. 105
Ludden, D. 132, 139
Lumumba, Patrice 36
Lumumba-Kasongo, Tukumi 34
Lynch, M. 1
Lyons, M. 68

MacGaffey, Janet 94, 98
Machel, Samora 36
Mackie, P. 68
Madonsela, Thuli 137
Mafeje, A. 29
Maffesoli, M. 197, 199
Maghreb 43
Magubane, B.M. 29
Maillard, J. de 95
Makhanya, Mondli 214
Makokha, J.S. 185
Malaquais, D. 86, 87, 97, 99
Malawi 41, 44
Maldonado-Torres, N. 27
Malema, Julius 151–2, 154–6 *passim*, 159, 163, 212
Mali 17, 187–96; ADEMA 189, 190; CNID 190; Conseil Supérieur de la Communication 189; Ministry of Communications 188, 189; Segu 190–2 *passim;* Transition Regime 187
Mamdani, M. 4, 5, 33, 35, 41, 106
Mandela, Nelson 151–2, 154, 155, 210
Mantashe, Gwede 212
Marcello 89
Maré, G. 214, 217
marginalisation xvii, 12, 49–53 *passim*, 60, 66, 79, 81, 85–103, 120, 121, 127, 141, 143, 153
Marishane, L. 212
market, hawkers, Muthurwa 12, 65, 68–82 *passim*
Maroleng, Chris 147
Martin, Guy 34–6 *passim*
Marx/Marxism 32, 38, 109
Mason, A. 206–8 *passim*, 210, 211
Masselos, J. 132
Mauritania 44
Mazrui, Ali 38–9, 41
Mbeki, Thabo 43, 54, 55, 211
Mbembe, A. 6, 7, 9, 32, 37–8, 136, 149, 150, 178, 219
McClintock, Anne 149
McCloskey, D.N. 98
McCormack, D. 205
McDonald, P. 209
McKay, A. 105, 108
McMurray, D. 1
Mdletyana, Mncedisi 130
Médecins Sans Frontières 55
media 14, 17, 128–33 *passim*, 139, 170–2 *passim*, 179, 185–9 *passim*, 192, 205–9 *passim*, 214, 218, 220, 221; – Appeals Tribunal 209
mediation 51–3, 58–60 *passim*, 128, 136, 186, 187, 192–200 *passim*
Meles Zenawi 43
memory 151, 176, 221
Mengistu, Haile Mariam 41
mercantilism 27, 29
Mexico City 78
Meyer, Birgit 197, 198
Mhlambi, Innocentia 14–15, 127–46

Middle East 8, 43 *see also individual country entries*
Mignolo, W.D. 28, 30
military regimes xix, 4–5, 14, 168, 169, 174, 175
Miller, C. 30
MINECOFIN 113
minibus traffic 65, 70, 73, 76, 77, 81
Mitchell, D. 68, 76
Mitchell, W.J.T. 1
Mitulla, W. 68, 69
Mkandawire, T. 42
Mngxitama, Andile 14–15, 127, 128, 132, 139–44 *passim*
Mntu, Citizen 219
mobilisation, citizen 10–11, 49–53, 56–61 *passim*, 129
mobility 73, 75, 77; economic 105; social 112, 121, 122
Mobutu, Seseko 42
modernity/modernisation 29, 30, 32, 41, 85, 178, 179
Monga, C. 89
Moore, B. 170
Moorman, M. 186
Moosa, Riaad 135
Morley, D. 206
Morton, S. 131, 133, 139
Motshekga, Angie 138
movements 40, 41, 51–6 *passim*, 60, 81, 127, 128, 140–3 *passim*; liberation 5, 16; Mungiki 81, Occupy xvi–xvii, 1; student 41; women's 40, 41; youth 40
Mozambique 30
Mudimbe, V.Y. 29
Mugabe, Robert 44
Muiruri, P. 68, 69
Muiu, Mueni wa 34–6 *passim*
Murithi, Timothy 43
Murray, Brett 157
Museveni, Yoweri xviii, 43
music xiv, 2, 14–17 *passim*, 20, 37, 167–81, 185, 186, 192, 196–9 *passim*; Afro-beat 167, 170
Musila, Grace A. 15, 147–66
Mwesige, P.G. 185
Myers, G. 66
Myers, M. 185

9/11 27
Nairobi 11–12, 67–82; CBD 67–71, 73–7 *passim*; City Council 68, 71–5 *passim*
Namibia 30
nation-building 3, 169, 186, 208, 210, 213, 218, 221
'national conference phenomenon' 41
nationalism 30–5 *passim*, 38, 42, 127, 128, 132, 144, 159, 167, 179, 208
nativism 32, 38
NATO 28, 30
Ndayambajwe, J.-D. 112
Ndjio, Basile 12–13, 85–103
Ndlovu-Gatsheni, Sabelo 10, 27–48
Nedbank 136
neo-liberalism 5, 10, 11, 18–20, 27–9 *passim*, 43, 87, 127–30 *passim*, 132, 134, 143, 179
Netherlands 86, 90
networks 57–9 *passim*, 78, 80, 81, 113, 195–6, 204, 205, 221
New Frank Talk 140
New Partnership for Africa 43
Newbury, C. 105, 106, 122
Newell, S. 206
NGOs xiv, xvi, xvii, xix, 3–5 *passim*, 9, 41, 49, 51–3 *passim*, 57, 58, 129
N'Gouabi, Mirien 36
Nguesso, Sassou xviii
Nigeria xix, 1, 9, 14–16 *passim*, 30, 43, 85–100, 167–81 *passim*, 186; Hausa-Fulani 89; Ife 176; Igbo 89–90; Zaria 176
Nijenhuis, K. 187
Nkondlo, Dr 130
Nkrumah, Kwame 33, 36, 40
Noah, Trevor 134–5, 150, 154–6, 158–62 *passim*
North Africa 1, 8, 43, 44, 221 *see also individual entries*
North America 96, 187; Euro-American factors 29–30, 44
Nyamnjoh, F.B. 32, 185, 187
Nzimande, Blade 212

Obadare, Ebenezer xix–xx, 1–23, 148, 150, 167

Obama, Barack 154
Obasanjo, Olusegun 43
O'Hanlon, R. 132
Olaniyan, T. 167, 179
Olaoluwa, S. 176
Olukoshi, A.O. 34
one-party rule 3, 34, 41
Ong, A. 79
Opoku-Mensah, A. 185
oppression xiv, xvi, 16, 33, 105, 107–11, 114–21 *passim*, 175–6, 219
origins 187, 196–7
Oring, E. 136
Osaghae, Eghosa 43
otherness 149, 164, 169
Ottaway, M. 43
Oyono, Ferdinand 153–4

Padmore, G. 31
'Pajero Brigade' xix
pan-Africanism 31, 43; Parliament 43
Pandey, Gyanendra 88
participation 14–17 *passim*, 42, 49, 51–3, 56–60, 127–46 *passim*, 170, 171, 187, 190–1, 200 *see also* audiences; radio
patrimonialism xiii, xv, xviii
patronage 27, 42, 52
peasants 8, 37, 57–9, 105–18 *passim*, 121–2
Peel, M. 93
Pereira, Nihal 66
Perry, J. 100
Pheko, Lebohang 147
Phemelo 142–3
Pieterse, E. 81
Pillai, P. 206, 207
Pillay, S. 141
Pinkerton, A. 205
Piper, L. 53–6 *passim*
Pliyega, Riah 136–8 *passim*
Podium Comedy Merchants 135, 136
politics xiii–xviii, 1–3 *passim*, 5, 9, 14–15, 17, 40, 52–6, 60, 65–84, 88–9, 127–46, 161, 163, 186–92, 200, 205, 207–9, 216–17, 220, 221; analysis 14–15, 127, 128, 132, 139–44 *passim*; consciousness 19,106–22 *passim*; oppositional xvi–xix *passim*, 1, 19, 37–41 *passim*, 104, 106, 164, 189–90, 208, 218
poverty 57, 87, 105, 107, 111–12, 153
power xii–xiii, xv–xvii *passim*, 4, 6–7, 11, 14–15, 18–20, 27, 28, 37–9 *passim*, 105, 110, 111, 148–50, 168–71 *passim*, 177, 179, 204–6 *passim*, 209, 220, 221; abuses of 15, 57, 59, 129, 144
powerlessness 20, 110, 111, 120
praise songs/texts 39, 41, 195
Prakash, G. 8, 132, 134, 139
press 14, 18, 208–15 *passim*; *Mail & Guardian* 212, 213, 215; *Sunday Times* 212, 214
Primedia 136
Probst, P. 5
protest xvi, 1–4 *passim*, 8,9, 30, 54, 55, 110, 117, 128–9, 133, 141, 152, 167, 176
Prunier, G. 106
public sphere 14, 16–18, 135, 147, 185–225 *passim*
Purcell, D. 205
Purdekovà, A. 109

Quijano, A. 27

race/racism 14, 15, 29, 128, 140–4, 147–66 *passim*, 205, 208, 211, 213, 216–17, 219, 221
radicalism 132–5, 140
radio 14, 16, 17, 185–201, 205; Foko 190; Siko 190, 191, 193–4; talk 16, 17, 185, 186, 192–6
rainbow nation 15, 127, 128, 144, 148, 150, 153–5 *passim*, 164
Randall, V. 185
Ranger, T. 2, 30
Rasmussen, J. 73, 81
Rawlings, Jerry xviii
rebellion/insurgency xvii, xviii, 5, 7, 8, 12, 28, 30, 65–6, 80, 122, 221; Bambata 30; Maji Maji 30; Ndebele-Shona 30
reconciliation 104, 109, 208, 216, 217

Redmond, A. 118
Refaie, E. El 206, 207
reform 3, 28, 189
Reidenbach, R. 95, 98
religion 4, 27, 42, 49, 197
Reno, W. 78
repression xvi, xvii, 27, 33, 121, 134, 148
resistance *passim*; discursive 14–16, 125–81; embodied 1–13, 65–124; everyday 9, 16–18, 104–24, 185–221
responsiveness, state 51, 53–6, 59, 60
Reyntjens, F. 104
rights, 11, 31, 34, 49–54, 58–60 *passim*; human 1, 28–30 *passim*, 33, 40–2, 140, 175, 177, Universal Declaration 33
riots 8, 122
Robin, D. 95, 98
Robins, S. 38, 39, 54
Robinson, P. 41
Robson, P. 57
Rodney, W. 30
Roque, S. 57–9 *passim*
Rosenthal, K. 127, 128
Rothchild, D.S. 3
Roy, Ananya 66–7, 78
Ruddock, A. 207
Rwanda 13, 19, 43, 104–24; economy 13, 104, 105, 111–12, 118; Hutu 13, 104, 106, 108, 118–20 *passim*; RPF 104, 105, 107, 118, 119; Tutsi 13, 104, 106, 108, 109, 116, 118; Twa 108; unity and reconciliation programme 13, 104, 109

sabelo njoko 217–18
Said, Edward 31, 169
Samuelson, Meg 159
Sandys, Duncan 35
Sankara, Thomas 36
Sanneh, Kelefa 168
São Paulo 65
Sarkar, S. 132
satire 37, 127, 131–9 *passim*, 147–65, 204–22 *passim*
Sayer, D. 186
Schulz, Dorothea 17, 185–203
Schutz, A. 168
Scott, James 8–9, 12, 92, 110, 139, 169, 170
secession 37
Seirlis, Julia 148, 151, 161
Sekoni, R. 136
Selebe, Senzo 213–14
Selebi, Jackie 136, 138–9
self-determination 33
Semenya, Caster 155, 158–9
Sen, A. 41, 95, 98
Senegal 44
Senghor, D. 185
Séraphin, G. 87, 91
sex/sexuality 150–1, 156–61
Shackleton, S.-J. 212
Shaik, Shabir 139, 211, 212
Sharp, J. 205
Simone, A.M. 66
Sivaramakrishnan, K. 110
Skocpol, T. 7
slavery 14, 16, 27, 29, 30, 32, 40, 177
Smith, D.J. 87, 89–91 *passim*, 93, 99
Snoxell, S. 68
sociality 189–96
Socpa, A. 89
Sogge, D. 56
Sony, Warrick 218
Sophie 116
South 210
South Africa 10–11, 14–16 *passim*, 18, 30, 43, 50, 51, 53–6, 60–1, 127–66, 176, 177, 204, 207–22; ANC 14–15, 54, 127–32 *passim*, 136, 138, 140, 141, 155–6, 158, 209, 213, 214, 217, 218, Youth League 151, 154, 211, 214; Anti-Privatisation Forum 127; BEE 136, 160; Communist Party 55, 132, 211; Constitution 54, 209; COSATU 55, 132, 211; Democratic Alliance 158, 159; economy 54, 128, 160; GEAR 128; Group Areas Act 153; Illegal Gatherings Act 210; Immorality Act 156; National Party 133, 208; National Police Commissioner 129, 136–9 *passim*;

National Prosecuting Authority 210–12 passim; NCO 133; NEDLAC 133; politics 54–6, 127–46; Protection of Information Act 209, 211, 212; Public Protector 129, 137; RDP 128; SABC 129, 130, 143, 147, 149, 153, 208; SAPS 128, 129; UDF 209–10; Umkhonto we Sizwe 214; *see also* TAC
Southern Rhodesia 30
sovereignty xiii, xx, 6, 19, 27, 34, 35, 44, 54, 175
Soviet Union 33
Soweto 176; Electricity Crisis Committee 127
Spain 135
Sparks, C. 207–9 *passim*
Spittler, G. 5
Spitulnik, D. 186, 188, 192–5 *passim*
Spivak, Gayatri 67, 131, 133, 169
state *passim;* post-colonial xii–xiii, 9–13 *passim,* 19, 29, 32–42, 65–124, 179, 220; 'quasi' 6, 40; -society relations xiii, 1, 3–5 *passim*, 7, 8, 18–20, 34, 36–42, 49–61 *passim*, 67, 77, 80, 104–22, 128–33 *passim*, 175, 176, 190, 208, 209, 220–1
Steinmetz, G. 186
stereotypes 15, 149–52, 156–64 *passim*
Sterne, Jonathan 187
Strange, S. 95
Street, John 178
strikes xvi, 81, 129, 132, 152, 163
students 1, 41, 176
subalterns 8–9, 12, 15, 16, 66–8, 78–82 *passim*, 129, 131–5 *passim*, 139, 175, 178
subjectivation 28, 30, 33, 37
subjectivity 1, 3, 5, 67, 168, 193, 200, 206
Swaziland 44
Sypher, Wylie 161
Syria 221

taboos 15, 107, 108, 148–50 *passim*, 164, 165
Tanzania 30
Taussig, M. 1
taxation 12, 76
Taylor, Robert H. 39–40
technology 17, 37, 187–8, 206
Teer-Tomaselli, R. 208, 209, 214
television 14, 130, 147, 193
Terblanche, N. 211
Terreblanche, Eugene 147, 149
terrorism 27–8, 30
theatre 186
Thomson, Susan 13, 104–24
Thrift, N. 219
Tilly, C. 7, 128
Tomaselli, K. 208, 209, 214
Touré, Amadou Toumani 187
Touré, Sekou 35, 40
trade 29; street 11–12, 67–82
trade unions xvi, 31, 40, 55; COSATU 55, 132, 211
tradition 4, 189, 191, 192, 196, 199, 200
Tranberg-Hansen, K. 68, 76
transparency 17, 41, 104, 187, 190
Treatment Action Campaign 10, 51, 54–6, 127
tricksters xvii, 12–13, 85–103 *see also feymen*
Tunisia 34, 42, 44
Turino, T. 186

Uche 90
Ufheil-Somers, A. 1
Uganda xviii, 38, 43, 44
UK 33, 86, 140, 170
Umfundisi, Bàba 215
UN 14, 16, 33, 104, 177–8; Charter 33; Security Council 16, 177
UNDP 104, 112
unemployment xvii, 43, 44, 54, 87, 107
unlaughter 218
UN-OHRLLS/UNDP 104
Urban, G. 198
urban factors 11–12, 57, 65–84 *passim*, 87
US 1, 28–30 *passim*, 33, 36, 96, 195; Pentagon 28
Uys, Pieter-Dirk (Evita Bezuidenhout) 133–4

Van Hoorn, I. 214
Vavi, Zwelinzima 132, 212
Verrips, Jojada 197
violence xv, xvii, xviii, 5, 30, 35, 106, 112, 115, 120, 121, 129, 176, 178, 213; sexual 157–8, 218
Visagie, Andre 147

Walraven, K. van 5, 30
war, civil xvii, 56–7; Cold 3, 16, 18, 27, 33; guerrilla xviii; against indiscipline 175; liberation 56, 175, 176; Ndebele 30; on terror 28; Second World 33
Warner, M. 187
Warnier, J.P. 98
Washbrook, D. 132
Washington consensus xiii, 3, 27, 29
Wasserman, H. 170
water 49, 57
Watkins, M. 161
wealth 13, 91, 94, 106
Weaver, Simon 164
Weber, Max 95
welfare 4, 51, 54, 57
West, Harry 170
West, M.O. 31
West Africa 30, 40, 85–103 *see also individual country entries*
White, B. 186
whiteness 151, 152, 161, 163
Wikipedia 134
Willems, Wendy xix–xx, 1–23, 134, 162
Williams, Raymond 193
women 8, 40–2 *passim*, 69, 72, 74, 112, 157–9 *passim*, 190, 193
Worby, Eric 39
World Bank 3, 19, 27, 104
World Trade Organisation 27
Wright, E.O. 52

Young, C. 33, 35, 40, 42
youth xvii, 11–13 *passim*, 20, 40, 42, 44, 85–103, 190, 193

Zaire 42
Zambia 41
Zapiro, Jonathan xvi, 18, 158, 204, 207, 209–21 *passim*
Zartman, Ira William 34
Zeleza, P.T. 31–2
Zille, Helen 158–9
Zimbabwe xix–xx, 9, 30, 34, 42, 44, 134, 162, 185; ZBC 134
Zobel, D. 195
'zombification' 37
Zuberi, Nabeel 170–1
Zulu 137, 186
Zuma, Jacob xvi, 18, 128, 132, 136, 138, 139, 154–8 *passim*, 163, 210–21 *passim*
Zuma, Mvikeni kaNzamala 214